Young Children and the Arts

Nurturing Imagination and Creativity

Young Children and the Arts

Nurturing Imagination and Creativity

edited by

Carol Korn-Bursztyn

Brooklyn College

INFORMATION AGE PUBLISHING, INC.
Charlotte, NC • www.infoagepub.com

Library of Congress Cataloging-in-Publication Data

Young children and the arts : nurturing imagination and creativity / edited
by Carol Korn-Bursztyn.
   p. cm.
 Includes bibliographical references.
 ISBN 978-1-61735-743-5 (pbk.) – ISBN 978-1-61735-744-2 (hardcover) –
ISBN 978-1-61735-745-9 (ebook)
 1. Arts–Study and teaching (Early childhood) 2. Creative ability in
children. I. Korn-Bursztyn, Carol, 1953-
 LB1139.5.A78Y68 2012
 372.5–dc23

                               2011052470

Printed in the United States of America

DEDICATION

I dedicate this book to Uriel and Julian,
whose creative energies inspire and delight.

CONTENTS

PART I

EXPERIENCE, CREATIVITY AND IMAGINATION IN THE EARLY YEARS

PART II

IMAGINATION AND THE ARTS: CASE STUDIES FROM THE FIELD

ACKNOWLEDGEMENTS

This book has deep roots in my own professional development as an educator and psychologist. I would like to thank my teachers at Oranim, particularly Malka Haas, whose singular commitment to the arts in early education and to understanding young children's needs was deeply inspirational. I would also like to thank the families, children and staff at the Early Childhood Center at Brooklyn College, with whom I worked for many years, for teaching me about how imagination informs and shapes reality.

My colleagues in the School of Education at Brooklyn College, and in the PhD Program in Urban Education at the Graduate Center of the City University of New York are a continued source of intellectual and creative inspiration. I would also like to thank my graduate students at Brooklyn College and at the Graduate Center for their generosity in sharing ideas and experiences. I would also like to thank my teaching artist and other arts colleagues from various New York City institutions with whom I've worked closely in teacher education, and in sharing ideas about the role of the arts in the lives of children and adults. I would especially like to thank all the contributors to this volume, whose collective wisdom is a source of enrichment.

I would like to thank Brooklyn College for providing me with the time to complete the manuscript, and PSC-CUNY for providing me with support to conduct the field research that resulted in this book.

I would like to thank George Johnson and the editorial team at IAP for their helpful suggestions and guidance in producing this book.

Finally, I'd like to thank Alberto Bursztyn, my partner, best friend and collaborator for his unwavering support and encouragement.

PREFACE

Young Children and the Arts: Nurturing Imagination and Creativity examines the place of the arts in the experiences of young and very young children at home and in out-of-home settings at school and in the community. *Young Children and the Arts: Nurturing Imagination and Creativity* offers an approach to integrating the arts in early education that draws upon both the theoretical and the applied. It presents a comprehensive approach to the arts that is aligned with early childhood developmentally appropriate practice and that combines an exploratory, materials-based approach with an aesthetic education approach for children from birth to eight years of age. It addresses how the arts are foundational to learning, and how teachers, parents and caregivers can nurture young children's developing imagination and creativity.

Young Children and the Arts: Nurturing Imagination and Creativity presents valuable guidelines for early childhood teachers, families, caregivers and community organizations who seek to introduce young children to participatory experiences in the visual arts, dance, music, and storytelling/theater. The models presented emphasize a participatory approach, introducing young children to the arts through activities that call for engagement, initiative and creative activity. The models presented are suitable for adaptation to specific locales and situations and explain how educators can work collaboratively with children, artists, cultural arts organizations, families, and communities to bring the arts into early childhood classrooms.

INTRODUCTION

Young Children and the Arts: Nurturing Imagination and Creativity presents an integrated model for the arts in the early years that explores the intersection of creative expression, experience, and the arts in the early years. It offers an approach to integrating the arts in early education that draws upon the theoretical and the applied, and presents models suitable for adaptation to classrooms, homes, and community based settings. This model also demonstrates how educators can work collaboratively with children, artists, cultural arts organizations, families, and communities to bring the arts into settings where young children live and learn.

Young Children and the Arts: Nurturing Imagination and Creativity examines the role of the arts in the lives of young children, and their impact on the development of children from the preschool years through age eight. It addresses how the arts (visual, performing, and literary) are foundational to high quality early education and suggests implications for how the arts can inform and impact educational practice. The book draws on children's engagement with the arts in their own creative use of materials and ideas and also in their response to works of art. In this model the classroom and the community are sites of creative activity across multiple learning modalities including schools, early childhood centers, homes, and community cultural arts organizations and venues.

Young Children and the Arts is divided into two parts. The first, *Part I: Experience, Creativity and Imagination in the Early Years*, written by Carol Korn-Bursztyn, introduces the reader to the importance of developing young children's creativity and imaginative capacity and addresses how early childhood settings and families can facilitate this process. The two opening chapters, *Defining a Place for the Arts in Early Education* and *Families and Communities: Supporting Imagination and Creativity in the Early Years*, examine, respectively, the intersection of high quality early childhood education and the arts, and the policy implications for broadening children's experiences in the arts by posing and responding to a series of questions.

The third and fourth chapters take a psychological bent that explores the connections between young children's development and the arts. *On Creating Meaningful Experience: A Relational Approach to the Arts* (Chapter 3) introduces and explores the connections between young children's psychological processes, developing capacity for relationships, narrative, and the role of meaningful experience. A developmental line for imagination, with the social imagination paving the way for the capacity for symbolic representation in language and storytelling, musical or embodied representation, and iconic or pictorial representation is traced in *Cultivating Imagination and Creative Thinking* (Chapter 4).

Part II: Imagination and the Arts: Case Studies from the Field, authored or co-authored by colleagues, presents vignettes of applied experience with young children by practitioners across a range of art forms, including the visual arts, theater, literature, music, and dance. Chapter 5, *Joy in the Making: Young Children and the Visual Arts* by Kirsten Cole, provides parents and teachers with a language for understanding and describing the importance of young children's work in the visual arts, and describes strategies and practices for fostering meaningful experiences in the visual arts. Chapter 6, *Museum Visits with Young Children: A Teaching Artist's Perspective*, based on an interview with Barbara Ellmann by Judith Hill Bose and written by Carol Korn-Bursztyn, explores museum visits by teachers and parents with children, from early childhood through the elementary school years. The chapter poses a series of questions, leading the reader from the initial steps of considering a museum visit, to planning and preparing experiences that can enrich and deepen children's experiences.

Chapter 7, *Art-Making with Young Children with Disabilities*, co-authored by Dana Freed and Alberto Bursztyn, explores the impact of the visual arts on the development of children with autism. Chapter 8, *Integrating the Theater Arts: Creativity and Inclusion* by Barbara E. O'Neill, presents adult-led storytelling and other forms of theater arts as activities that can be used to foster an inclusive, developmentally appropriate early childhood classroom environment. The chapter provides readers with the tools to create their own approaches to integrating the theater arts into their work with children with and without disabilities. In Chapter 9, *Playworlds and Early Literary Arts Education*, Beth Ferholt introduces the concept of playworlds, a pedagogy based on Vygotsky's theories of play, art, imagination, and creativity in which children and adults engage in adult–child joint play.

In Chapter 10, *A Journey of Musical Collaboration,* Judith Hill Bose describes a collaborative journey into the study of music with young children in which she explores live musical performances through a case study of children's own music making and reflection-in-action. A detailed description of the collaborative process in which activities and experiences were co-designed with early childhood teachers provides an up-close view of the applied work. Andrew Aprile discusses creative approaches to African music education for young and very young children in Chapter 11, *Music-making with Young Children: African Orff and Rhythmic Intelligence.* He explores the possibilities of multicultural music education and proposes that African music proves a promising starting point for the development of children's rhythm and musicality. Herman Jiesamfoek, in Chapter 12, *Dance and Play,* takes on the contemporary challenges of encouraging children to leave digital media aside, and of helping their parents and teachers support spontaneous physical movement and dance. Jiesamfoek provides five cross-cultural vignettes of children engaged in spontaneous physical play: three in New York City, one in the Netherlands, and one in a Surinamese Bush Negro village.

PART I

EXPERIENCE, CREATIVITY AND IMAGINATION
IN THE EARLY YEARS

CHAPTER 1

DEFINING A PLACE FOR THE ARTS IN EARLY EDUCATION

Carol Korn-Bursztyn
Brooklyn College
and City University of New York

ABSTRACT

This chapter examines the place of the arts in the early childhood years by posing and responding to a series of questions that address early childhood education and the arts. A review of best practices in early childhood education provides a framework for exploring the arts for young and very young children in school and in home and community settings. The arts and early education are explored within a constructivist approach to early education.

INTRODUCTION

The following chapter will explore and define the place of the arts in early childhood settings. It will introduce and respond to five pragmatic questions that address the intersection of early childhood education and the arts at points of convergence, and at moments of tension. Nesting within each of the questions are subsets of questions and topics that provide con-

Young Children and the Arts, pages 3–20
Copyright © 2012 by Information Age Publishing

3

text and that help to frame an applied approach to creating arts suffused early childhood experiences. Taking a developmental approach, the early childhood years are defined here as beginning with birth and extending through the eighth year. The arts are defined here as inclusive of dance, music, theater, the visual arts and literature.

The questions that follow begin with a general overview of early childhood practice, and an exploration of the place of the arts in the experiences of young and very young children both in and out-of-school. This is followed by an exploration of tensions in the field between competing models of early childhood practice and their implications for the arts in early education. Additionally, varied approaches to developing arts experiences with and for young children will be described, and arts programs consistent with best practices in early education envisioned for children from birth to age eight.

QUESTIONS

Question One

What constitutes early education? Where does early childhood education, both formal and informal, take place? How are early childhood teachers prepared?

- Child care: family child care, center based care—publicly and privately funded.
- Teacher credentials.

Early education denotes a broad range of ages and developmental levels, beginning with birth and extending through the eighth year. Early childhood education takes place in a wide variety of settings, including the home, family child care, publicly and privately funded center-based child care, faith-based institutions, and public and private schools. Head Start programs provide programs for low-income preschool and kindergarten aged children, while Early Head Start provides programs for pregnant, low-income women and their children from birth to age three.

A shortage of child care programs in both low- and middle-income neighborhoods for infants and toddlers has created a boon for private family day care providers, many of whom offer programs out of their private homes, at competitive rates. It should be noted, however, that unlike other professional categories for which states certify practitioners, the designation "teacher" is not protected by state or national licensure/certification. Though child care providers are routinely referred to as teachers, many providers do not hold early childhood teacher certification or licensure.

Teacher preparation across the nation is highly variable, ranging from providers with no higher education to teachers with master's degrees, or higher, in education. The level of academic preparation required for teaching young children varies state by state. In general, higher levels of academic preparation are required for publicly financed pre-K, Kindergarten, first and second grade, while requirements in the private sector are often considerably lower. Programs for infants and toddlers tend to employ caregivers with limited formal academic preparation. Highly qualified teachers are in short supply, due in large part to the low pay early childhood educators typically earn in family- and center-based child care.

Efforts to professionalize the practice of early education have focused on provision of in-service professional development training and on developing career ladders to assist caregivers in obtaining higher education leading to teacher certification. Professional development activities are largely unregulated and occur with less frequency than desirable, especially in the private sector. Teacher preparation is highly salient to the practice of early childhood education, and especially to an orientation to the arts. Higher levels of teacher preparedness are more closely associated with what the field considers to be best practice in early education.

Question Two

What are key principles and prevailing theories in early childhood education, and why are these important to nurturing imagination and creativity in young children?

- What constitutes high quality early education? What is meant by the imagination? By creativity?
- What is Developmentally Appropriate Practice? (National Association for the Education of Young Children)
- Piaget's theory of intellectual development.
- Vygotsky's theory of development.
- Gardner's theory of multiple intelligences.
- Sternberg's triarchic theory of intelligence.

The National Association for the Education of Young Children (NAEYC), the accrediting body for early childhood teacher education programs and for early childhood settings where children are served, sets benchmark standards for high quality early childhood education. These standards are nationally recognized for quality early education and care programs for young children, and for culturally and linguistically sensitive developmentally appropriate practice or DAP. DAP provides guidelines according to child age and developmental level for curriculum development, and for matching adult expectations to children's developmental needs and achievements.

A developmentally appropriate curriculum, for example, provides for a classroom environment in which young children's social-emotional, physical, creative expression and aesthetic development are all furthered. It provides for cognitive development, specifically in the areas of language and literacy, mathematical and scientific thinking, and family and community studies. Especially relevant to the arts is the strong emphasis that NAEYC places on fostering play, child-directed activities, and social interaction.

Consistent with standards for high quality early education, the arts in early education place a premium on child initiative, rather than teacher-directed activities. In the visual arts, for example, this takes the form of unstructured and varied materials in a well ordered environment in which materials are carefully selected and organized within children's reach. Dance in a DAP classroom, for example, involves children moving in highly individual ways to music, rather than learning a series of dance steps. High quality early childhood programs place a premium on activities that encourage, rather than hinder, the development of imagination in children. A multi-sensory curriculum in which children are encouraged to see, touch, hear, smell and taste are key to the development of imagination in the early years. In the early years, experientially-rich activities are primarily sensory in nature. Rich experience, those experiences in which children act upon what their senses have engaged, are central to developing imagination in the early years.

Imagination is tied to the real world in which children live; it is both reality-bound and a process that encourages exploration of both materials and ideas. Children make meaning through imagination by first gaining direct experience through sensory engagement, and later, through their revisiting and embellishing experience in play or with artistic media. As noted in Chapter 2, imagination is a function of a growing capacity for reflection on experience and for independent thinking. In early childhood, reflection occurs in action—through the marks, sounds, and images that children produce. By providing opportunity to visit and revisit experience in thought and through action, imagination helps children understand their experience and give expression to their embodied understanding.

When young children participate physically in an experience—when they move to music they are listening to or pretend to hold an imaginary instrument like the musician they see on stage, or join in during a story-telling performance—they develop ability to reflect on experience, ability foundational to growing cognitive ability. This is a point often lost in the current zeitgeist of early literacy, where paper-and-pencil skill development exercises substitute for child initiated, physical activity. An example is provided by an early childhood director who complains of an unruly three year-old who refuses "to do his work"—tracing letters and shapes—and crawls under a table in protest.

While imagination in the early years reflects mental processes, young children's creative acts give expression to growing capacity to act in the world. Their creative acts provide an entry point into understanding how the mind develops in the early years. Like imagination, creativity is associated with children's experiences in the real world. Not to be confused with imitative activity—itself a precursor to creativity—creative acts provide expression of children's embodied understanding, as informed by their imaginative process. Good early childhood programs provide ample opportunities for children to engage their developing imaginative capacity in creative efforts. They provide rich experiences for young children and provide multiple means by which children can reflect upon their experience in action. Teachers and caregivers talk with children, read books about common experience, and provide them with the creative arts materials through which they can reflect-in-action on their experiences in the real world.

Early childhood developmentally appropriate practice is grounded in Jean Piaget's theory of cognitive development (1936/1963,1937/1954, 1929/2007), which emphasizes both the principle of developmental readiness and the role of children's self-directed activity in developing cognitive capacity. Children construct understanding of natural phenomena by acting on the world; their thinking and the ways in which they understand the world change qualitatively as they grow.

Piaget's theoretical approach to cognitive development provides the underpinnings of constructivist theory, a highly influential approach to the teaching of math and science in the childhood years. At each stage of development, Piaget proposed, children re-organize and re-structure their understanding of the world, in accordance with their developmental achievements. Children's spontaneous remarks and productions provide insight into their developing minds; each stage of childhood—and especially early childhood—is qualitatively different from that which preceded it.

Early childhood classrooms that take a developmental-interaction approach most closely approximate Piaget's theory as applied to education. These classrooms are busy, yet highly organized, environments where children are encouraged to take initiative, act autonomously, and engage in creative activity. Play and active exploration are encouraged, and arts activities are a regular feature. The role of teachers and other adults is to support children's interest by providing materials and a warm and intellectually lively presence. The adult presence is supportive, helping children develop and sustain an inquiry-oriented attitude towards learning, while negotiating the complex task of building social relationships with others. These early childhood classrooms are consistent with developmentally appropriate practice—and are on the wane in both the public and the private sectors.

Writing roughly at the same time as Piaget but unknown to him at the time, a Swiss genetic epistemologist in the early 1920s and 1930s, Lev Vygotsky, a Russian psychologist, emphasized the role of language and the imagination in the development of thinking in the early years (1962, 2004). Vygotsky's major contributions were his emphasis on the capacity for language as a distinguishing feature of the human species, the social and cultural embeddedness of human experience and learning, and his concept of the zone of proximal development or ZPD (Cole, John-Steiner, Scribner & Souberman, 1930/1978.)

Vygotsky's ZPD had its origins in his emphasis on the grounding of learning and the development of thought in the social and cultural environments in which children live and grow. He maintained that intellectual capacity occurs within a range: the lower limits represented by what a child can accomplish independently and the upper limits by what the same child can accomplish under the guidance of an older figure—a teacher, another adult or an older child. Vygotsky's theory leaned heavily on a viewpoint that placed social interaction at its core. The child's environment was, he posited, inherently social, and steeped in the cultural context in which the child lived.

From a Vygotskian perspective, social interaction is a central component of a constructivist approach, which emphasizes children's activity, including interactions with others, as part of the human learning environment. Ironically, Vygotsky's zone of proximal development is often presented within the context of direct instruction, rather than the active, social-constructivist approach to concept development his work supports.

The role of language occupied another significant component of Vygotsky's theory. He proposed that language enabled the development of thought and the capacity for imagination. An early advocate of the Russian Revolution (later bitterly disappointed by Stalinism), Vygotsky's emphasis on language was connected to a project of personal and social freedom. By dint of imagination, people were freed from the constricting realities of their lives and able to imagine other ways of being. He traced the imaginative capacity to early childhood, where imagination, rooted in reality and not fantasy, laid claim to real experiences in children's lives. In this, Vygotsky took issue with Freud's (1930/2010) emphasis on the pleasure principle and wish fulfillment in early childhood, affirming that the child's imagination was firmly rooted in lived experience, rather than instinctually driven or infused with desirous fantasies or wishes.

Vygotsky proposed that intelligence is shaped by one's cultural milieu and by what society deems valuable. He argued against isolation of those children deemed different for physiological, psychological or cognitive reasons, and emphasized the compensatory abilities that arise from such deficits. Implicitly building on Vygotsky's contributions, Howard Gardner's

(2000) theory of multiple intelligences, or MI, similarly challenged the idea of intelligence as a fixed entity, and posited that diverse abilities represent diverse intelligences.

Much beloved by early childhood teachers for whom multiple intelligences resonate with their observations of child behavior, MI has had disappointingly little relevance to actual classroom practice. A casualty of the charge to increase children's discrete skill performance in areas deemed directly relevant to scholastic achievement, MI has fared a fate similar to that of the arts in education. Like an arts-based approach to education, MI posits multiple points of entry into learning, dependent upon each child's unique profile. Of the eight multiple intelligences currently posited by Gardner (linguistic, logical-mathematical, spatial, bodily-kinesthetic, musical, interpersonal, intrapersonal, naturalistic, and possibly existential and spiritual intelligences), six are directly applicable to the visual and performing arts: these are bodily-kinesthetic, visual-spatial, linguistic, interpersonal, intrapersonal, and musical intelligences.

Robert Sternberg's (1985) practical or "street smart" intelligence most closely resembles Vygotsky's notion of culturally and socially situated intelligence. Following Gardner (2000, 2004), Sternberg also takes issue with intelligence as a fixed entity given to measurement through intelligence tests that heavily rely on linguistic capabilities, which he calls analytical intelligence. Sternberg's triarchic theory of intelligence recognizes creative intelligence, the ability to draw on prior knowledge and skills to deal with new challenges, as one of three forms of intelligence (analytical, creative/ synthetic and practical intelligences).

Question Three

What are the prevailing tensions in early childhood education, and how do these tensions impact the arts?

- Disagreement about the aims of early education, especially about how to best prepare children for school, or school-readiness.
- Social/emotional development versus academic skill development.
- Play-based, exploratory curriculum versus teacher-directed activities.
- High structure and control (limited mobility and choice) versus flexible structure (greater mobility and choice).
- Obedience to adult authority versus initiative and (fear of) defiance.
- Limited scope of arts.

Contemporary revision of curricular practices in early childhood education focuses on skill development in discrete content areas. This is a significant departure from the early childhood professional practice of following an integrated curriculum that is inclusive of children's affective and developmental needs. In the early childhood classroom, this has meant an increased emphasis on a fairly narrow range of academic skills acquisition— primarily literacy, and secondarily, numeracy. Many New York City school districts, for example, call for extended blocks of time devoted exclusively to literacy and mathematics skill development; teachers report that they must scramble to find time for mandated social studies and science lessons.

This trend is accompanied by a concurrent decrease in emphasis on social skill development, play and creative endeavor, including the arts. It is not unusual to find that when offered, the creative arts are squeezed in-between bathroom/wash-up and lunch times. Even Kindergarten has been reconfigured as preparation for the lengthy regimens of skill development instituted in first grade. Pre-Kindergarten, or what was referred to in more leisured times as "nursery," serves the purpose of preparing children for Kindergarten.

Child care, public and non-public, unsurprisingly has come to resemble prep school for pre-Kindergarten. Greater emphasis on the importance of early education has led to pronounced tensions in the field, especially between advocates of play-based curriculum and proponents of direct instruction of early reading and numeracy skills. Early literacy underlined the importance of language development and early exposure to print literacy for all children, but also resulted in a tilt away from social/emotional development towards academic skill preparation. In many early-childhood settings, school readiness activities have resulted in an emphasis on teacher directed activities, and a decrease in children's mobility in the classroom. Diminished opportunity for play has resulted in fewer opportunities for children to learn how to resolve frictions with peers in order to keep playing.

The phenomenon of decreased opportunity for play intersects with the areas of greatest concern and anxiety for teachers, especially beginning teachers—teacher authority and classroom management. This has great impact on the arts, which have suffered marginalization in programs for toddlers through classes for first and second graders. There is widespread apprehension among both early childhood teachers and child care providers that the arts will lead to disruptive behavior, loss of teacher-control, and in the visual arts, mess. The specter of messiness provokes teacher fear that the arts will provide license for irresponsible freedom, and that the invisible lines that mark the boundaries of acceptable behavior will be blurred. Messiness and the risk of disorder provoke teacher (and administrator) dread of a breakdown of adult authority, commonly expressed as fear of children "going wild" or "out of control."

Teacher apprehension has resulted in a severely limited scope of the arts offered in many early childhood classrooms. Activities that require a minimum of movement, such as storytelling, for example, are favored. Activities that involve movement, such as dance and music that might give the appearance of disorder and loss of teacher control, are avoided. Paint and clay have been edited out of many classrooms; crayons and markers, are favored, as are teacher-prepared cut-outs, particularly in advance of holidays.

As noted earlier in this volume, the arts provide a metaphor for tension between freedom and boundaries in education. The reluctance to dip into the messiness and perceived disorder of the arts is a stand-in for concerns about the optimal balance between freedom and structure, expression and boundaries. High quality early childhood pedagogy is an aesthetic practice that requires its teacher/practitioners to develop proficiency in creating the structures that children need in order to work freely.

When young children, for example, become familiar with art materials and with the procedures and expectations that govern the use of various art materials, they learn that freedom to explore and create takes place within a structure and framework that their teacher guides. Familiarity with arts materials—learning their properties and becoming skillful in their use—is an important first step for children. The skillful teacher or other adult creates a learning environment in which children can learn the procedures that govern autonomous activity, such as where to get fresh paper and where to place completed artwork, and how to replace brushes in paint holders. The framework that the teacher creates provides a framework or structure within which children learn how to exercise autonomy and freedom responsibly. The arts provide many clear examples of how environments may be organized to support children's growing sense of autonomy, ability to make choices, and to develop ideas freely and without constraints.

Question Four

What is art for young children? What are the relationships—and what are the tensions—between art making and aesthetic education in the early years?

- Art making; tension between process and product; unstructured and structured.
- Aesthetic education.
- Metaphoric thinking, critical thinking and the arts.

There is often a significant disconnect between what is considered best practice in early childhood pedagogy—which provides pride of place to the arts and to play—and actual, field-based practices. While the National Association for the Education of Young Children (NAEYC) offers national accreditation for early childhood center-based programs based upon adherence to standards of best practices in early education, accreditation is wholly voluntary. Teachers and caregivers often know less about the arts and about how to structure arts experiences for young children across the early childhood age spectrum than they wish. While typically favorably disposed to the arts, they are often hesitant to engage in activities with which they have little experience and about which they have many fears. Teacher education programs tend to offer limited instruction in how to work in the arts with young children, while in-service professional development activities typically address school readiness and classroom management techniques.

Two significant tensions in early childhood education find their fullest expression in the arts. These are the tensions between child-initiated and directed activity, and between process-oriented and product-oriented activity. Both of these tensions are fully and readily observed in the visual arts, which is often the only art form represented in classrooms, albeit in limited and sometimes distorted form. The visual arts in early education have traditionally focused on exploration of materials and on free and unhindered expression with unstructured materials such as paint, clay, crayon and other media. As noted earlier, fewer opportunities are provided to children in early education today to work with materials that appear messy to teachers and child care providers, such as paints and clay.

The second, related tension in early childhood education is between process and product. Early childhood pedagogy has long emphasized process over product in children's art, and children's initiative rather than teacher-direction. In practice, a heavier teacher-hand has the often desired effect of limiting childish spontaneity, creating fewer possibilities for mess. Teachers often spend inordinate amounts of time pre-cutting shapes and duplicating forms for children to color in anticipation of crafts activities. The children, it should be noted, are generally enthusiastic about these activities. Structured and limiting as they are, they offer greater opportunity for spontaneity and expressiveness than the drill and practice regimens of school readiness activities.

Music in early childhood pedagogy is closely associated with movement, early instrumentation and song. However, in many early childhood classrooms today, music is presented as background, rather than foreground. Teachers are often ill-prepared to work with music as a foreground experience. Song is applied in the service of classroom management, as in the "clean-up song," during transitions between activities, or not at all. Instruments, where available, are typically not readily available for exploratory activity, but are locked away in cabinets. Similarly, few opportunities for dance are typically provided; teachers and caregivers are largely unfamiliar with how to work within this art form, and as noted elsewhere, are loathe to risk children moving in unpredictable ways.

In recent years, as community arts organizations and museums have expanded outreach into early childhood classrooms, aesthetic education has offered an alternate approach to the historic emphasis on materials-based practice in early education. In the aesthetic education approach, the focal point of study is a work of art, typically created by an adult artist. There is an inherent tension between aesthetic education and early childhood tradition. Early childhood educators may be reluctant to introduce works of art by adult artists into early childhood classrooms out of concern that a) children's experiential learning will take a back seat to teacher-directed activity, and b) adult-created works will be valorized at the expense of children's own artistic productions.

Aesthetic education with young children typically involves partnership with a cultural arts organization, and the in-class presence of a teaching artist. In this approach close study of a museum-quality work of art involves collective looking and talking about what the children observe, and the meanings that they derive from their observations. Experiential learning through materials-based exploration is an important adjunct to close study of works of art. Work with art materials, movement, storytelling, sound and music optimally precede and follow structured group activities. These are best co-developed and co-led by teaching artists and classroom teachers, though as a result of insufficient opportunity for joint planning, these are often developed and led solely by teaching artists.

Depending on the age of the children—and on the inclinations of teacher and teacher artist—the arts based activities that follow may be entirely unstructured, or some adult-direction may be provided. Optimally, selection of the work of art as well as planning for arts activities should be related to the children's interests; often these are related to curriculum under study. Aesthetic education, too, treads a fine line between honoring the arts as disciplinary practice, and as supportive of other, primarily curricular aims that are external to the arts.

Cultural arts organizations, teaching artists, and museum educators often provide a mix of approaches to the arts, with some organizations tilting more in the direction of close study of works of art, while for others, the tilt is towards materials-based, experiential work. The arts, both materials-based, and aesthetic education-based, provide an important function in the development of creative thinking, as noted in Chapter 2. In the section that follows, I present a vision of arts-suffused experiences for children in the early childhood years, from birth through age eight that integrates a materials-based, experiential approach as well as an aesthetic education (AE) approach.

Question Five

How can arts experiences be created for and with young children, birth through age eight?

- The arts and children ages birth through two years.
- The arts and children ages three through five.
- The arts and children ages six through eight.

The arts and children ages birth through two years.

Child development in the first years of life can be viewed through the lenses of growing intentionality, social relatedness, and beginning capacity for symbolic representation. It should be noted that the ages presented in this essay are rough approximations only; there is great individual variation in young children's development, especially for children with special needs. The years from birth to age two mark the beginnings of intentionality and deliberate action, as indicated by active exploration, movement, and early language development, beginning with production of sound. The years from birth through the second year are also characterized by growing body-awareness, and by a developing sense of social awareness of oneself in relation to others. Cognitive development in the first two years of life is rapid, with capacity for symbolic functioning first manifested during these early months and years.

The achievement of early language marks the very young child's growing capacity for symbolic function. Language serves a dual role: it both stimulates and creates capacity for symbolic representation. As language develops, children's play begins to take on greater symbolic meaning. Concurrently, young children begin to gain greater understanding of themselves in relation to others, especially to their caregivers. Dramatic play first emerges in toddlers, typically as enactments of care-giving acts, an early mimesis of their own experiences of being cared for—and an early identification with care-giving figures.

Appreciation for storytelling and theater arise from young children's early symbolic attempts at recreating and reenacting early experience from the positions of both the one who provides, and the one who receives care. In the very early years, narrative and storytelling introduce children to theater by telling and retelling narratives that resonate with young children's own lived experience. Early narrative development in young children is linked to their growing experience of story. The development of early narrative ability overlaps with early education's approach to early literacy, which also seeks to develop young children's storytelling ability. There is also overlap between young children's early experience of creating theater in their dramatic representations of early experience, including imitation of social interactions and scripts, and the emphasis on play in developmentally appropriate early childhood practice.

The arts offer both a means of participating in shared human experience and a means of symbolic representation. Mark-making is the earliest symbolic means by which older infants and young toddlers leave a visual imprint of their presence, whether these are handprints in cereal at meal-time, in play-doh (a precursor to clay), or in the sandbox. Taking an experiential, materials-based approach, activities that promote sensory exploration and that enable babies and toddlers to act on the world—and to appreciate the results of their actions—are characteristic of both exploratory play and early art-making.

Children who grow with a sense of love and security display greater exploratory behavior, which leads to increased cognitive development. Activities that further exploration or what is known as exploratory play, whether this consists of exploring the properties of musical instruments, crayons, sand, water or objects, furthers cognitive development in young children. Consequently, experiences that are meaningful and that lead to intellectual growth are those that meld emotionally significant experience with opportunity for exploration and experimentation in a safe, supportive, and intellectually stimulating environment.

An early aesthetic education approach to the visual arts with babies and young toddlers draws on their inclination to attend visually to their environment. Selection of works of art for the very young children needs to be undertaken with great care. They need to be of high interest in order to encourage sustained attention. Simple pictures of recognizable figures and objects are, for example, intrinsically interesting to very young children as they grow in their capacity for symbol formation. When children can hold, point to and mouth pictures of faces, people and simple, everyday objects, they embody study of abstract images, becoming familiar with symbolic representations of everyday events.

The aesthetic education approach described here is complementary to an exploratory, materials-based approach that is characterized by children's unfettered exploration of and use of materials that can provide the means of leaving their mark on the world. The role of aesthetic education with very young children is to expand children's experiential worlds, and to deepen their understanding through encouraging reflection in action. This approach may be applied to various art forms, including visual arts (as noted above), music, dance, and theater. Music and dance in an early arts program can readily combine elements of experiential-based arts with aesthetic education experiences.

Very young children respond to sound and music with their own movement and sound production. Not only do very young children spontaneously move to music they hear, they also move in response to dancers' movements. An aesthetic education approach that introduces very young children to works of art may well draw on an early capacity to mimic what others do, and to feel what they feel, too. An approach to music and to dance that integrates experiential learning through doing with the aesthetic-education practice of introducing works of art, can provide a powerful approach to the arts with very young children.

In general, arts education for very young children is largely the domain of small, private entrepreneurs who offer programs of variable quality. Music literacy for young children is largely in the hands of private, commercial interests. Music for infants, for example, is marketed with the aim of enhancing measured cognitive functioning, rather than for its value as disciplinary knowledge. Interactive programs that engage babies, young toddlers and their parents or caregivers in early arts activities are rare within center-based child care programs. Early arts for infants and toddlers should optimally be based upon an experiential, interactive approach that incorporates exploratory and sensory-based learning, in a warm, supportive environment. Adding an aesthetic education tilt, very young children can also be introduced to works of art in music and dance, the study of which is through the children's own embodied, physical activity.

The arts and children ages three through five.

The period of development between the ages of three and five is marked by rapid development of early symbolic ability, and capacity for social interaction with a widening circle, especially including peers. Language skills and narrative ability develop quickly; children are increasingly able to give language to emotions, and can revisit, embellish, and re-enact scripts of everyday life through symbolic play and art-making. Art making remains primarily process-oriented for children, though this period is marked by children's growing awareness of art-making as both process and product.

As children become increasingly self-aware, they become more aware of themselves in relation to others. Friendships gain in importance, and play becomes gradually more socialized. With developing capacity for symbolic representation, play in the years between three and five becomes increasingly creative. By this, I mean that their play, referred to in early childhood parlance as dramatic play, bears the imprint of a growing capacity to work and rework everyday experience in the imagination. Symbolic or dramatic play is the representation of children's growing capacity for imagination and its expression in creative play.

The creative play of young children is typically inflected by the scripts of their everyday lives, and by narratives of their own invention. As children's language becomes more sophisticated, their ability to use symbols, or what Vygotsky termed symbolic function, increases as well. This has the effect of a growth in capacity to represent lived experience more fully and in richer detail in both narrative and in dramatic play. When children are introduced to theater, they often display their familiarity with this genre through active audience participation. Children from three to five increasingly act upon their physical environment. They also typically seek social interaction and enjoy active audience participation and interactive performances.

Young children who experience delays in exploratory behavior or in ease of social interaction can benefit from an approach to the arts that encourages active exploring and creating with materials, story, sound, and movement, and that promotes guided interaction with others. Incorporating an aesthetic education approach through introducing works of art in the varied art forms has the added benefit of helping young children understand art as activity participated in by children and adults, rather than the exclusive domain of childhood. Often, the resonances of children's interactive, experiential learning together with their experiences with works of art are recognizable in the children's own creative activities.

An aesthetic education approach linked to materials-based practice in the visual arts can add a social component to early arts learning in the visual arts. When children are encouraged to explore materials and to create artwork independent of adult directives, they quickly develop familiarity with the tools and materials of the visual arts. Similarly, an approach to developing performing arts literacies in music, dance, and theater optimally draws on children's activity and active exploration of music and dance through active listening, responding, making music, and dancing.

Following an aesthetic education approach, children's active responses, earlier described as reflection in action, are engaged in language, as well. Aesthetic education experiences provide opportunities to engage children in guided conversation about works of art. Guided conversation based on the children's observations or noticing helps them to translate reflection-in-action to reflection-in-language. This helps children develop capacity for symbolic representation. In young children, it should be noted, the two processes of reflection-in-action and reflection-in-language are typically intertwined. Young children commonly embody their observations, leaping up to point to a detail in a painting or to mime a dance movement or gesture, even as their gestures may be accompanied by language.

Reflection-in-language is closely aligned with growing capacity to inhibit action and to self-regulate behavior. Introducing children to the vocabularies of the arts enhances their developing capacity for symbolic representation. Introduction to the musical concept of notation, for example, was quickly recognized by a group of three year-old children as akin to writing, an activity with which they were familiar from their the early literacy practice of writing and displaying children's stories and responses to group activities.

Development of music literacy in young children optimally begins with developing close familiarity with the art form. Taking an experiential learning approach, young children can be introduced to unstructured opportunities to interactively hear and respond to music with their bodies (clapping, stomping, tapping) and with an assortment of simple instruments. As in the visual arts, familiarity with materials occurs alongside growing visual literacy. It precedes deliberate teacher or teaching-artist led close study of works of art. As children become increasingly comfortable with music, they can benefit from aesthetic education activities that focus on a work of art and that build on children's ability to notice and to respond. As noted earlier, introduction of a vocabulary specific to music enhances children's conceptual development, and it has the added pedagogic benefit of creating cross-disciplinary connections.

Movement is the first language of childhood. It is through movement that children first explore their surroundings, and through movement that they develop a growing sense of body awareness, and a capacity to self-regulate their physical responses. Dance provides an opportunity for children to explore what their bodies can do in space, to acquire greater awareness of their bodies and of the spaces that they and their peers occupy. Like music, dance experiences teach children to listen carefully, and to be mindful of the space occupied by others. Through active engagement in dance exploration, children learn not only how to initiate movement, but also, importantly, how to stop moving, too.

Growing capacity to reflect upon experience, in movement and in language, lends support to integration of experiential-based arts learning with aesthetic education. Taking an experiential approach, as children grow in their capacity for symbolic representation, they can represent their feelings in movement and dance. From an aesthetic education perspective, study of a dance performance through movement, reflection-in-action and in-language can deepen children's dance literacy, while strengthening their capacity for creative thinking.

The arts and children six through eight.

The years between six and eight see rapid development of symbolic function, as reflected in children's artistic productions, which become increasingly representational of both lived experience and fantasy. During these years, children begin to appreciate art as both process and product. As a result of growing capacity for self awareness, some children may become increasingly critical of their own efforts in comparison with the work of others. This is especially pronounced in the visual arts, especially in settings where the arts serve as illustration.

An integrated approach to visual arts literacy addresses both the primacy of children's creative work and their growing participation in social and cultural life. Six to eight year-old children, who have experience with a broad range of arts materials (such as paints, media for drawing, clay and collage) are increasingly able to benefit from learning approaches to painting, drawing, collage, and sculpture. Close study of works of art have the benefit of helping children see their own creative efforts as being connected to the cultural life of a society in which they are active participants. At the same time, an aesthetic education approach that introduces children to an interactive approach to museums, galleries, and digital media can help create meaningful arts experiences that can inspire young artists.

Music learning in the years between six and eight may also be addressed in an integrative manner, with a dual emphasis on music making coupled with close study of music performance. Experiential learning is deepened by access to instruments; some children are ready for beginning instruction in instrumental technique. Both experiential and aesthetic education approaches to music literacy have in common an emphasis on the place of music in people's lives. Music learning is readily connected with community and social studies curriculum in the early grades, and especially with consideration of the cross-cultural phenomenon of music and dance.

Similarly, dance literacy may be addressed through an integrated approach that combines dance and movement experience with an aesthetic education approach that takes up close study of dance performance. Children between the ages of six and eight are expected to be proficient at taking turns and capable of working in small groups. In reflecting on a performance, children in this age range are better able to reflect on their observations in language. Greater capacity for recall will help children to remember sequences of movements they have observed, and to revisit these in creating their own dance movements. While younger children will require some adult assistance to sequence some dance movements as a group, children at the upper limits of the early childhood range (age eight) will likely be able to work cooperatively to create a performance.

CONCLUSION

Arts-suffused experiences are consistent with early childhood educational practice that fosters curiosity, exploration, experimentation, and dramatic play. The arts have in common with best practices in early education, an emphasis on child-initiated activity, rather than adult-directed activity. Early arts programs should, like high quality early childhood programs, take a participatory approach, introducing young children to the arts through activities that call for exploration, initiative, social engagement, and creative activity. In the chapter that follows, I will explore how innovative arts policy can support early arts initiatives across diverse settings in which young children and their families live, work, and learn.

REFERENCES

Cole, M., John-Steiner, V., Scribner, S., & Souberman, E. (Eds.). (1978). *L.S. Vygotsky mind in society: The development of higher psychological processes.* Cambridge, MA: Harvard University Press. (Original work published 1930)

Freud, S. (2010). *Civilization and its discontents.* Eastford, CT:Martino Fine Books (Original work published 1930)

Gardner, H. (2000). *Intelligence reframed: Multiple intelligences for the 21st century.* New York: Basic Books.

Gardner, H. (2004). Audiences for the Theory of Multiple Intelligences. *Teachers College Record, 106*(I), 212–220.

Piaget, J. (1954). *The construction of reality in the child.* New York: Basic Books. (Original work published 1937)

Piaget, J. (1963) *The origins of intelligence in children.* New York: W.W. Norton & Company, Inc. (Original work published 1936)

Piaget, J. (2007). *The child's conception of the world.* Lanham, MD: Rowman & Littlefield Publishers, Inc. (Original work published 1929)

Sternberg, R. (1985). *Beyond IQ: A triarchic theory of human intelligence.* Cambridge, UK: Cambridge University Press.

Vygotsky, L. S. (1962). *Thought and language. Studies in communication.* Cambridge, MA: MIT Press.

Vygotsky, L. S. (2004) Imagination and creativity in childhood. *Journal of Russian & East European Psychology, 42*(1), 7–97.

ADDITIONAL RECOMMENDED READINGS

Ayman-Nolley, S. (1999). A Piagetian perspective on the dialectic process of creativity. *Creativity Research Journal, 12*(4), 267–275.

Burton, J. (2000). The configuration of meaning: Learner-centered art education revisited. *Studies in Art Education, 41*(4), 330–345.

Dewey, J. (1990). *The school and society & the child and the curriculum.* Chicago: The University of Chicago Press. (Original work published 1932)

Dewey, J. (2005). *Art as experience.* New York: The Berkeley Publishing Group. (Original work published 1934)

Eisner, E. W. (2004). Multiple intelligences: Its tensions and possibilities *Teachers College Record, 106*(1), 31–39

Eisner, E. (1991). What the arts taught me about education. *Art Education, 44*(5), 10–19.

Goleman, D. (1997). *Emotional intelligence.* New York: Bantam Books.

Isenberg, J. P., & Jalongo, M. R. (2000). *Creative expression and play in early childhood* (3rd ed.). Upper Saddle River, NJ: Merrill/Prentice Hall.

Isenberg, J., & Quisenberry, N. (1988). *Play: A necessity for all children.* A position paper. Association for Childhood Education International. Olney, MD: Association for Childhood Education International.

Jackson, P. (1998). *John Dewey and the lessons of art.* New Haven, CT: Yale University Press.

CHAPTER 2

FAMILIES AND COMMUNITIES

Supporting Imagination and Creativity in the Early Years

Carol Korn-Bursztyn
Brooklyn College
and City University of New York

ABSTRACT

This chapter presents a series of questions that address how families and communities can support arts initiatives for young children. It considers policy implications for broadening children's experiences in the arts in the home, community, and in early childhood settings, including child care programs. The Reggio Emilia (RE) approach is described as an example of arts-suffused early childhood experience that links early education settings with families and communities.

INTRODUCTION

The following chapter will pose six pragmatic questions addressing arts initiatives for young children, and how these may be supported by families and

Young Children and the Arts, pages 21–36

communities. Following each question are related sub-questions and topics that provide context for considering each general question. The questions that follow begin with a consideration of the role of innovative arts policy in broadening young children's arts experiences in the home and in the community, as well as in early education and child care programs.

Exploration of the place of the arts in the experiences of children both in and out-of-school/child care, and the policies that can support the arts for young children, follow. The Reggio Emilia or RE approach (Edwards, Gandini & Forman, 1993) is described as an example of an arts-suffused early childhood educational environment that incorporates families and communities in both the philosophy and pragmatics of everyday life in and outside of the classroom. Finally, the role of families and communities in developing and promoting arts suffused experiences for and with young children will be addressed.

QUESTIONS

Question One

How can innovative policy help to broaden the experience of the arts for young children, families, teachers and caregivers, particularly in underserved communities?

- Where should arts initiatives be located?
- What might a comprehensive arts initiative in early childhood look like?
- How can an early arts initiative be linked to other early childhood initiatives?
- How can the differences between approaches to the arts as tools or as disciplinary knowledge in their own right be addressed?
- How can cultural arts organizations promote connections between early childhood settings and community arts organizations?

Innovative policy in the arts can play a leading role in providing a framework for a comprehensive approach to the arts for young children from infancy through age eight, in school and out-of-school, at home and in the community. It is especially critical that the arts become part of the conversation of what constitutes high quality early education and why this is important to the education and well-being of children and families. To be effective, arts policy needs to address the forms of education, formal and informal, that shape the experience of young children from the cradle through the childhood years.

Optimally, policy should address the places where young children typically spend the greatest number of their waking hours. For many, this means at home in the care of family members, with informal child care providers, or in child care centers. Clear, comprehensive, and informed early childhood arts policy can help to frame the curriculum structures, including the curriculum content to which young children will be exposed, in new and expanded programs for young and very young children. Additionally, innovative arts policy can provide direction for research and development efforts to design arts programs for young children and their families in community organizations, and creative media technology applications.

To be maximally effective, a comprehensive and focused arts policy needs to be portable—easily able to travel across the diverse settings of home, school, child care, and community institutions—including those that provide direct services to children and families, such as libraries, health and wellness centers, and social service agencies.

Innovative arts policy, for example, might support a broad-based early arts initiative, and accompanying family and community arts initiatives, that can be introduced across the diverse settings in which young children and their families live, work, and learn.

An early arts initiative based upon best practices in early childhood pedagogy would take a participatory approach to the arts, developing young children's arts literacies by introducing them to the arts through activities that call for engagement, initiative and creative activity. An early arts initiative can reside comfortably alongside, and intersect with other early childhood education initiatives, most notably in early literacy and family literacy.

While early literacy directly addresses early childhood pedagogy, family literacy programs advance the comprehensive aim of supporting child literacy by furthering parental literacy, and by introducing parents and other family members to ways in which they can directly support their young children's developing literacy abilities. Acknowledging the significant role that families and communities play in young children's learning in- and out-of-school, an accompanying family and community arts initiative signals that learning in the early years takes place in multiple settings, and underlines the role of families in supporting and joining their young children in arts learning.

Though it bears some commonalities with early literacy, early arts learning comprise a set of arts literacies distinct from early literacy goals. Both early arts and early literacy initiatives incorporate complex sets of literacies. Early literacy represents a set of distinct but related proficiencies, most notably language (receptive and expressive) and print literacy. For example, letter recognition, name and word recognition, print-sound connections, growing familiarity with books and with a variety of writing tools and materials. The early arts also represent a collective set of literacies, including visual arts, music, theater, and dance literacies. It assumes the arts as disciplinary knowledge distinct from other early childhood content areas. Both early arts and early literacy initiatives have in common an emphasis on the central role of families and communities in supporting and participating in children's learning.

Early literacy and early arts initiatives optimally draw on a developmental approach that emphasizes skill development in accordance with developmental age expectations and with children's individual abilities. Both early arts and early literacy initiatives, when based upon principles of effective early childhood practice, emphasize and capitalize on children's interest, and their active exploration, initiative, and creative efforts.

The changing face of early education, a response to increased pressure to prepare young children for the academic rigors and achievement testing that lie ahead, has resulted in a largely instrumental approach to the development of language and literacy in the early years, and by extension, to the arts as well. Increased pressure for early academic skill development has effectively transformed the arts from disciplinary knowledge integral to early childhood practice to a tool for furthering learning in other content areas, especially early literacy and reading skills. The arts are typically called upon as tools to illustrate early attempts at writing, to enhance motivation or render subject matter more interesting, and as a restful alternative to the stress of early academics and consequent decreased opportunity for play.

Tension between the arts as tools to teach curriculum content, and the arts as disciplinary knowledge and curriculum content is the end product of the altered role of the arts in early childhood, and of the general anxiety about learning—and measurement of learning—in the early years. While the tension between the arts as tool or as disciplinary knowledge is commonly remarked upon by arts specialists and teaching artists working in early childhood settings, it is all but invisible to early childhood teachers. The primary preoccupation of early childhood teachers is with the pressures of the downward extension of formal academic preparation to the early years, and diminishing opportunities for play. The arts under any guise are a welcome distraction for both children and teachers.

Partnerships between schools and cultural arts organizations have done much to introduce early childhood teachers to the arts as an integral part of everyday early childhood classroom experience. However, a desire on the part of cultural arts organizations to render themselves useful in times of budgetary constraints, when their contributions may be viewed as expendable, has resulted in a close linking of the arts to curricular content, rather than as disciplinary knowledge in their own right. Restructuring of New York City's public school system, which empowered principals to make budgetary decisions, may prove a cautionary tale. Schools that had long partnered with cultural arts organizations discontinued these partnerships in favor of spending on literacy programs and test preparation.

When cultural arts organizations partner with schools, they typically work with children no younger than four year olds; it is less common for teaching artists to work in programs with toddlers and three year old children. Where available, arts programs for babies and young toddlers are provided by local, private providers for parents or caregivers and babies. Few guidelines, however, exist for how the arts can be introduced to the very young, or how arts experiences can be created for very young children and their caregivers.

It is especially useful to consider here arts programs and curricula, such New York City's Department of Education's well-crafted Blueprints for the Arts in dance, music, visual arts, and theater,[1] constructed for use in the NYC public schools with children from pre-K (four years) through grade twelve. The early years between birth and age three, identified as particularly significant to neurological development, early learning, and social emotional development are largely omitted in the professional literature on the arts in education. This is likely due to the absence of federal, state or city department of education oversight of programs for children in the first three years of life.

Recent rapid expansion of universal pre-K programs has resulted in more inclusion of curricular guidelines for four year olds, resulting in redefinition of public education as Pre-K through 12, rather than K–12. There is high need for development of resources in the arts specifically designed to introduce babies and toddlers to participatory experiences in the visual arts, dance, music, and storytelling/theater. It is critical that guidelines and supportive materials be readily available to early childhood teachers, families, caregivers and to community organizations in the public sector. Dissemination must encompass print, broadcast, and interactive media, and through offerings in community venues, including child care centers.

Question Two

How prepared are early childhood educators to engage in the arts?
What supports and professional development are required for
teachers and administrators? How prepared are artists to work with
very young children?

- What is the place of the arts in early childhood settings?
- How capable do teachers feel they are in introducing the arts in their classrooms?
- What supports are required for teachers and administrators?

- How capable do teaching artists feel in working with young and very young children?
- What supports are required for teaching artists?

Teachers and caregivers are typically under-prepared to work in the arts with young children. While they tend to view creative arts activities, and especially play, quite favorably, they are hesitant to engage in activities with which they have relatively little experience. This reluctance is exacerbated by a prevailing climate in schools and childcare centers of school-readiness, which is commonly viewed by teachers and administrators as antithetical to creative activity. The erosion of play has warranted a good deal of well-deserved attention from the field of early childhood education. Recent research in neurobiology (Panksepp, 1998a, 1998b, 2007) that points to the salutary effects of rough-and-tumble play on cognitive development has bolstered the field's claims about the importance of active play (though most teachers actively inhibit rough-and-tumble play). The diminishing role of the arts in early education, in contrast, goes relatively unnoticed.

Early childhood teachers, especially those who teach in public school, frequently complain that the administrators who oversee their programs have little to no familiarity with early childhood education. While many teachers hold a positive but limited view of how to work in the arts, their supervisors often perceive the creative arts as a diversion from the serious business of academic readiness and skill development. Arts education, albeit limited, is provided in most teacher education programs, but it is a rare offering in school leadership programs.

Although early childhood education has deep roots in the arts, field-based practices have diverged so broadly from the field's historic background that introducing a coherent, early arts initiative would require a re-culturing of many early childhood settings. Schools, even small schools and child care centers, are complex settings—and exceedingly resistant to change. Teachers and administrators would benefit from ongoing participation in professional development seminars and mentoring relationships in the arts. The support and involvement of key stakeholders in these settings are critical to change efforts. Teachers need to feel reassured that their attempts to introduce change will be supported by their administrators, peers, and the children's families. Outreach efforts to parents and families to involve them in arts learning are important to the success of early arts initiatives.

A program of professional development for teachers might include both an ongoing seminar series and collaborative work with teaching artists within the classroom setting. Seminars for teachers might incorporate a case study approach in which teachers and teaching artists implement what they are learning. They can bring their notes, observations and the children's artifacts back to the group for discussion and further development. It is important that the group leader have experience in both early education and in working in the arts with young children (or that there be two group leaders, one proficient in early education and the other in the arts).

Collaborative work between early childhood teachers and teaching artists has benefits that derive from an equitable relationship in which each party is expected to learn from the other. Teachers learn how to introduce and develop the arts in their classrooms, while teaching artists learn how to develop their teaching practice with young children. This is especially salient for teaching artists, many of whom have little formal background in teacher education. When teachers and teaching artists do not work collaboratively, teachers often withdraw when artists enter the room, and when the arts partnership ends with change in administration or loss of funding, the gains made are soon lost.

Artists and teaching artists who work collaboratively with teachers need to develop familiarity with early childhood practice, and to develop an appreciation for how collaborative work in a classroom differs from studio work with children. Early childhood education takes a developmental approach to education that differs, often markedly, from approaches to education in the elementary and high school years. Developmentally appropriate practice assumes understanding of both child development and early childhood pedagogy. It underlies all educational practice with young children, and should inform approaches to working with the arts. It is especially important that artists understand the tensions in early childhood education between teacher-directed and child-initiated activity, and between structured and unstructured activities.

School leaders can also benefit from case-based seminars and mentorship for arts-based school change, together with other early childhood administrators. It should be noted that many directors of child care centers and private preschools have little to no formal education in school leadership. Coaching on how to introduce and support change in their settings can be helpful for this group. Periodically, joint seminars within which administrators join teachers and teaching artists can further the agenda of school change, regarding the place of the arts.

Question Three

What is the Reggio Emilia approach?

- What is the Reggio Emilia approach?
- How are families and communities reflected in this approach?
- What is the place of local forms of artistic expression in an early childhood arts experience?

The Reggio Emilia or RE approach (Cadwell, 2002; Edwards et al., 1993), named for Reggio Emilia, is a small, prosperous city in Emilia Romagna, a region in northern Italy known for political activism. It was founded in the aftermath of World War II by parents who wanted to build a school for their children that would provide an antidote to fascism and that would ensure a democratic society. Impressed with the parents' ideas about the place of collaboration and critical thinking in young children's education, Loris Malaguzzi joined his work in creativity as a way of thinking about and responding to their efforts.

Educators working in the RE approach eventually developed a set of guiding principles that centered on children's creative expressiveness, or symbolic languages, and partnerships among teachers, parents, atelieriste or art educators, and pedagogiste or pedagogical coordinators. Parents continue to play a central role in RE; they are involved in all aspects of school life—including curriculum development. As a result of Reggio Emilia's success in building successful home-school partnerships, RE has even played a leadership role in labor market examination of principles of social management.

The RE approach is an evolving, highly experiential approach that involves continual study of children, teacher learning and research, and close collaborative work among teachers, parents, atelieriste and pedagogiste. Teacher learning is central to RE. Teachers, atelieriste and pedagogiste regularly meet to study, discover and nurture the children's fluency with symbolic languages, and to consider long-term projects or progettazione. There are no curriculum guidelines or manuals. Learning is experiential and is centered on the child's interest, curiosity and initiative. In this, the RE approach follows Deweyan and Piagetian approaches that highlight children's activity in the construction of knowledge and in their understanding of natural phenomena.

In the RE approach, ideas for long term projects come from the children's own inquiries, or from teachers' and parents' observations and ideas. These are closely linked to local communities. The RE approach privileges local forms of knowledge production, making this approach especially relevant to multicultural communities. Ongoing collaborative seminar sessions are a regular feature of RE preschools and child care centers, and these are sites of lively discussion and planning. They take the place of both formal academic preparation and professional development activities (the position of early childhood teacher in Italy appears to require little in the way of formal academic preparation). While the RE approach is highly experiential, children's engagement with art materials (especially in the visual arts) and exploration of local forms of knowledge suggest that an aesthetic education approach to study of works of art that focus on local, cultural traditions in the arts can be readily incorporated into long-term projects.

Extensive documentation of the children's activity and development is key to collaborative team discussion and to meetings with parents. The environment in RE is also considered a pedagogic tool. Classrooms are awash in light, filled with plants, and in each room—even in rooms for infants and toddlers—is an atelier (studio) and a mini-atelier. These spaces offer children a wide variety of materials and opportunities to engage expressive, symbolic languages, where they can work individually and in groups.

The RE philosophy has proven attractive to American educators, who resonate with its focus on children as self-directed learners who learn best through multi-sensory experience (touching, seeing, hearing and through physical movement), who need to have multiple opportunities and ways in which to explore and express themselves, and who thrive in relationships with other children, their teachers, and especially their families. Interest in RE first became strong in the 1990s as American educators became familiar with RE philosophy and tried to incorporate aspects of their approach to the arts in early childhood settings. Parental interest today, particularly among urban, educated families with background or interest in the arts, is growing. Concern among parents about the impact of their children's precocious entry into competitive academic environments has kindled a growing resistance to the rhetoric of school readiness and nursery as prep school.

Despite the widespread enthusiasm for this philosophical approach among teachers and parents, RE has not had widespread impact on the shape and form of programs for young children in this country. Early childhood programs are largely offered in the U.S. through an agglomeration of private venues, for which parents pay out-of-pocket or through government vouchers. (By contrast, early childhood education has enjoyed the support of contemporary Italian law for the past forty years; in 1968, Italy established preschool education for all three to five year olds, and in 1971, and again in 1999, Italian law called for increased provision of infant-toddler care.) In Italy, Reggio Emilia continues to play an advocacy role, and is credited with contributing to legal recognition and protection of access to high quality early education and care programs as a right of all Italian children and families.

Question Four

How can families be involved in the arts in early education? Which community venues might support the arts in the early years?

- How can parents become partners in developing early arts literacy?
- What cultural events do families participate in outside of the early childhood setting?

- How can arts programming for children and families build an interest in pursuing cultural arts activities outside of school?
- What kinds of activities can families and children participate in together? Where do these take place? How can local community organizations play a role in promoting the arts in early education?

It may be useful to consider an early arts initiative within the context of an agenda of change, which makes use of multiple ways of reaching families and community members, and that creates grass roots organizations in which families can take leadership positions. A broadly conceived early arts initiative might address early arts literacies in schools and child care centers, and in community institutions, and even in broadcast and interactive media. A key step in building an early arts initiative is to conduct situated research of the communities where the initiative will be housed, as part of the planning process. Regional differences should be apparent in program development at each site, in response to differences in population, community resources, local traditions and customs. It is valuable to know how families spend their time when not at work or school and the kinds of cultural events in which they participate. A comprehensive early arts initiative might, for example, have a community component, in which programs for children and families are offered at the local institutions that families frequent.

An early arts initiative might borrow from Reggio Emilia's integration of families and communities into the curriculum and structure of preschools and infant-toddler child care centers. Parents can be invited to take part in program development and in arts learning. Following a contemporary trend in educational programming that addresses children and adults as learners, programs for children should include a parent learning component in which parents not only learn about their children's activities, but further their own knowledge of the arts. Study of communities, including the arts that emerge from these communities can be an integral part of an aesthetic education approach to close study of works of art in dance, music, theater and the visual arts.

Question Five

What might be the impact of participation in an arts-based educational programming in the early years on indicators of child outcomes in childhood and adolescence? What is the impact of participation for parents, teachers, and artists?

- What is the impact on children's creative problem-solving ability?

- How have children and adolescents who participated in arts programming as young children fared (according to academic and
  sociological indicators)?
- What is the impact of participation on parents' relationships with
  their children? On the parents' own arts literacy?
- What is the impact on teachers' professional practice of participating
  in arts initiatives? On artists who work in early childhood settings?
- How can schools reconsider "parent participation" to include family
  involvement in community based arts programming?

Planning for assessment of the impact of a broad based early arts initiative is integral to the planning process. It would be useful to develop a
series of assessment measures, employing both quantitative and qualitative
methodology, for each component of the initiative. Some of these possible
questions are listed above. Longitudinal research of the young children
and their families who participate in the initiative, especially those who continue in the initiative for several years, can help to measure the long term
effects on children's academic and social functioning.

Helping to connect parents with their children's learning has demonstrated impact on children's academic careers. In schools, parent participation often translates into parent-teacher conferences, typically concerning
problematic behavior. The arts present occasions for creating opportunities
for parents and children to engage in constructive activity and in learning. Joining adult and child attention is important in the early years for
children's developing cognitive ability, and is significant to the continued
development of attachment relationships between parents and children.

Introduction of an early arts initiative to schools and child care centers is
likely to represent opportunity for significant institutional change. It can be
anticipated that a comprehensive arts initiative will impact on teacher and
administrator attitudes, educational practice, as well as increased educator
participation in the arts. While some effects may be almost immediately
measurable, some of the ways in which educators may be affected are likely
to change over time. An important question to ask concerns the anticipated
duration of changed attitudes and practices, and the supports required in
order to sustain long term change.

Similarly, the impact on artists of working with children and families in
a variety of settings bears investigation. As artists, for example, learn about
schools and about early education, they are likely to incorporate new ways
of thinking and working into their teaching practice. It is likely that this will
leave a mark on their professional identities.

Question Six

How can broadcast and interactive media play a constructive role in promoting the arts?

- What constitutes educational broadcast programming for children?
- What are criteria for good games?
- How can broadcast and interactive media help to develop early arts literacy in young children?
- How can broadcast and interactive media promote interaction between children and parents or teachers or caregivers? Between children and siblings or peers?

Early literacy and family literacy programs have their roots in the deep cultural impact that the introduction of Sesame Street in the 1970s (Stanley, 2009) brought not only to children's television, but to the borders between adult and child programming, and between school and home as sites for learning. Sesame Street seeded the educational ground for the early literacy and family literacy projects that emerged in the following decades. It was innovative because it appealed to both children and to their parents—and it provided out-of-school linguistically rich experience for all children. The program's visual appeal and subtly comedic undertones appealed to both children and parents, whether or not their homes were print rich, or whether or not English was spoken as a second language.

Sesame Street's success in appealing to both children and to diverse adult audiences, including highly educated parents and those with more limited formal education, set the stage for the development of public awareness of the benefits of linguistically and print-rich environments for young children. Specifically, introduction of key elements of early literacy, including letter and letter-sound recognition, to children who might otherwise not gain sufficient exposure to print materials or to the English language in their homes resulted in significant gains for, especially, children growing up in poverty.

Research in child development, and specifically in the neuropsychology of brain development, has over the past decade fueled a concern—even a passion—for early literacy. This has resulted in a boon to publishers of children's books and to manufacturers of games and toys, including computer programs and hand-held devices, all purporting to develop young children's early literacy skills and beginning reading (and to a lesser extent, numeracy) skills. Few educational guidelines are widely available for families, teachers, and caregivers, though, to gauge the educational quality of broadcast and interactive media for young and very young children widely marketed as promoting "school readiness." Though many items bear an imprimatur of "educational," this term is unregulated and has largely contributed to the commercialization of early childhood. The largely unregulated (educational) market has had its greatest impact on families who can least afford to squander resources.

Hoping to gear their children towards successful scholastic careers, many families stock their homes with computer software and hand-held games in an effort to promote skills marketed as educational. Young children consequently have fewer opportunities to engage in exploratory and imaginative play, or in arts-based activities. From a parental perspective, media technology has the added advantage of avoiding the noise and mess of arts activities. Increasingly the arts are viewed as quaint throwbacks to an earlier time when childhood was unhurried, and crayon and paintbrush were the technologies of the early years. Even children whose homes are not stocked with a plethora of media technology are familiar with broadcast and interactive media. The child care centers they attend are likely to be the recipients of public funds, including universal pre-K funding, and are likely to offer computers and software for children in their classrooms, as well as selected broadcast media in the late afternoon.

Though the field of early education largely frowns on broadcast media in favor of active play in early childhood settings, regular viewing of television programs such as Sesame Street is an informally sanctioned component of full-day and extended-day child care programs, especially in low-income neighborhoods. Wide availability of DVDs and the ease of streaming video has made viewing of commercially available children's programming a staple in many child care centers, especially late-afternoon viewing by tired toddlers, preschoolers and their exhausted caregivers.

There is need for high quality broadcast and interactive media for young children that can introduce arts literacies to young viewers, their families, and caregivers, while encouraging active participation, exploration, and co-operation. The arts offer children an opportunity for both individual initiative and social experience. When children engage, for example, in making music, they need to learn to listen to each other, and to take turns. They learn how to be an audience, and also learn the pleasures of listening and responding in the company of others.

Research and development efforts in broadcast and interactive media to develop arts literacies in the early years might consider the place of the creative tension between individual initiative and social experience that is central to how young children learn. Games that help to develop arts literacies in children should be highly interactive, providing opportunity for young children to explore and to exercise initiative. Games should also promote collaborative effort. While a child may wish, at times, to play independently, games should permit cooperative activity with another child(ren) or with an adult. The National Association for the Education of Young Children's

Guidelines for Developmentally Appropriate Practice or DAP (NAEYC, 2009) provide a touchstone for product development, aligning new games and other products with best practices in early childhood education.

CONCLUSION

The field of early childhood education could greatly benefit from a focused, comprehensive initiative in early arts that will reach children and families where they live, work, and go to childcare and school. A comprehensive initiative would need to be highly flexible, so as to reflect the diverse needs of communities, and also to reflect the individual needs of the children being served. Such an early arts initiative might take the form of collaborative ventures involving museums, libraries, cultural arts organizations, community centers and institutions.

School administrators are often unfamiliar with the arts in education, and can benefit from case-based seminars and mentorship in the arts. Outreach to families to involve them in arts learning is important to the success of early arts programs. Artists who work collaboratively with teachers also need to develop closer familiarity with early childhood practice. They need to appreciate how classroom work differs from studio work with children. It may be useful to consider multiple ways of reaching families and creating grass-roots organizations in which families can take leadership positions.

Although early childhood education has deep roots in the arts, as noted elsewhere, practices have diverged so broadly that introducing arts initiatives in schools and child care centers requires a re-culturing of many early childhood settings. Schools and child care centers, whether small or large, typically resist change. Key stakeholders, including teachers, parents, administrators and other staff are critical to the change efforts that introducing and sustaining arts initiatives in schools call for. Teachers need to feel reassured that their efforts will be supported by administrators, peers, and families.

Community-based arts initiatives that are flexible and that reflect the needs of young children, their families and communities are an important adjunct to in-school arts experiences. Community-based arts initiatives often involve collaborative ventures among museums, libraries, arts organizations, and other community institutions. Additionally, there may well be a role for broadcast and interactive media that can bring the arts into the homes of families with young children. Early childhood is garnering increased media attention; it is likely that comprehensive early childhood initiatives will be formed within the coming months and years. It is therefore critical that the arts have strong representation in future discussions about the expansion of early childhood programs.

NOTE

1. NYC Department of Education: *Blueprint for the Arts: Music, Grades Pre-K–12* 2004/2008; *Blueprint for the Arts: Visual Arts, Grades Pre-K–12* 2007; *Blueprint for the Arts: Theater, Grades Pre-K–12* 2005; *Blueprint for the Arts: Dance, Grades Pre-K–12*.

REFERENCES

Cadwell, L. B. (2002). *Bringing learning to life: A Reggio approach to early childhood education.* New York, NY: Teachers College Press.

Edwards, C., Gandini, L., and Forman, G. (Eds.). (1993). *The hundred languages of children: The Reggio Emilia approach to early childhood education.* Norwood, NJ: Ablex.

National Association for the Education of Young Children (NAEYC). (2009). *Position paper: Developmentally appropriate practice in early childhood programs serving children from birth through age 8.* Washington, DC: Author.

Panksepp, J. (1998a). *Affective neuroscience: The foundations of human and animal emotions.* New York: Oxford University Press.

Panksepp, J. (1998b). Attention deficit hyperactivity disorders, psychostimulants and intolerance of childhood playfulness: A tragedy in the making? *Current Directions in Psychological Science, 7,* 91–98.

Panksepp, J. (2007). Can play diminish ADHD and facilitate the construction of the social brain? *Journal of the Canadian Academy of Child & Adolescent Psychiatry, 16,* 57–66

Stanley, A. (2009, November 8). Same street, different world: 'Sesame' turns 40. *New York Times, Arts.*

ADDITIONAL RECOMMENDED READINGS

Bodilly, S. J., & Augustine, C. H. (2008). *Revitalizing arts education through community-wide coordination.* Santa Monica, CA: Rand Education (commissioned by The Wallace Foundation).

Bruner, J. (1986). *Actual minds, possible worlds.* Cambridge, MA: Harvard University Press.

Chapman, L. (2005). "No child left behind in art?" *Arts Education Policy Review, 106*(2), 1–17.

Eisner, E. W., & Day, M. D. (Eds). (2004). *Handbook of research and policy in art education.* Mahwah, N.J.: Lawrence Erlbaum Associates, Inc.

Gandini, L., Etheredge, S., & Hill, L. (Eds.). (2008). *Insights and inspirations from Reggio Emilia: Stories of teachers and children from North America.* Worcester, MA: Davis Publications, Inc.

Greene, M. (2001). *Variations on a blue guitar: The Lincoln Center Institute lectures on aesthetic education.* New York: Teachers College Press.

Korn-Bursztyn, C. (2003). The arts and school reform: Case study of a school in change. *Teaching Artist Journal, 1*(4), 220–227.

Lewin-Benham, A. (2005). *Possible schools: The Reggio approach to urban education.* New York: Teachers College Press.

McCarthy, K. F, Ondaatje, E. H., Zakaras, L., & Brooks, A. C. (2004). *Gifts of the muse: Reframing the debate about the benefits of the arts.* Santa Monica, CA: Rand Corporation.

Tepper, S. J., & Ivey, B. (Eds.). (2008). *Engaging art: The next great transformation of America's cultural life.* New York: Routledge.

Zakaras, L. & Lowell, J. F. (2008). *Cultivating demand for the arts: Arts learning, arts engagement, and state arts policy.* Santa Monica, CA: Rand Corporation.

CHAPTER 3

ON CREATING A MEANINGFUL EXPERIENCE

A Relational Approach to the Arts

Carol Korn-Bursztyn
Brooklyn College
and City University of New York

ABSTRACT

This chapter explores the relationships among young children's psychological processes, developing capacity for relationships, and the role of meaningful experiences. Children's narrative and storytelling are described as outcomes of their participation in meaningful experiences, while the arts are presented as an important venue for creating emotionally meaningful experiences that can further young children's curiosity, emotional and cognitive development, while furthering their narrative abilities.

Young Children and the Arts, pages 37–49
Copyright © 2012 by Information Age Publishing
All rights of reproduction in any form reserved.

INTRODUCTION

In this chapter I explore the relationships among a) psychological processes in the early years, b) the child's growing capacity for relationships with others, and c) the place of emotionally meaningful experience in children's lives. I describe the role of parents and teachers in creating meaningful experience in which children can explore, experiment, share interest, and develop initiative. Meaningful experience emerges from a relational matrix of children and parents, and later between children themselves and between children and teachers. This relational matrix, and its place in creating meaningful experience with and for children, is described in the section that follows as formed by the interplay among the processes of attachment, joint attention, and separation-individuation.

This chapter further explores how children's narrative and storytelling are an outgrowth of their participation in meaningful experiences. The arts are presented as an important venue for creating emotionally meaningful experiences that can further young children's curiosity, emotional and cognitive development, while furthering their narrative abilities.

Learning in the early years is profoundly intersubjective and experiential. From their earliest experiences of learning to read parents' faces for interest and response, children who have met with sufficiently matched responsiveness—not too consistently matched, nor too distracted—learn to read and respond socially to the world. Learning to read the world, beginning with the world as represented by the human face, is an early pre-verbal form of reading—a reading of sign and intention that will precede by years a decoding of the symbolic system of written language. It is an interpersonal act marked by mutuality: learning to read the signs and emotions revealed by the other sets the stage for children and parents to engage in activities that require joint attention—those everyday events and activities in which child and parent join interest.

Observing, looking, listening, and feeling are all foundational to how young children learn about the world and make meaning of their experience. Pointing to and naming the world are social activities that build upon young children's desire to participate in an endlessly interesting world, a world that is peopled with others in ever-widening dimensions. Language and relationships with others surrounds such experience. Naming objects in a world that is seen, felt, smelled, and talked about signals the growing role that language and social interactions will increasingly play in the construction of narratives of children's experience.

Paradoxically, this openness to the world is later often viewed as a distraction from the real business of schooling or its junior version, "getting ready" for school. The awareness and attention that children bring to their environment are often dismissed as distractibility, "off-task" rather than "on-task" behavior. Children's attentiveness to the environment, however, provides an important avenue by which they develop the ability to focus and to sustain attention. A common goal of caregivers and teachers is to minimize distractibility, and to increase the amount of time spent on an activity, especially if that activity is quiet and involves the child either sitting or lying down. The capacity to focus attention on a task or phenomenon—whether that task involves the child's active mastery of a climbing apparatus, quiet play with a puzzle, or focused attention on an ant on the ground—is an important part of the developing motor and cognitive abilities. However, what we often think of as distractibility in young children often indicates alertness and openness—an attitude towards the world that is essential for learning, and that is, optimally, increasingly self-directed.

Children's ability to take in the environment by deploying this ability to focus and to shift attention serves an important early function that connects children to the caring adults in their lives, and that connects them to their surroundings. Research in neuropsychology suggests the significance of mirror neurons in our ability to understand and to react to social experience. Arnold Modell, in his 2003 book *Imagination and the Meaningful Brain*, traces the roots of empathy to physiology, observing that this is an unconscious process, unmediated by cognitive awareness. Within hours of birth, infants open their mouths in response to observing an adult opening her mouth. Where the infant's gaze meets lively engagement and interest on the part of the other, she is more likely to keep on looking, responding to the other's face with matched reactions of interest and attunement. In this matched responsiveness, Modell suggests, lay the roots of empathy.

In contrast, infants turn away, breaking gaze and interrupting their visual focus in response to too much or too little stimulation. When stimulation becomes too great, or when the infant's gaze meets with indifference in the parent's face, turning away serves a self-regulating or self-soothing function. When the parent's face registers preoccupation or distress, infants are more likely to turn away, matching the adult's low-keyed affect with diminished responsiveness and withdrawal of interest and attention.

Reciprocal engagement is meaningful for both children and adults. It helps children build capacity for sustained interest and attention, is intellectually stimulating and emotionally gratifying, and builds capacity for empathy. Contemporary infant research points to the intersubjective nature of relationships between infants and their primary caregivers, revealing coordinated patterns of responsiveness, with each partner influenced by and responding to the other's non-verbal cues. The capacity to focus on and respond to each other not only shapes the infant's attachment to the parent/caregiver, as noted widely in the developmental literature, including Daniel Siegel's work (1999, 2007), but gives rise to mutually constructed patterns of attachment of child to adult and of adult to child. In the section below,

I describe the impact of attachment on the relational worlds of young children, and its impact on children's growing sense of agency and initiative.

CREATING EXPERIENCE: CONTRIBUTIONS
OF ATTACHMENT AND JOINT ATTENTION

Early work by theorists including John Bowlby (1969/1982)and Mary Ainsworth and her colleagues (Ainsworth, Blehar, Waters, & Wall, 1978) suggested that attachment emerges first in interactions between children and their parents; it is formed out of ties of love that bind children to adults, and adults to children. Attachment serves the function of helping children anticipate their parents' reactions, particularly when they are in need of soothing. Secure attachment, which rests on the expectation that parents will be available and can effectively soothe, is central to children's ability to self-regulate negative emotions in stressful situation.

Significantly, children who are securely attached explore more; they develop purposive behavior, manipulate toys and other objects, and in general, are curious about and display initiative in exploring their surroundings. Exploratory behavior in early childhood is critical to developing an attitude of curiosity and engagement in the world; this in turn results in greater learning and cognitive development. Securely attached children anticipate that the world is full of good things and experiences that can be shared with others.

Rather than flowing solely from parent to child, patterns of attachment are co-constructed between parent and child, and impacted by the residue of personal and cultural patterns of attachment in the parent's life, as well as by the child's developmental condition. When infants, for example, present with developmental conditions such as Autism Spectrum Disorder (ASD), their parents can become physically and emotionally drained from the effort of sustaining a high level of positive engagement in the absence of reciprocity. This can lead to less synchronous or matched interactions between these babies and their parents.

As a result of social impairments that are typical of children with autism, Rutgers and her colleagues (Rutgers et al., 2007) concluded, it may be more difficult for parents to correctly read their children's attachment needs and signals. This may lead to more insecure patterns of attachment when compared with typically developing children, or with children who present other clinical conditions, such as mental retardation or language disorders. Level of cognitive functioning is an important variable here, too. Children with stronger cognitive functioning or, what researchers refer to as mental development, as contrasted with chronological age, tend to be more securely attached to their parents than children with ASD and mental retardation. Children with ASD, in turn, appear to be less securely attached than children who present with mental retardation, but without autism.

What emerges from the attachment research with typically and atypically developing children is the connection between facility of social interaction and the establishment of secure attachment. Children who grow in an environment that is nurturing and responsive to their needs and sensitivities want to learn about the world, and to create meaning from their experiences. However, children who do not easily engage with others can face challenges to developing the kinds of reciprocal interactions that lead to patterns of secure attachment. It should be noted, however, that while attachment patterns first emerge in infancy, these are not fixed and immutable. Rather, with facilitating educational and therapeutic experiences, children and their parents can develop more secure and confident relational patterns. For example, interventions such as Stanley Greenspan's (1992) Developmental, Individual-difference, Relationship-based model (DIR) that build on emotional interactions that are positive in nature, warm and encouraging of children's initiative, promote cognitive and emotional growth. The DIR model builds capacity for joint attention in children who present with deficits in social capacities or skills as a result of developmental disorders.

Joint attention calls up experiences of attachment and calls upon attachment histories between children and their parents, and between children and their teachers or caregivers. Typically, children edge closer to adults who join their interest and attention to theirs, seeking a proximity that suggests attachment behavior. Joining of interest on the part of child and adult is a product of, as well as a symbolic representation of, the physical proximity-seeking behaviors that characterize attachment. While joint attention is implicated in children's developing cognition and especially communicative competence, it plays a complex role in the psychological lives of children and parents. While joint attention is an outgrowth of early attachment relationships between children and parents, it focuses on phenomena outside of the parent-child interaction. Joint attention draws on attachment patterns, but signals the growing role of parents and educators in leading children into active engagement in the world.

Joint attention, or the capacity of children to join their attention with that of another, plays a central role in young children's growth. It is increasingly noted for the significant role that it plays in furthering young children's development across a broad spectrum of areas, including attention capacity and social and emotional growth. I will focus, here, on experiences of joint attention involving the adult–child dyad as a precursor to experiences of joint attention between children and other adults, and between children and their peers. Experiences of joint attention, co-constructed by children and responsive adults, including parents, teachers and caregivers, lay the groundwork for children's capacity to attend to and interact meaningfully with others, and also marks the earliest stages of communication.

Joint attention rests upon mutual investment of interest and provides grounding for the development of children's capacity for sustained attention. It is a fully collaborative act, and assumes that the object of joint attention—whether reading a book together or observing ants crossing the pavement—is of interest to both partners. Joint attention also provides a template for reciprocal engagement with caring and nurturing adults who find interest in what it is that the children find interesting, and who can, together with children, co-create shared meaningful experience. Jerome Bruner (1990) observed that joint attention is foundational to children's language learning and cognitive development. For example, when parents and children gaze out a window together and talk about what they see on the street, or when a teacher holds a young child on her lap and reads a picture book in which they are both interested, these dyads are engaging in joint attention. Language surrounds activities that call for joint attention. This not only supports children's growing literacy skills, but, on a deeper level, supports children's intellectual development by furthering their interest in and curiosity about the world.

Joint attention lays the foundation for how children develop understanding of how minds work, known in the developmental literature as theory of mind. Children's growing ability to understand how their own minds work, and to grasp that others have minds of their own too, is rooted in early experiences of joint attention. When children experience a meeting of minds, such as occurs when child and adult both focus their attention on a common interest, their understanding of how minds work grows. Dawning awareness that others have minds that work in ways that are different from one's own helps children self-regulate, or modulate their own behavior. It also helps develop capacity for empathy and for the kinds of empathic behaviors that undergird social interactions with others. For these reasons, it is highly desirable that young children repeatedly engage in meaningful, shared experiences that incorporate joint attention and, significantly, mutual pleasure and enjoyment. Joint attention is at the core of meaningful, shared experience between adults and children. When adults and children join attention within the context of warm, pleasurable exchanges, they co-create experiences that are meaningful and enriching for both partners.

When parents create emotionally meaningful shared experience with their children, they deepen bonds with their children, furthering the mutual process of attachment that began in earliest infancy. A parallel role for teachers of very young children is to create opportunities for emotionally meaningful shared experience between themselves and the children in their care, and, increasingly, between the children themselves. In this manner, they further the children's capacity for forming multiple attachments, a capacity that will help buffer them as they grow, enhancing resiliency. In the section that follows, I will describe the characteristics of emotionally meaningful experience, and how this may be co-constructed by adults and children.

CO-CONSTRUCTION OF EMOTIONALLY MEANINGFUL EXPERIENCE

Psychologically, joint attention also serves the purpose of triangulation—introducing a third dimension into the attachment-dominated experience of child and parent, or child and caregiver. It appears for the first time as an object or phenomenon that is external to the relationship between the dyad, and that captures the attention of both. An important characteristic of the object of joint attention is that it is external to the bodies of the child/adult dyad; the physical gesture that best characterizes joint attention is reaching for the object, moving away from, rather than clinging to the dyadic partner.

Meaningful experiences of joint attention between young children and adults serve an almost paradoxical function. While deepening attachment relationships through the building of co-constructed, emotionally meaningful experience, joint attention opens the dyadic relationship to the world outside of the child/adult dyad. It opens up the early intense preoccupation of child with parent and of parent with child, and allows for the possibility of new objects, interests and passions. The role of toys, other objects and foci of attention are especially significant here. Joint attention both heralds and furthers the process of what Margaret Mahler and her colleagues in 1975 (Mahler, Pine, & Bergman, 1975/2000) referred to as separation-individuation, a process that describes the child's first tentative steps into the world beyond parents, a world that is revealed through active exploration and experimentation. The process of separation-individuation emerges out of the early relationship, or attachment, between child and parents; its vicissitudes are flavored by the quality of that relationship.

Parents and educators play an important role in furthering children's interests by encouraging their initiative. Following and joining in the children's interests, they co-create experiences and provide opportunities for children to explore and experiment in a purposive manner. The world of objects and natural phenomena provides a gateway for babies and young toddlers from exclusive reliance on the body—their own and that of the parent or caregiver—to developing interest in a wider world. The natural environment—even in an urban setting—provides a compelling variety of opportunities for joint attention, and for the exploratory activities that lead to developing initiative. An emotionally meaningful experience between parent and child might take the form of following the child's reaching for a leaf or acorn, or following a toddler's tracking of the small movements of sidewalk ants. The experience includes looking together, sharing in the child's excitement of new phenomena, and most importantly taking pleasure in the interaction—matching the child's affect or emotional tone, or for children who are especially low-keyed, bringing the positive emotional level up a notch through warm interactions.

Children invite parents and teachers to join in their interests, and to take part in the pleasures of initiative and purposeful activity. Creating meaningful experiences with children, however, places special demands upon adults. Joint attention and interaction can present challenges for many adults who can quickly lose interest in what young children find interesting, or who insist that children follow their interests. It demands of adults—whether they are teachers, caregivers or parents—that they invest their full attention in the object or phenomenon in which the child has interest, and that they find interest in children's interest. Following the Latin root of education, educar—to lead, it asks of adults that they also lead children into the world, introducing them to new experiences in which both can find interest and share in learning.

Everyday, emotionally meaningful experiences of shared attention and purpose help children take pleasure in interaction and further their capacity for relationships with others. Children's interest in the world is deepened by their experience of engaging with responsive adults with whom they share common interests, and with whom they engage in jointly or co-constructed activities. Emotionally meaningful experience in which both child and adult share attention, turn-taking and initiative, and in which they share pleasure in interacting, reassures children of their bonds with parents and trusted caregivers, and helps them anticipate that their worlds will be enlarged through their relationships with others.

In summary, joint attention between child and parent, and between child and teacher or caregiver, furthers attachment, an important component in children's learning and psychological development. It also serves as a precursor to the role that shared activities and conversation will provide as a marker and means of furthering individual attachment processes and group affiliations throughout the life cycle. The ability to join one's attention to another's contributes to the capacity for play—a complex endeavor that calls upon the capacity to read the other's intentions and desires, to take turns, to share initiatives and ideas, have fun, and in playing, create emotionally meaningful experience. Joining adult attention to a child's attention for sustained interaction and play, though, presents challenges for many parents and teachers.

CHALLENGES TO CREATING EMOTIONALLY MEANINGFUL EXPERIENCE

Co-creating emotionally meaningful experiences with children means that adults re-learn finding interest in everyday phenomena, and perhaps most important of all, take pleasure in joining their interests to those of children. Joint attention, a foundational component of meaningful shared experience, demands that adult agendas, tasks, and preoccupations be set aside, and it means unplugging from cell phones and social media. It demands of adults that they follow children's lead, scaffolding and extending children's interests, while finding interest in that which children find compelling. Shared attention lays the foundation for the capacity for sustained attention, an ability linked to the quality of children's interactions with others.

Adults are faced with the challenge of learning to look anew, to view familiar experience as unfamiliar, as seen through the eyes of the small child. Adult capacity to notice anew and to create experience out of the phenomena of everyday life is critical to the process of developing children's ability to direct sustained attention and to think though phenomena they experience. It can be a daunting task, though, for many well-intentioned adults to suspend familiarity with everyday phenomena, and to follow a child's lead in taking up what they notice and attend to. It requires a revisiting of one's own early childhood experience by following the child's perspective, and joining in the focus of her attention.

Some parents, including individuals who work in highly creative fields, report feeling bored when they exclusively follow their children's lead in play. Even as they celebrate their children's ideas and initiatives and take care not to seize leadership from their children, they find themselves retreating emotionally and intellectually as they inhibit their own creative contributions. One father, a visual artist, remarked, "It drives me crazy—I find it so incredibly boring to sit on the floor and just go with what (the children) are doing ... I'm thinking about my work and itching to get back to it and they're so into (play with blocks and action figures) and full of ideas ... I feel guilty like I should be enjoying this." A mother honestly confronted her spontaneous reaction to the suggestion that she spend dedicated floor time talking and playing with her language-delayed toddler. "It's so boring ... I was imagining putting Anna in the stroller and strolling around the neighborhood, stopping in at galleries, showing her the sights. That's not what you mean, though ..."

Adult boredom, with consequent emotional withdrawal, is an important footnote to considerations of joint attention between parents and their children, and between teachers and their young students. Following John Dewey (1932/1990), who in 1932 raised question about the advisability of following the child's lead to the exclusion of contributions by the adult/

teacher, I suggest that creative engagement calls for initiative by all parties. In order for adults to be engaged with children in creating experiences, they must also be involved as respectful co-creators of that experience, careful not to intrude upon children's initiative or usurp their authority at play, while joining in and contributing their own ideas to the construction of shared experience.

In contrast, withdrawal of interest on the part of parents and caregivers as a result of boredom may have a dampening effect on children's experience of adults as an interested party to their ideas and experiences. In turning joint attention of child and adult to natural phenomena and shared experience, children and adults engage in turn-taking, with each drawing from and building on the contributions of the other in such a manner as to sustain interest and attention, and importantly, provoke curiosity.

ON ASKING QUESTIONS: NURTURING INTEREST AND CURIOSITY

Young children are careful observers of their surroundings and highly attuned to changes within their physical and emotional environment. In the early childhood years, adults can help young children construct understanding of their experiences by helping them learn to make observations and to talk about what they have seen and experienced. Children's curiosity about the world and attentiveness to both natural phenomena and human interactions create multiple opportunities for teachers and parents to help children give language to their observations, and to co-create emotionally meaningful experiences. When adults and children observe the natural environment together, for example, opportunities to explore mathematic and artistic concepts, such as line and shape are created. Engaged adults not only name what is jointly observed, but guide children's developing ability to notice by asking questions that draw upon the children's observations, supplemented by the adults' observations, too.

Growth in the capacity to understand and to use language provides an important means by which children understand and can share experience. Children's developing capacity for language serves a communicative function of understanding and being understood by others. It provides a second important function, as a tool for constructing narrative with which experience can be shared through the creation of stories that encode personal and shared experience. The development of both communicative and narrative skills draws upon children's physical, sensory, and emotional engagement with the world, beginning first and foremost, with the human environment.

Observations encoded in language are important to children's growing capacity to create narratives about their experiences, helping them to make sense and create meaning of their experiences. Children's capacity for close study of their environment invites educators and parents to listen carefully, to engage in conversation that will deepen children's understanding, and to encourage their questions and comments. The capacity to ask questions emerges from the gap between what is known, and what one needs to know. Imagination in the early childhood years works to fill these gaps, playing an important role in the development of the capacity for critical thinking. This is readily observed in young children's questions about their own origins— and their theories about how they came to be in the world.

In his 1998 book, *The Beast in the Nursery*, Phillips notes the urgency that underlines children's questions, and observed that the child "is addicted to, driven by, what he doesn't know" (Phillips, 1998, p. 11). Referencing Sigmund Freud's seminal work, Adam Phillips reframes what James Strachey, in his 1976 translation of Freud, referred to as the sexual researches of children, observing that children are prolific generators of theory, and that children's need to know, indeed their passionate interest in life may be tracked to an elemental curiosity about their origins. Referring to "children's fantastic sexual speculations," Phillips cites Freud, who observed, in *On the Sexual Theories of Children*, that children's "false sexual theories . . . each one of them contains a fragment of real truth, and in this they are analogous to the attempts of adults, which are looked at as strokes of genius, at solving the problems of the universe which are too hard for human comprehension" (Freud, cited in Phillips, 1998, p. 12).

Children experience the world intensely, with all of their senses and with all of their being. Out of the intensity of their sensual life, children make art—imagining what they don't know, and in imagining, creating theories and inventing stories. The vignette that follows, recounted by an early childhood teacher, Ms. M., who studied her young students' responses to her own increasingly apparent pregnancy, demonstrates the driving need to know and the exuberant theorizing of a class of fifteen five year old girls. It demonstrates, too, how children's observations, questions and theories are grounded in particular social and cultural contexts; these are enacted in stories and improvised play scenarios, and accompanied by a running narrative in which the children sift through their understandings of social conventions.

As her pregnancy progresses, Ms. M. observes that the children put dolls under their shirts; as the weeks go by, she comments, "more and more children in the class are having a baby, being a baby or delivering a baby." The teacher notes that the children's questions and developing theories increasingly turn to what she calls "getting a baby." A snippet of conversation among a small group of five-year-old-girls follows.

    Renee: I want to be the mommy.
    Mimi: Nobody wants to be the birthday girl.

Dana: Me—and I get to hold the baby because it's my birthday. It's baby's birthday and my birthday together. These are my beautiful shoes that I'm wearing. OK mommy, these are my shoes—I bought it. Mommy set up the table for my birthday. *[A brief argument among the girls breaks out as they set the table.]*

Mimi: Teacher, I am the bride.

Dana: We need to clean the table. OK, I'm the flower girl. I'm mommy; I'm the birthday girl.

Mimi: Now you're getting married. My mommy didn't get married and have a baby. She prayed and prayed and then she had a baby. Right, Jeanna? Mommy doesn't get married with a baby? [Jeanna responds inaudibly.]

Mimi: Teacher, Jeanna thinks that a mommy gets married with a baby. Could a mommy marry a baby?

Dana: Yes

Mimi: Dana, you can't just get married like this. You don't marry a baby, you have to pray and pray for a baby.

Language and the construction of narrative are closely connected with how one comes to make sense of personal, emotionally meaningful experience. In the chapter that follows, the connections among emotionally meaningful experience, children's early construction of narrative, and developing storytelling capacity are explored for their contributions to the development of creative thinking and the imagination.

CONCLUSION

The arts in the early years are consonant with children's need to realize or make concrete the concepts that they are exploring through everyday, meaningful experience. Opportunities to work with art materials, to listen to and make music, dance, create one's own stories and dramas, are all means by which young children reflect in action on their lived experience. Parents and teachers can, together with children, co-create opportunities for emotionally meaningful experiences by drawing on the arts—engaging in active exploration of art materials, music, dance, and storytelling.

The arts provide an important venue through which children and adults can share opportunities for joint attention that bring them closer, drawing on and developing earlier patterns of attachment. When arts experiences are emotionally meaningful for children and adults, these can facilitate development by encouraging initiative and curiosity. The arts, as meaningful emotional experiences that are co-constructed with helpful adults, can help children develop narrative ability through conversation about their ideas and impressions, leading to heightened symbolic capacity. Emotionally meaningful arts experiences provide opportunities for exchange of ideas though verbal and non-verbal means, and for emotionally satisfying occasions of both shared interest and individual expression.

REFERENCES

Ainsworth, M. S., Blehar, M. C., Waters, E., & Wall, S. (1978). *Patterns of attachment: A psychological study of the strange situation.* Oxford, England: Erlbaum.

Bowlby, J. (1982). *Attachment and loss: Vol.1. attachment* (2nd ed.). New York: Basic Books. (Original work published 1969)

Bruner, J. (1990). *Acts of Meaning.* Cambridge, MA: Harvard University Press.

Dewey, J. (1990). *The School and society & the child and the curriculum.* Chicago, IL: The University of Chicago Press. (Original work published 1932)

Freud, S. (1953/1976). *The Standard edition of the complete psychological works of Sigmund Freud.* J. Strachey & A. Freud (Trans). New York: Norton. (Original work published)

Greenspan, S. I. (1992). *Infancy and early childhood: The practice of clinical assessment and intervention with emotional and developmental challenges.* Madison, CT: International Universities Press.

Mahler, M. S., Pine, F., & Bergman, A. (2000). *The psychological birth of the human infant: Symbiosis and individuation.* New York: Basic Books. (Original work published 1975)

Modell, A. (2003). *Imagination and the meaningful brain.* Cambridge, MA: MIT Press.

Philipps, A. (1998). *The beast in the nursery: On curiosity and other appetites.* New York: Vintage Books.

Rutgers, A. H., van IJzendoon, H., Bakermans-Kranenburg, M. J., Swinkels, S. H. N., Van Daalen, E., Dietz, C., . . . van Engeland, H. (2007). Autism, attachment and parenting: A comparison of children with autism spectrum disorder, mental retardation, language disorder, and non-clinical children. *Journal of Abnormal Child Psychology, 35,* 859–870.

Siegel, D. J. (1999). *The developing mind: How relationships and the brain interact to shape who we are.* New York: Guilford Press.

Siegel, D. J. (2007). *The mindful brain: Reflection and attunement in the cultivation of well-being.* New York: W.W. Norton.

CHAPTER 4

CULTIVATING IMAGINATION AND CREATIVE THINKING

Carol Korn-Bursztyn
*Brooklyn College
and City University of New York*

ABSTRACT

This chapter traces a developmental line for imagination, with the social imagination paving the way for the capacity for symbolic representation in language and storytelling, musical or embodied representation, and iconic or pictorial representation. In this chapter, the role of imagination in the development of metaphoric and creative thinking in early childhood is discussed. The resulting relationships among children's storytelling, imagination, creative thinking, and the arts is explored.

INTRODUCTION

In this chapter I propose a developmental line for the growth of the imagination in childhood, and suggest that the social imagination is the earliest form of imagination to emerge. While the social imagination first emerges in early childhood, optimally, it continues to develop throughout the life cycle. Empathy builds on the child's growing capacity for social imagina-

Young Children and the Arts, pages 51–67

tion, and is rooted in children's real experiences of being responded to consistently and with sensitivity by their caregivers—parents, teachers, and other significant adults. The social imagination both anticipates and marks the growth of other forms of symbolic functioning, including capacity for symbolic representation in language and narrative, in physical, musical or embodied representation, and iconic or pictorial representation.

Imagination is also implicated in the development of metaphoric and creative thinking in early childhood. In this chapter I will explore how metaphoric thinking and creative thinking develop in the early years, and how these forms of thinking are related to the growth of children's storytelling and imagination. This chapter will take up the relationships among children's storytelling, imagination, creative thinking, and the arts.

HOW DOES IMAGINATION DEVELOP?

Imagination is inherently relational, rooted in the early social interactions between infants/toddlers and their parents and caregivers. Face-to-face interactions through which infants see themselves reflected in the responsive face of the other assure that children will recognize and respond to the affective expressions of others (Legerstee & Varghese, 2001). The roots of empathy can be found in the profoundly social nature of mutual engagement and emotional connection between child and adult. Mutual engagement, referred to as attachment in the developmental and psychoanalytic literatures by various writers, beginning in the late 1970s including Ainsworth and her colleagues (Ainsworth, Blehar, Waters, & Wall, 1978), Bowlby (1969/1982), and Bretherton and Mulholland (1999), and continuing more recently in the work of Fonagy and his colleagues (Fonagy, Gergely, Jurist, Target, 2002), fuels the development of the social imagination in childhood.

The social imagination grows out of the intricate web of relationships in which human experience is grounded. Its manifestation is capacity to imagine the experiences and lives and of others. It draws on developing capacity for empathy, beginning with recognition of the self in the other through repeated positive mutual interactions with trusted attachment figures. Expressions of early empathic response in childhood begin with experiences of affect contagion, as when one child's weeping induces another child's tears. As children grow, they become better able to differentiate between their own experiences and the experiences of others. Empathy may be considered a developmental process that optimally continues to unfold throughout the lifespan. Its expression differs at various life stages in accordance with environmental opportunities for identification with empathic others, as well as availability of attachment figures who can provide a secure base from which one can develop both a capacity for autonomy and for relationships with others. Growing capacity for empathy drives the development of social imagination.

The social imagination reveals an early capacity to hold the other in mind, and with repeated satisfying experience, tolerate the less than perfect matching of children's desires with adult responses. The developing social imagination gives rise to an increasingly realistic image of parent or teacher as separate individuals with unique ideas, perspectives and desires that not infrequently are at odds with children's ideas and wishes. Growing awareness of separateness is typically met with ambivalence; children both strive developmentally for increased autonomy and protest the distance that this implies. In trying to bend a parent's or teacher's will to their own, young children simultaneously assert and deny their growing sense of individual identity and differentiation from others.

More mature forms of empathy involve not only identification and mirroring of affect or emotion, but also growing cognitive capacity to maintain one's own position as separate and unique. The social imagination calls for not only incorporating the experience of the other into one's own subjective world; it requires acknowledging the separateness of the other. Following what the philosopher Emmanuel Levinas in 2000 referred to as the face-to-face, encounters with the other involve both a subjective experience of the other as similar to, and as different from the self. This phenomenon, in which empathy is joined with feelings of separateness or distance, is foundational to Levinas' philosophy of ethics, and relevant to an engaged, responsible pedagogy. The social imagination emerges from these everyday oscillations between identification with others and cognitive capacity to establish and maintain one's own individual boundaries and sense of self.

What Levinas (2000) refers to as distance may be conceptualized as psychological differentiation in which the difference between self and other is felt. Borrowing from Margaret Mahler, Fred Pine, and Anni Bergman's (1975/2000) book, *The Psychological Birth of the Human Infant,* in which they describe a developmental trajectory of separation-individuation, emotional growth in the early years can be said to turn on the pivotal role of the psychological experience of feeling both closeness and distance between self and other. In 1971/2000, Heinz Kohut similarly posited that empathy alone is insufficient for emotional growth. He described "mirroring" as the experience in which the self is reflected in the other and pointed to the inevitable breaks in mirroring that lead to differentiation of self from other. Growth in capacity for caring relationships, Kohut (1984) proposed, emerges from the developing ability to tolerate both closeness and distance.

Feeling of distance between self and other is also critical to developing cognitive capacity. In a similar vein, Wellman, in 2002, observed that the developmental phenomenon known as theory of mind suggests both expanding capacity for understanding one's own mind, and for understanding that others may have different beliefs and intentions. The social imagination, I maintain here, serves a bridging function between self and other, between one's own position and the imagined experience of the other. It is a prerequisite for engaged action in the world, and for developing a sense of responsibility for the lives of others. Nurturing the social imagination can therefore be viewed as an ethical response to the responsibility of teaching, a pedagogy based on responsibility for one's students. Nurturing the social imagination in children is foundational to a responsive and responsible pedagogy, and foundational also to an educational ethos that encourages children to develop and to act from a position of identification and concern for others.

While there is broad agreement about the importance of imagination in furthering creative problem-solving, there is relatively little emphasis on how imagination might be nurtured. This is especially the case regarding the social imagination, which resides at the locus of pedagogy and ethics. There is need to cultivate a pedagogic imagination that can envision how the social imagination can embrace and act upon the perceived similarities that undergird empathy, as well as the perceived differences that speak to distance between individuals. The social imagination, formed by relational experiences of closeness and distance, is also critical to understanding and enacting inter-cultural encounters where moments of empathy as well as distance predominate.

The social imagination is the first form of imagination to emerge in childhood: it emerges from real relationships between children and responsive, trustworthy parents, caregivers, and teachers. Rooted in early physical experience, the social imagination anticipates and paves the way for other forms of imagination that involve symbolic representation in language and narrative, or in physical, embodied or visual form. For example, children's narrative and emerging storytelling ability and early representation of lived experience, including affective or emotional experience, in art media are all symbolic means by which experience, including affective or emotional experience are represented.

Like Dewey (1932/1990), who in 1932 wrote that the purpose of education was for life as lived and not as preparation for life, Vygotsky (1934/1987), wrote that imagination was a process that was both reality-bound and that encouraged freedom without any constraints of practicality. In a work translated into English only in 2004, he laid out his ideas regarding the role of imagination in human life. For Vygotsky, the imagination represented a significant human achievement; by dint of imagination people were freed from the constricting realities of their lives and thus able to imagine other ways of being.

NURTURING IMAGINATION

Imagining provides the possibility of multiple responses to questions about the world. It provides a means for children to reflect on their experience, as through a kaleidoscope—each reflection, a refraction of experience, yielding a different story, painting or dramatic scene. Imagination is the tool with which young children investigate, and through creative acts they reflect on and derive meaning from their experiences in the world. The experimental and improvisational nature of children's play and narrative make these the theater of childhood, filled with the passions, theories, stories, comedies and tragedies of children's everyday lives. The arts provide pathways by which children can develop and express their theories about the world, and formulate the questions that will extend their understanding and ultimately challenge these same theories.

Increasingly, however, imagination and the kinds of creative activity that the arts call for exist on the margins of school life. Even in classrooms for young children, opportunities to play and to engage in the arts are relegated to recreation rather than integral to curriculum. Imagination is dismissed as daydreaming, peripheral to, and even at odds with the real purpose of school. Imagination continues to be the stepchild of skills-based learning, despite its recognition as central to the development of thinking in children by such diverse writers as Sigmund Freud (1901/1980), Jean Piaget (1929/1973), Lev Vygotsky (1932/1987; 2004), and Donald Winnicott (1971).

Imagination facilitates rather than derails thinking. It provides the spark by which theories are envisioned and enacted in the world. Through the creative acts that provide shape and form to children's theories, imagination provides the ground upon which the ability to reflect on lived experience first emerges. Dewey, in is 1902 essay, *The Development of Attention* (1902/1956), spoke to developing a "culture of imagination" in which children are afforded occasions where they can express and enter into an exchange with others about their experiences and understandings. As early as 1934, Vygotsky (1934/1987) unequivocally observed that "imagination is a necessary, integral aspect of realistic thinking" (p. 349), and that complex forms of understanding call for more complex forms of imagining. When imagination is invoked, different ways of being in the world and of making sense of experience become possible.

The arts occupy a special relationship in the development and expression of children's imagination. In her extensive writing and lecturing in the area of aesthetic education Maxine Greene (2004a, 2004b) has over the course of more than three decades pointed to the role of the arts in awakening interest, and in furthering social justice. More recently, her colleagues at the Lincoln Center Institute for the Arts in Education have written on the role of imagination in people's lives, in-school and out-of-school

(Liu & Noppe-Brandon, 2009). The arts provide an avenue through which children can re-imagine, revisit and reflect on their own experiences, and imagine the lives of others. The arts provide multiple entry points into the development and elaboration of imagination; creative acts in varied arts media and forms give expression to children's embodied understanding. In the section that follows, I explore the role of the arts in developing capacity for imagination and for the development of creative thinking.

THE ARTS AND IMAGINATION

The arts provide entry points into the development of multiple forms of imagination in children, from the social imagination to the more symbolic forms of imagination represented by children's narrative storytelling and other creative works of art. The arts, including dramatic play—the theater of childhood—provide opportunities for the kinds of inter-subjective encounters with others that help children develop capacity for social imagination. The arts, additionally, are an important means by which children learn to deploy abstract symbol systems, a necessary component of imagination.

Despite the centrality of the arts to the development of the imagination, the arts have a diminished presence in education, even in the early childhood years, where the arts have traditionally been prominently featured. For Vygotsky, the arts provided a liberating function by freeing one from the boundaries of a narrow reality. The arts, though, also function as metaphor for tension between freedom and boundaries. Reluctance to engage in the arts often serves as a proxy for concerns about the optimal balance between freedom and structure, expression and boundaries.

Responsible pedagogy requires that teachers learn how to create the structures that children need in order to work freely, and, importantly, how to manage freedom responsibly. Two significant tensions in early childhood education, though not exclusively, find their fullest expression in the arts. These are the tensions between child-initiated and directed activity, and between process-oriented and product-oriented activity. Decreased opportunity to engage in the creative arts and in the social interactions that can nourish a growing social imagination intersects with teacher anxiety about classroom management.

The specter of messiness provokes fear of child initiative—in other words, the arts will provide license for irresponsible freedom, with resulting breaching of boundaries. Messiness and the risk of disorder provoke dread of breakdown of adult authority, commonly expressed as fear of children "going wild" or "out of control." Activities that require a minimum of movement are favored over those that involve child initiative and movement or that might give the appearance of disorder. Music, dance, paint, and clay have been edited out of many classrooms; crayons and markers are favored, as are teacher-prepared materials, especially in advance of holidays.

A second, related tension is between process and product. Progressive pedagogies have long emphasized process over product in children's art-making, and children's initiative over teacher-direction. In practice, teacher-directed activity allows fewer possibilities for disorder, but has the effect of quashing children's spontaneity. Teachers often spend inordinate amounts of time cutting out shapes and duplicating forms for children to color. The children, it should be noted, are generally enthusiastic about these activities. Limiting as they are, they offer greater opportunity for choice and expressiveness than the drill and practice regimens of many skill development activities.

The changing ethos of education, a response to increased pressure to prepare children for the academic rigors and achievement testing that lie ahead, has effectively transformed the arts from an avenue for developing imagination to a tool for furthering learning in other content areas. The arts are typically called upon as tools to illustrate early attempts at writing, to enhance motivation, to render subject matter more interesting, and, for the youngest children, as a restful alternative to the twin stressors of early academics and decreased opportunities for play. Tension between the arts as tools to teach curriculum content, and as entry points into the development of the imagination is the end product of the diminished role of the creative arts in education, and of generalized anxiety about learning and its measurement.

Partnerships between schools and cultural arts organizations, and between institutions of higher education and cultural arts organizations (Korn-Bursztyn, 2003, 2005) have done much to introduce teachers to the arts as an integral part of classroom experience. In a case study of a partnership between a New York City elementary school and an arts organization, Korn-Bursztyn (2005) traced the impact of the partnership on the school's culture, pedagogy and children's interest and enthusiasm for both the arts and the curricular connections their teachers introduced.

The arts provide opportunities for the kinds of intersubjective experiences in which children enact their understandings of the social imagination. For example, when children engage in co-generative dialogue about works of art, including those they have created, they provide and encounter opportunities for empathic understanding, and for learning how minds and individual subjectivities differ from each other. Such encounters provide for a possibility of what Gadamer referred to as a merging of horizons (see Warnke, 1987), a process that involves an imaginative leap in creating new possibilities out of social understandings.

Metaphoric thinking, and the capacity for creative thinking that metaphoric fluency gives rise to, are closely related to the growth of the imagination. In the section that follows, I will explore the relationship among the imagination, the arts, and creative thinking.

FOSTERING CREATIVE THINKING

The early years are increasingly gaining recognition as a critical time when attitudes towards learning are shaped and the foundation for academic skill development first laid down. It is also a time when intellectual curiosity and the cognitive skills that enable sustained inquiry begin to emerge. This makes young children prolific questioners who bring this compelling need to know to their everyday lives. Even the casual observer of young children will soon be struck by the desire of children to learn about the world, and by their intuitive understanding that one gets to the root of how and why the world works by asking questions, imagining possibilities, and by doing. These three characteristics—asking questions, imagining, and doing—provide the underpinnings for the development of critical thinking in early childhood.

Asking questions, imagining, and doing are also foundational to the arts in early education. The arts draw on young children's affinity for asking questions, exploring and experimenting—activities that are consistent with an inquiry based approach to learning that can enhance children's capacity for imagining and playing with possibilities. The arts are consonant with young children's need to concretize or make real what they explore, learn and imagine. They offer the possibility of drawing upon young children's impulse to do and to create, grounding this within an approach to critical thinking that places curiosity and inquiry, experimentation and experiential learning, imagination and its expression at its core.

The capacity to ask questions emerges from recognition of the gap between what one knows and what one needs to know. Imagination in the early childhood years fills these gaps and plays an important role in the development of young children's critical thinking processes. Imagining provides opportunity to play with alternate responses to questions about the world and presents children with multiple ways of expressing their understandings of how the world works. For young children, imagination is not a flight of fancy or escapist entertainment, but rather, it serves the function of facilitating reflection by helping children to step back from active engagement with the world, and through their creative acts, making meaning of their experiences.

Imagination, and the creative acts that lend shape and form to its expression, provide the ground upon which the capacity to reflect upon personal experience first emerges.

Reflection undergirds creative thinking; it provides the mechanism by which experience may be considered, first self-referentially, and later, from multiple vantage points. We see this first in very young children's self-talk, in the murmurings of young children before they fall asleep and in toddlers' early play; the child is subject, the perspective predominantly "me." Somewhat later, the observant listener will note the multiple roles and voices that can be heard in toddlers' and preschoolers' self-talk and play. Engaging in imaginary conversations between several subjects, young children can move gracefully between these voices, adopting the pitch, mannerisms, and likely perspectives of the varied characters represented.

Echoes of a de-centering process, a process that will continue throughout the child's life and that is critical to the lifelong development of the capacity to engage in creative thinking, can be discerned here. In assuming multiple roles and in adopting multiple voices, young children signal a growing capacity to step outside of their own vantage points and consider, albeit briefly, the perspectives of others.

IMAGINATION, STORYTELLING AND THE ARTS

In his 1990 book, *Acts of Meaning*, Jerome Bruner reflects on how an individual's sense of self arises out of the continual process of making meaning. Describing the self as a story or narrative sequence that we tell about our lives, he points to the influence of experience and the impact of historical circumstances on the stories we tell about ourselves. Narrative, or the capacity to tell stories, is central to human experience. We create storied accounts that lend meaning to our own lives and to the actions of others. The narratives that we construct, beginning in childhood, arise out of a matrix of relationships with others, and are informed and shaped by the meaning that we make of our life experiences.

Sarbin, in 1986, proposed that the human need to impose structure on experience leads to the organization of experience in story-like form. Over the past several decades, children's narratives have been examined from different perspectives, including the linguistic, social, and developmental. From a linguistic perspective, children's narratives have been examined for syntactical and grammatical structure. From a social perspective, children's stories have been studied for how they symbolically represent the scripts of everyday life, while reflecting the linguistic and social codes of the culture. From a cognitive perspective, the stories that children tell have been studied for what they imply about development, while the educational literature has focused on the contributions of storytelling experiences to children's language development, including the acquisition of English as a second language.

Children's growing communicative competence helps them give language to experience, taking an active role in creating understanding and meaning out of experience.

Their self-talk reveals the impact of the social and linguistic codes that surround and constitute everyday life for children. Self-talk, a particular genre of children's storytelling, fills a number of different functions for the growing child. For the young child, talking to oneself upon going to sleep or upon awakening provides a self-soothing function, helping children regulate their reactions to what are often complicated transitions between wakefulness and sleep. Self-talk accompanies dramatic or pretend play, particularly the solitary or parallel play of the young child, offering a running narrative that reveals the social and cultural expectations that undergird the everyday lives of children.

An excerpt from a narrative soliloquy by a three-year-old boy named Sam follows, illustrating how the stories that children tell take up the social and cultural values and expectations of the particular environments in which children grow. Here, the socially desirable role of initiative and action intersects with social expectations, marking the border between babyhood and "big boy" status. Sam takes on multiple voices, playing both adult and child roles, alternating between a deep, mannish voice, and a young child's sing-song, high-pitched register. The brief narrative that begins as an ode to heavy work machines merges with his growing experience as a listener and teller of stories.

[Child's voice]: One tractor-shovel
Two tractor-shovel
That other tractor-shovel. Give me the . . .
Three tractor-shovel.

[Man's voice]: I have a question.

[Child's voice]: Oh oh. I can't let it go down and I can grab it like like a . . . Look! See that—I—and I couldn't do it. I almost grabbed it but it didn't bounce . . .
See I can do it. I can do it.
Matter of fact, I can do it without dropping it.
I can do it. I can do it.
See I can do it 'cause I could.

[Man's voice]: You are a big boy, you can.

[Child's voice]: Look, look like that monkey goes. He plays with books. And I don't play with books. I read them. It can say *Big Wheels* by Ann Rockwell. Wheels make us, help us drill up the street and dig up the street.

Children's growing capacity to create narratives contributes to the development of reflective capacity, an ability to reflect on experience through representation and transformation. At their core, children's narratives hold nuggets of lived experience. These narratives, though, are not faithful accounts of everyday experience, hewing to linear conventions of sequence and time, but rather, are filled with associations to meaningful experiences, daydreams, and the contents of their imaginations. An example, taken from a different conversation around Vincent Van Gogh's *The Starry Night*, points to the highly idiosyncratic turn a conversation among a group of three-year-old children takes as they point to what they notice and imagine, and strain to see what their peers are seeing in the painting and in their own imaginations.

> **Davey:** (pointing to the dark swirling clouds): Snow—going to . . . rain! Clouds drop it. Clouds dropping on my head right here!
>
> **Kate:** A snowball. I know one here—my mommy's umbrella.
>
> **Davey:** A snake! Going down there and going down . . . This spider over there—sleeping!
>
> **Sarita :** A house. I see a spider and a snake in there . . . scratching me!
> I'm shouting for my mom.
>
> **Don:** A spider going home, going home he's sleeping. Spider going to bed. She's got a blanket . . . That's his house.
>
> **Davey:** There's a house—going down there. He's going with my father.
>
> **Edward:** The spider's sleeping there.
>
> **Davey :** I don't see a spider.
>
> **Edward:** (with nose to painting) In here, in here.
>
> **James:** A snake is round and round . . . he's sleeping.
>
> **Sarita:** I'm scared—spider catching me. I go in my house and sleep. This is my house (points to building in painting) and that's my mom. I'm sleeping here. I'm scared and (there's a) monster in my closet!
>
> **Sarita:** (points to the same building again) This is (very softly) my Sri Lanka. Gods are fighting for me. Monsters don't like fighting.
> My moon, my mother, and father and friends.

Later, Sarita takes her mother by the hand to show her *The Starry Night* reproduction that earlier in the day was introduced to her class. Pointing to the spire atop the building, she murmurs, "My Sri Lanka." Her mother, smiling, confirmed that her daughter's association was, in all likelihood, a reference to the emotionally meaningful experience the family had six months earlier, when they visited the family's native city of Kandy. The spire to which her Sarita pointed, her mother observed, resembled the ancient Buddhist temple in Kandy, with which her daughter was greatly impressed.

TRANSLATING AND TRANSFORMING EXPERIENCE IN THE ARTS

Children's narratives, however, are not always crafted in the verbal register. Their stories, which include bits of lived experience, are richly mined with artistic media. Sometimes, a kinesthetic movement rather than a visual stimulus evokes an association to an experience. For example, some months after his class worked with a teaching artist to look at and respond to Van Gogh's *The Starry Night*, a three-year-old boy leaped excitedly from the table where he was helping to stir cake batter round and round with a wooden spoon, and ran across the room to where a reproduction of the painting hung on a wall. Pointing to the swirls of blue paint, he stirred the air vigorously—as he had the batter a few moments earlier—and exclaimed, "Look, it's just like this."

The arts are a rich resource for the transformation of experience into expression. Like early childhood practice, the arts center curiosity and inquiry, experimentation and experiential learning, imagination and expression. The arts provide another function significant to the development of the capacity for reflection in young children—a capacity to consider situations and problems from multiple vantage points. The arts foster a multimodal and multi-perspectival approach to reflection and to the creation of personal knowledge about the world. They do so by providing an entry point into reflection on personal experience, a key component in the development of critical thinking.

The arts provide another function significant to the development of creative thinking in young children. They foster a multi-modal approach to reflection and to the creation of personal knowledge about the world. They do so by providing, first, a point of entry into reflection on one's own personal experience, a key component in the early development of critical thinking. The point of entry that the arts provide young children to reflect on their experience is first and foremost multi-sensory and multi-modal. Opportunities to work with art materials, to hear and to make music, to be in the company of dancers and to dance, to witness storytellers and to create one's own story dramas are all means by which young children reflect-in-action on their own experience. Reflection on experience is key here to the early development of creative thinking; by reflecting-in-action children build personal ways of learning about and knowing the world.

By providing multiple entry points into learning, the arts address a broad range of abilities, talents, and learning styles. This is highly meaningful to early childhood educators, other professionals, and parents who seek to support their children's learning by attending to and drawing upon the multiple, sensory-rich ways that children have of experiencing, learning about, and developing theories about the world. Drawing upon diverse sensory modalities, Howard Gardner, in 1983, first proposed a theory of multiple intelligences (MI)—multiple sensory- and experiential-based forms of intelligence, suggesting multiple entry points into experiencing and learning about the world. His wide body of work in MI (2000), over the past two decades, invokes the sensual nature of children's learning.

Young children call upon their perceptual and physical experiences, translating these across haptic, visual and auditory modalities, that is, from the visual to the gestural and performative. In this manner young children formulate and express early conceptual understanding, playing with concepts across art forms and learning modalities. The arts provide a means for children to respond to and to create new experience by giving form to ideas generated by children's own creative acts. Through the act of creating, lived experience is given shape, form, and expression. For example, immediately following activities in which binary concepts including high and low, fast and slow were studied in a music workshop, Jesse sat down at an art table, folded a clean piece of drawing paper diagonally, and with great focus, deliberately drew with a single black crayon a triangle on each of the two panels. Filling one triangle in with his crayon, he announced: "A light and a dark tent," and put his crayon down. Perhaps inspired by the binary concepts explored earlier that morning in the music workshop, Jesse deliberately created stark shapes, a study in binaries, and different from the more elaborate, representational drawings he typically produced.

Through the visual arts, music, dance, and drama, young children explore their own experiences and encounter the experiences, creative productions and perspectives of others. When, for example, children engage in dialogue with their peers and teachers about a work of art, they encounter other views that may or may not be similar to their own. Such dialogic experiences provide children with opportunities for gentle, de-centering experiences in which children hear and respond to the different perspectives of their peers, learning to acknowledge the reality that other people have different perspectives.

Unlike occasions in which differences of viewpoint, as in who gets the tricycle first, result in playground tussles, the arts provide opportunities for children to encounter and to respond to different ways of seeing the world in an affect-rich, but less emotionally charged situations. When young children de-center, they move beyond their own impressions, making room for the possibility of other perspectives. De-centering experiences are invaluable for the development of creative thinking, which implies the ability to step outside of one's immediate impression to consider alternate ways of perceiving the world.

TRANFORMING EXPERIENCE: METAPHORIC THINKING AND THE ARTS

The arts provide another important function in the development of creative thinking. They create a bridge between the representational and the semiotic, a means by which young children can move between representation of meaning in pictorial form and linguistic expression, and between the representational and the symbolic. Research in children's developing metaphoric thinking suggests that metaphoric understanding, for example, expressed in children's visual representations of experience, often precede the linguistic.

Children's drawings, for example, often contain story-fragments and emotions for which words have not yet been formed. Anger and frustration become stomping feet and heavily inked lines; narrative follows affect and its expression. The arts provide a bridge between affect and expression, and between experience and its symbolic representation or transformation. The transformative nature of the arts, which makes possible the transformation of lived experience into its representation in the visual arts, dance, music, drama, and literature, points to its importance in developing metaphoric thinking in young children.

Metaphoric thinking calls upon the capacity to step outside of one's immediate experience of an event and to transfer that understanding to an entirely different set of circumstances. The arts provide an opportunity for young children to make connections between experiences by calling upon multiple modes of representation, including, but not limited to, the linguistic. When young children become familiar with the processes, materials, and representative works of specific art forms, their expressive repertoires are extended and enhanced. The arts provide opportunity for young children to move, for example, between the physical experience of dance, or gesture and movement, to its visual representation in line and shape, or in language. They help children give form to ideas generated by the imagination, inspired by creating and responding to works of art. Through the child's creative acts, what was unformulated experience is now given shape, form, and expression.

Metaphoric thinking has another, related cognitive benefit linked to language and literacy development. The capacity to understand and use metaphor is related to children's ability to comprehend and think critically about text. Fluency in metaphoric thinking, especially where this involves linguistic expression, is implicated in higher order reading skills in the middle childhood years. Metaphoric thinking informs and shapes reading comprehension, the most sophisticated of reading skills, and that which is most closely associated with language-based critical thinking abilities.

In summary, the arts in the early years provide opportunities to extend teacher understanding and parental support of the early foundations of critical thinking. Work in the arts can contribute to adults' ability to appreciate children's thinking when it diverges from the expected and to imagine new ways of working with curriculum. For the adults in the lives of young children, engaging in the arts provides a means of joining children in making meaning of the world. Significantly, the arts provide opportunity for both adults and children to observe and reflect on those gaps between the known and the unknown that imagination and creativity fill.

The arts provide opportunity to formulate questions and to consider possible worlds and perspectives that might otherwise be missed. Imagination is germane to what Maxine Greene (see 1978; 2004) refers to as "wide awakeness," an orientation towards the world that leaves one open to the possibilities that observation, experience and creative thinking may bring. Young children are, by nature, wide-awake in their approach to life. Teachers and parents can appreciate and re-learn from their children a wide-awake approach to everyday life, that offers the possibility of re-engaging adults with their own imaginative and creative processes (see Singer, 2009).

CONCLUSION

The contemporary over-emphasis on testing and measurement of mastery of academic content has depleted education of its broader social mission and potential. The arts call for movement from dialogue to enactment; in doing so they provide opportunities for children to act upon their growing understandings of intersubjective experience through embodied activity. This chapter traces the relationships between the development of the social imagination and creative thinking, and explores the role of the arts in furthering children's development. It calls for re-imagining early childhood practice in which the imagination and the development of creative thinking are centrally located. Arts initiatives grounded in an approach that privileges nurturing imagination and the development of creative thinking can address a critical shortcoming in the lives of many young children.

REFERENCES

Ainsworth, M. S., Blehar, M.C., Waters, E., & Wall, S. (1978). *Patterns of attachment: A psychological study of the strange situation.* Oxford, England: Erlbaum.

Bowlby, J. (1982). *Attachment and loss: Vol.1. Attachment* (2nd ed.). New York: Basic Books. (Original work published 1969)

Bretherton, I., & Mulholland, C. (1999). Internal working models in attachment relationships: A construct revisited. In J. Cassidy & P. Shaver (Eds.), *Handbook of attachment* (pp. 89–111). New York: Guilford Press.

Burton, J. M., Horowitz, R, & Abeles, H. (2000). Learning in and through the arts: The question of transfer. *Studies in Art Education, 41*(3), 228–257.

Bruner, J. (1990). *Acts of meaning.* Cambridge, MA: Harvard University Press.

Dewey, J. (1956). The development of attention. In the child and the curriculum and the school and society. Chicago: The University of Chicago Press. (Original work published 1902)

Dewey, J. (1990). *The school and society & the child and the curriculum.* Chicago: The University of Chicago Press. (Original work published 1932)

Fonagy, P., Gergely, G., Jurist, E. L., & Target, M. (2002). *Affect regulation, mentalization and the development of the self.* New York: Other Press.

Freud, S. (1980). *On dreams.* New York: W.W. Norton & Co. (Original work published 1901)

Gardner, H. (1983). *Frames of mind: The theory of multiple intelligences.* New York: Basic Books.

Gardner, H. (2000). *Intelligence reframed: Multiple intelligences for the 21st century.* New York: Basic Books.

Greene, M. (1978). *Landscapes of learning.* New York: Teachers College Press.

Greene, M. (1993/2004a). The artistic-aesthetic curriculum: Leaving imprints on the changing face of the world. In M. Greene (Ed.), *Releasing the imagination: Essays on education, the arts, and social change* (pp. 177–185). New York, NY: National Association of Independent Schools.

Greene, M. (2004b). *Releasing the imagination: Essays on education, the arts, and social change.* New York: National Association of Independent Schools.

Kohut, H. (1971/2000). *Analysis of the self: Systematic approach to treatment of narcissistic personality disorders.* Madison, CT: International Universities Press.

Kohut, H. (1984). *How does analysis cure?* Chicago: University of Chicago Press.

Korn-Bursztyn, C. (2003). School change and the arts: A case study. *Teaching Artist Journal, 1*(4), 220–227.

Korn-Bursztyn, C. (2005). Crossing institutional cultures: Brooklyn College and Lincoln Center Institute for the Arts in Education. In M. Holzer & S. Noppe-Brandon (Eds.), *Community in the making: Lincoln Center Institute, the arts, and teacher education* (pp. 45–57). New York, NY: Teachers College Press.

Legerstee, M., & Varghese, J. (2001). The role of maternal affect mirroring on social expectancies in three-month-old infants. *Child Development, 72,* 1301–1313.

Levinas, E. (2000). *Entre nous: Essays on thinking-of-the-other.* New York: Columbia University Press.

Liu, E., & Noppe-Brandon, S. (2009). *Imagination first: Unlocking the power of possibility.* New York: Jossey-Bass

Mahler, M. S., Pine, F., & Bergman, A. (2000). *The psychological birth of the human infant: Symbiosis and individuation*. New York: Basic Books. (Original work published 1975)

Piaget, J. (1973). *The child's conception of the world*. St. Albans, NF: Granada Publishing. (Original work published 1929)

Sarbin, T. R. (Ed.). (1986).*Narrative psychology: The storied nature of human conduct*. New York: Praeger Publishers.

Singer, J. (2009). Researching imaginative play and adult consciousness: Implications for daily and literary creativity. *Psychology of Aesthetics, Creativity, and the Arts, 3*(4), 190–199.

Vygotsky, L. (1987). The imagination and its development. In R. Rieber & A. Carton (Eds.), *Problems of general psychology & thinking and speech*. New York: Plenum Press. (Original work published 1932)

Vygotsky, L. (1987). Lecture 5: Imagination and its development in childhood. In R.W. Rieber & A. S. Carlton (Eds.). *The collected works of L.S. Vygotsky, Vol.1* (pp. 339–349). New York: Plenum Press. (Original work published 1934)

Vygotsky, L. S. (2004). Imagination and creativity in childhood. *Journal of Russian & East European Psychology, 42*(1), 7–97.

Warnke, G. (1987). *Gadamer: Hermeneutics, tradition and reason*. Sanford, CA: Stanford University Press.

Wellman, H. M. (2002). Understanding the psychological world: Developing a theory of mind. In C. Goswami (Ed.), *Blackwell handbook of childhood cognitive development* (pp. 167–187). Malden, MA: Blackwell.

Winnicott, D. W. (1971). *Playing and reality*. New York: Basic Books, Inc.

PART II

IMAGINATION AND THE ARTS:
CASE STUDIES FROM THE FIELD

CHAPTER 5

JOY IN THE MAKING

Young Children and the Visual Arts

Kirsten Cole
City University of New York

ABSTRACT

Scholarly research and anecdotal evidence suggest that young children's growth and learning are deeply enhanced through engagement with the visual arts. Working with visual arts media offers opportunities for young children to connect joyfully with their learning and to express their complex understandings of the world. The visual arts support the development of children's narrative capacity and provide opportunities for expression of complicated emotional realities. Arts-rich early childhood classroom presents many opportunities for collaboration and community building, yet parents and teachers often feel unprepared as to how to encourage young children's engagement in the visual arts. This chapter provides parents and teachers with a language for understanding and describing the importance of young children's work in the visual arts, and describes strategies and practices for fostering meaningful experiences in the visual arts.

Young Children and the Arts, pages 71–90

71

VIGNETTE

I teach art education classes to future early childhood teachers. One afternoon, when my son Max was two and a half, I brought him to the art studio classroom where I teach. To occupy him while I prepped materials, I set Max up with paints in the primary colors, a brush, water, a sponge and a tray. While setting out the materials I wondered aloud, "What colors do you think you can make?" and let him get to work. As he painted I checked in occasionally, making comments that reflected the choices and discoveries I saw him making.

He worked quickly through several sheets of paper, sometimes applying a few strokes before being ready to move on, sometimes applying layer after layer, shape after shape, until the page was soggy with an olive brown mass of paint swirls. As he painted he talked to himself, declaring the colors that were appearing on the page or narrating the story behind the shapes and lines he created. His paintings evolved continually as he assigned new meanings, added new shapes and mixed new colors.

After some time, I noticed that Max had become conspicuously silent. I looked across the room and saw a look of utter absorption on his face. I walked over to his work space and heard him whispering gleefully "Purple...purple...purple!" As I got closer I saw that he had dumped the red and blue paints out on his tray and mixed up a vivid purple. He repeated a cycle of dipping his sponge first in the water, sopping up paint, then squeezing the sponge with his fist. With utter fascination, Max observed the purple water flowing through the spaces between his fingers, down his forearms and clothes and onto the floor below. So consumed with his discovery of this radiant color he didn't seem to mind or even notice getting wet. "Purple...purple...purple!"

INTRODUCTION

Anyone who has observed young children deeply engaged in art making, has had the chance to witness what psychologist Mihaly Csikszentmihalyi, in his seminal 1990 book *Flow: The Psychology of Optimal Experience*, described as the concept of flow—that is, the complete joyful absorption in an activity. Max's discovery of the richness of purple, achieved through his own experimentation and sensory experience of the paint, resulted in a complete immersion in his early understandings about color, the mixing of pigments, the liquid and viscose properties of the paint. While I had set the parameters for his exploration, Max made these discoveries on his own. Even at that early age the opportunity to learn autonomously was a source of palpable satisfaction for him.

When considering the learning opportunities that the visual arts offer young children, I recall an idea I first heard expressed by education philosopher Patricia Carini, in her 2001 book *Starting Strong: A Different Look at Children, Schools and Standards.* Carini asserted that we must recognize that all children are born striving to make sense of the world. This concept, though simple on the surface, pushes back against the current structure of the education system, in which we continually sort and classify children by increasingly narrow standards. Though perhaps not its intention, the ubiquity of high stakes testing as a means to measure the success of the school system leads many to believe that some children can learn well while others cannot. Given the right circumstances, however, all children can activate their desire to make sense of the world and to learn. Working in the arts provides a powerful tool for creating learning opportunities for all children. As parents and teachers we must provide rich and varied opportunities for such engagement.

In this chapter I will describe the kinds of learning that the visual arts promote and share some strategies for supporting young children's engagement with the visual arts. The goal of this chapter is not to suggest specific projects. There are many such resources already, and often such guides suffer from being overly prescriptive and teacher directed. Rather this chapter will discuss the ways in which the visual arts are critical in early childhood, and how parents and teachers can foster experiences in the visual arts. The following four topics will be addressed:

- Growth, learning and the arts
- Knowing the learner in order to facilitate experiences with the visual arts
- Responding to children's work
- Aesthetic education for young children

Before I begin, a brief note about my own background in the arts. I remember my excitement as a young maker, drawing portraits of my neighbors, sculpting abstract forms in clay, using scraps to build imagined worlds. As I grew, however, I began to believe that I did not have that ineffable talent for art that others had. Like most children I found that my opportunities for engagement with the arts receded as I made my way through school. Finally, in adulthood, I took a night class in art-making with found materials, rediscovered the joy in making, and returned to school. MFA in hand, I began working as a teaching artist at an afterschool program in Brooklyn and as a museum educator leading workshops for visiting school children. Currently I am a doctoral candidate in the PhD Program in Urban Education at the Graduate Center, CUNY, and teach art education classes to teacher education candidates and teachers, while parenting two young children.

Working at the intersection of these roles—as teacher, learner, artist, and parent—I continually learn and relearn the joys of making art. While I have worked with young children in a variety of settings, in this chapter I will refer often to observations of my son, Max. Working alongside him over the past five years, I have had the opportunity to witness the evolution of a young art maker.

GROWTH, LEARNING AND THE ARTS

Fortunately, in the realm of early childhood education, the visual arts are still generally recognized as an integral component of the curriculum. Even at a time when budget cuts in public education have decimated support for the types of learning that are not assessed on high stakes tests, most early childhood classrooms still provide for access to some basic art materials: crayons, markers and play-doh. With additional knowledge of the visual arts, early childhood teachers may extend children's experiences with materials to include construction from recycled materials, clay, and paint. Unfortunately, with each passing year that a child spends in school, art recedes further from the curriculum. It is rare, for example, to find a dedicated easel and paint area in a fifth grade classroom. In early childhood, however, the arts are still recognized as a critical entry point for activating the learning and growth of young children.

As teachers we draw on what we have gathered through our life experience and our professional training to inform our teaching. Some of us enter the classroom recalling meaningful experiences in the visual arts, while others of us do not have such memories to draw from. Much of what passes for art education in the early childhood curriculum is overly prescriptive and teacher directed. Rows of identical turkeys, cut from handprints and colored with an identical palette may brighten many an early childhood classroom. However, they do not represent the deep engagement in the visual arts that we can and should provide to young children. Additionally, in some classrooms, access to art materials is seen as a time-filler, peripheral to "real" learning, or a reward for completion of "real" work. As parents and teachers, we must communicate our value for the visual arts and their role in children's lives by making them an integral part of the curriculum.

ENGAGING ALL KINDS OF LEARNERS

One reason the visual arts are critical for children at all stages of learning, but particularly in early childhood, is that they provide an entry point to engage different kinds of learners. As Howard Gardner's 1983 theory of multiple intelligence highlights, each of us learns best through different intelligences. While some children and adults respond well to verbal or written materials, others need to experience and communicate their learning through move-ment or music or the arts. When we limit children's education to early literacy activities such as early reading and writing, we reduce opportunities for many learners to make sense of the world. This is particularly true for children with special needs. As many an art, music or physical education teacher will tell you, it is often the "problem child," the one with labels and diagnoses, who shines in their class. When children are given the opportunity to engage their intellect through more active and multiple pathways, these students show capacity for focus, leadership and perseverance that their classroom teachers may not see during the rest of the school day.

In addition to engaging multiple types of learners, the visual arts also of-fer opportunity for flow—for joyful absorption in the discoveries that lead to learning. In that joyful state, the motivation for learning becomes inter-nalized. Eleanor Duckworth, in her 2006 book *The Having of Wonderful Ideas and Other Essays on Teaching and Learning*, described the moments when children teach themselves through discovery as "the having of wonderful ideas." She argued that our role as educators is to foster these types of expe-riences, times when children's curiosity and exploration fuels their learning process and yields the most meaningful learning. In these environments learning is intrinsic. Students move beyond the rote activity of providing answers for the teacher and are instead motivated by the excitement of seeking and responding to their own questions. Meaningful engagement with the visual arts enables this kind of joyful discovery and provides an excellent opportunity for parents and teachers to foster deep learning and intellectual development.

CONNECTIONS ACROSS THE CURRICULUM

Another critical argument for the visual arts in any classroom, but particu-larly the early childhood classroom, is the ways in which the arts invite and enable interdisciplinary learning. Young children, especially, ignore artificial distinctions between different subject areas. For example, a young learner might float seamlessly from her scientific observations of acorns to a narra-tive thread about the squirrels that gather them, which in turn leads her to demonstrate her knowledge about hibernation through a physical perfor-mance. Meryl Goldberg, in her 1997 book *Arts and Learning*, argued that we must recognize the arts as a methodology or tool for learning. Building in opportunities for children to develop and express their understandings of new concepts through the visual arts deepens and reinforces their learning.

Working with my son Max, I have observed him use the arts as a tool for expressing his burgeoning knowledge of complex concepts from na-ture. At age three and a half, Max spent one month in his pre-school classroom learning about the life cycle of the butterfly. Over the course of several weeks the class observed, drew and discussed the changes they were witnessing in the caterpillar habitat that hung in a corner of their room. Their study culminated in the release of the butterflies on a trip to a local garden.

At home one afternoon, Max worked steadily for over an hour, digging through a bag of recycled materials to assemble bits of egg carton, mesh, twine, pipe cleaners, tape and paper. The piece evolved over time, sparked initially by the properties of the egg carton, which seemed to evoke for Max a many-legged caterpillar. Once this phase of the piece was completed, he searched the right material to encase it in and decided upon plastic mesh to represent the chrysalis. Realizing he had neglected an earlier stage, Max added two, round, pipe cleaner eggs and finished by affixing a hand-drawn butterfly to the other side of the installation. When the piece was completed he insisted on string to hang it from the window, mirroring the chrysalises that had hung in his classroom (Figure 5.1).

Figure 5.1

At age four, Max followed up our reading of a book about how bodies work with a drawing of the circulatory system of a sheep. While showing me the completed drawing, Max excitedly traced veins drawn in deep blue and red leading to and from the sheep's heart and outward to the extremities. Clearly for Max and many other children, his work in the visual arts has helped to reinforce and communicate his understanding of complex scientific concepts.

Science is but one subject in which the visual arts can be used as a methodology for learning. For those interested in further reading, you may refer to the suggested readings at the end of this chapter. Authors who have written on the links between the visual arts and other subjects include Carol Korn (1998) on the connections between the visual arts and the development of narrative and literacy and Nancy Beal (2001) on the visual arts and social studies. Others teacher-researchers, including Karen Gallas (1994) and Julie Diamond (2008), have written on the ways in which the visual arts can be used as a thread to weave together all components of the early childhood curriculum. While it is also important for the arts to be permitted to exist for arts sake in the early childhood classroom, these authors described the myriad ways that the visual arts can be used as a tool for teaching and learning in all areas of the curriculum.

BUILDING COMMUNITY THROUGH MAKING TOGETHER

Kindergarten teachers like Vivian Gussin Paley (1998) and Julie Diamond (2008) have written eloquently of the power of the arts to build community in their classrooms. Anyone who has observed the hive of activity taking place in an early childhood classroom can tell you that painting, building and drawing can be highly interactive activities for young children. Children working individually alongside each other take regular breaks to look at each other's work, narrate the story that is emerging, ask questions, and make suggestions. Often these observations and conversations lead to collaborations that spring up organically, as children add to each other's pieces unhampered by the distinctions of "my work" and "your work."

Even within the adult (teacher education) classroom, I have witnessed the powerful capacity of the visual arts to build community. As part of the course I teach for pre- and in-service classroom teachers, we spend half of each session working with materials in the studio. Most weeks each student works individually, exploring a new material or building on the discoveries gained in the previous week. During our studio time, the students chat and laugh, share strategies with the material and comment on each other's work. It is during this half of the class that a warmth and collegiality grows. The atmosphere of the studio creates a culture of respect that serves us in the more traditional lecture/discussion half of the class, where rigorous but collegial debates arise as we respond to readings and new concepts.

Midway through the semester, I tell my teacher education students that we will be working on a group mural project. I begin with a quick slideshow of images of murals and a discussion of what murals are. I have the students count off to create groups so that they are now working in a group of new friends from around the room, rather than the comfortable habit of working with a neighbor. I give the students a large piece of butcher paper, paints, and collage materials and ask them to work together to generate an idea for a group mural. It is this week that the studio classroom really comes alive. The chatter and laughter are louder and lighter. Despite the levity, productivity is booming, with students collaboratively envisioning and creating complex pieces that fill them with enormous pride. When we share the pieces at the end of class, many students comment that working together they were able to accomplish much more than they could have on their own. Their reflections echo Vygotsyky's (1978) theories on the crucial role of social interaction and play in learning. The group mural project provides them with a rich and meaningful model of the power of collaborative work. While young children often arrive at visual arts collaboration organically, it is important to build in explicit opportunities for such group work in the early childhood classroom.

EXPRESSING FEELINGS THROUGH VISUAL LANGUAGE

Finally, the arts provide another language for young children to express their feelings and to make sense of the complex circumstances of their lives. During my pregnancy with our second child, I watched Max use his drawings to work through his anticipation of and reactions to the arrival of his baby brother. As my belly grew under his hands, Max created an almost daily series of portraits of our family. In many of these pictures I was the central figure, drawn as a giant circle with short lines protruding for my appendages, flanked on either side by narrow stick figures that represented Max and his father. Max would draw a small round figure in the middle of my circle self: "my baby" he explained. Following the birth of his brother Zeke, Max continued to draw his family portraits. Now, however, our newest member was often conspicuously absent. His father often loomed large and I was moved to the periphery of the page. Max would proudly display the pictures to visiting grandparents declaring, "Here's my family! Here's me and mommy and daddy." When asked if anyone was missing, Max would innocently reply, "No."

Finally one day, Max presented me one day with a picture of four bees floating above a flower, linked together by strong green lines from his mark-

Figure 5.2

ers (Figure 5.2). He told me that the drawing was of, "a family of bees, held together with string, so the baby doesn't get lost." I knew then, without his needing to tell me directly, that Max had made some peace with the new configuration of our family. Over the course of that year, I was relieved that Max's drawings gave him a visual language to express the complex, forbidden and nuanced responses that any young child might have on the arrival of a new sibling. His artwork opened up a safe space for him to anticipate, to erase, and eventually to embrace his younger brother.

KNOWING THE LEARNER IN ORDER TO FACILITATE EXPERIENCES WITH THE VISUAL ARTS

We have discussed the many ways in which the visual arts can and should play a central role in early childhood education. But how do we, as parents and teachers, facilitate meaningful experiences in the visual arts? Many of us are stymied by the perception that we must ourselves be talented artists in order to teach arts to children. In the later stages of artistic development there are certainly strategies and techniques that can be taught. In early childhood, however, the main requirement is a commitment to facilitating experiences with materials that allow children to come to discoveries on their own. In order to foster meaningful experiences, we must know the children we are working with. This knowledge strengthens our capacity to introduce children to materials and to set parameters that spark but do not inhibit expression and exploration.

Before we begin to work with young children it is crucial to consider what the child brings, both in his or her experiences with visual arts materials and in his or her intentions as a maker. Both Nancy Smith (1984) and Marianne Kerlavage (1997) have written excellent guides to gaining a deeper understanding of the phases that young children pass through as they grow in their experiences with the visual arts. These authors offer detailed descriptions and specific examples of the evolution of children's growth in their understanding of themselves as makers and the capacity that the arts have to communicate their intentions. Drawing on the work of Smith and Kerlavage, what follows is a brief guide to the phases you might see young children pass through.

One caveat, however, before we begin: As with other aspects of growth (physical, intellectual, social and emotional), children's artistic growth does not develop in lockstep or represent a set of rigid benchmarks determined by chronological age. Rather than measure children's growth and learning in comparison with age norms, parents and teachers must train ourselves to be close observers of children as individuals and to appreciate their growth in relation to their own development. That said, it is helpful for us to have a shared language for understanding the phases that we will likely see young children move through as they grow in their experiences as makers. The descriptions below will help you to understand and appreciate what you are seeing and to give you language to express the changes you are observing in each maker.

SENSORY EXPLORATIONS OF VERY YOUNG MAKERS

From birth to age seven, children's relationship to visual arts materials and their understanding of how the arts serve them grow in layers. Very young makers experience the visual arts as a purely sensory experience. Making marks in sand, squeezing mud, and stacking blocks are all profoundly satisfying and immediate experiences for young children. These explorations serve as the foundation for children's later experiences with visual arts materials. As children grow in their exposure to arts materials, they bring this interest in sensory exploration and experimentation to paint and glue and clay. Do not be surprised if very young children use materials in ways you did not anticipate or intend.

Planning to work with two year olds on collage for the first time, you might introduce them to an exciting range of textures and patterns, placing glue and several containers with different types of paper (e.g., tissue, construction, sandpaper) at each table for them to tear. You may find that some children may never affix the materials you provide to their page, consumed by the thrill of spilling glue out of its container, observing its viscosity, fascinated by how the glue flows differently than water. You should not consider this session a failure, as the children are making exciting discoveries about the property of glue. Use this experience to revise your plan for next time. Perhaps you may opt to provide a less distracting material like paste. Or you may decide to capitalize on their interest in exploring this material by adding paint to the glue. Whatever you decide, remember that children need time to experiment, discover and make their own choices as they work with a range of art materials.

Working in another material for the first time, the two and a half year old may spend an entire painting session mixing colors on the tray or using the brush to paint their bodies rather than the paper. Give these young scientists license to explore and experiment, even if their explorations do not result in the visible outcomes you were expecting. I have observed many parents watch with dismay as the distinct marks their young painters begin with are rapidly painted over, resulting in a soggy, olive-brown mass that drips off the edge of the page. We must remember that children's growth in the visual arts builds from the discoveries made through these early experiments. As adults working alongside children we hold very different expectations of the purpose of art making. Too often our attention is attuned to the end product rather than the process. From the child's perspective, the process *is* the product. What is paramount for them is the temporal experience of making discoveries and the evolving narrative that the process enables them to communicate. In focusing overmuch on the end product, we adults miss out on the complexity and richness that children's work contains.

Another common misunderstanding we often bring to our work in the visual arts with very young children is that we expect them to have the intention of working representationally. Very young children do not yet think of their explorations of materials as resulting in a representation of a thing in the world. We serve young children better when we resist the urge to assign our interpretation to young children's work. This is important for several reasons. We must remember that very young children are experiencing the materials as primarily a sensory experience. Building on these early explorations, children later begin to understand that they can use the materials to depict an experience or feeling. In the beginning of this phase of discovery, the story that they narrate will be fluid, not fixed.

As you watch a four year-old working with a piece of clay, he or she will delight in the mutability of the material. Working with it for the first time, children will use their hands to discover the properties of clay, which unlike its manufactured cousin play-doh, is earthy, silky, and dense and offers a surface that can be worked in more detail than play-doh. For classroom use, self hardening clays are available at a reasonable price and can allow children to make pieces that dry in the classroom and can be painted. This adaptable material lends itself to the evolving narrative of young children. Pounding it flat, a young maker may tell their neighbor how much they love to eat pancakes. The pancake is quickly rolled it up and reshaped into a dinosaur, which comes under attack by a larger dinosaur represented by their hands. This creature is then torn apart and reformed anew.

Even as a keen observer, you may find yourself unable to recognize each of these objects. In this early representational phase, the child will not be bogged down by such a fixed and final view of representation. Instead they will take pleasure in the fluidity of the narrative that the material enables. As you engage with the child about his or her work, set aside your adult expectations for a finished piece and appreciate the many twists and turns that the process of exploration fosters.

DISCOVERING THE VISUAL ARTS AS A LANGUAGE

About midway through early childhood, the child begins to understand the capacity the arts have to communicate his or her ideas and experiences to a viewer. The age when this discovery happens will vary by child, but it is often around the age of four that children begin to think of the visual arts as a tool for communicating. While you may have observed young children's early work in great anticipation of this phase, you might also find that it brings with it some new frustrations for the maker. The very young child engaged in sensory exploration of materials was not concerned with his or her work being understood. Children who are now working representationally may become frustrated that they are not able to depict a house or rocket ship or pineapple with the exact details they had in mind. For this reason, we need to be especially mindful of the ways in which we talk to children in this phase about their work. In addition to bringing some frustrations, however, this new phase of working representationally also brings great delight.

The visual arts offer young children a powerful tool as storytellers, and their artistic growth goes hand in hand with their growing capacities for articulating spoken and written narrative. This can be especially important for children who develop verbal language at a different rate from their peers. For children who speak later than their peers, their sense of narrative and their capacity for communication can be activated through their work in the visual arts. As children continue through early childhood, they grow in their use of strategies and details that allow them to depict the narratives that live in their imaginations and in their memories. Be aware, however, that the phases of artistic growth are not strictly linear. A seven year old who works with great sophistication and detail in his or her representational work may continue to take joy in the sensory exploration of a new material and in working abstractly.

CREATING OPPORTUNITIES FOR WORK

With a basic understanding of the phases of artistic growth, you can begin to think about how to set up meaningful visual arts experiences for children. If you are working with children in a pre-representational phase—in the time before they think of their art as representing a thing or experience in the world—your main task is to offer opportunities for the child to explore the sensory qualities of the material. Avoid the common mistake of thinking that very young children need to work representationally. This often results in adult-directed, cookie-cutter projects. Such projects may demonstrate that the children are capable of following directions, but yield little in the way of the deep learning that comes from exploring materials and making discoveries.

A quick (five minute) set up in which you ask engaging questions to introduce or re-introduce the material is all that is needed. Your questions should encourage exploration of the properties of the material and help prompt the children to think about the ways they can change it. For example, when working with three year olds in clay we might begin by asking the children, "How many ways can we change the clay with our hands?" After a brief exchange that elicits their observations or predictions about the material, you can remind the children of a few simple guidelines (e.g., "Do we eat clay?" "No!") and allow their discoveries to begin. For pre-representational makers, their experiences with art materials should be about enabling them to learn what the materials can do. This process of exploration lays critical groundwork for their later work, when they begin to think about what *they* can do with the materials.

For representational makers working with a new material, a period of exploration is also crucial. This gives the children a chance to experiment and observe the properties and the capacities of the material. For example, when introducing construction from recycled materials (cardboard, egg cartons, formcore, tubing, etc.), you might begin the session by asking the children to experiment with how many ways they can use glue and scissors to build strong connections between the materials. Be sure to devote adequate time to this process before moving into a phase in which they plan to represent an idea or experience. This period of exploration can also be framed with some basic guidelines.

Because working three dimensionally may be a new challenge for many children, I often suggest that they try to build something taller than it is wide. I also have them test the durability of their connections by asking them to turn the object upside down to see if any of the pieces fall off. Beginning with an exploration of a material develops their confidence and knowledge, which serves them well when they continue to use the materials to represent objects, figures, or personal experience.

As children grow, they may become overwhelmed by the task of deciding what to make. Our role as parents and teachers is to ignite that initial creative spark and to help them to envision and plan for their work before they begin. Once children have had a chance to make discoveries about what they can do with the material, we can offer open-ended topic questions to extend their work. My colleague Linda Louis (1999) articulated an excellent four-step process, *Topic Question, Personalization, Visualization* and *Transition to Work*, that gives parents and teachers a structure for sparking interest while encouraging freedom and choice in children's work.

Louis (1999) suggests that we begin each art making session by offering a *Topic Question*, which sparks the creative process. For example, beginning a painting session with your first grade class after a field trip to the zoo, you might pose the question, "If you were a zookeeper, what kind of animal would you most like to work with?"

As the children share their thoughts, you can help shape their ideas through the *Personalization* step, by asking questions that draw out the specific details of their experience. For example, many children may respond that they are most interested in the giraffes. You might follow up with questions such as; "What kind of an outfit would you wear to be a zookeeper? What might be in the giraffes' habitat? What colors will you need to mix in order to paint the trees?"

By probing in this way, you are leading children in the step of *Visualization*, helping them to develop their plan for a painting that represents their unique vision for representing their idea or experience.

Finally Louis (1999) recommends closing this brief session with a question that helps in the *Transition to Work*, which concretizes the first step of their art making by asking, for example, "Will you need to use a big brush or a small brush?" or "Will you hold your paper this way, vertically, or this way, horizontally?"

You can generate your own list of questions that spark a productive session with visual art materials, but be sure to consider whether your question is a good match for the material the children will be working in. Drawing on your own knowledge about the interests and experiences of the children will help you develop questions that are especially meaningful and relevant to them. Also, though, you may want to anticipate a few of the children's possible responses before you begin, do not be afraid to follow the children if they take your topic and run with it in a direction you did not plan for. The purpose of this initial dialogue is to generate enthusiasm and to help the children envision their work. If the children join you by expanding upon ideas for their artwork, this will only deepen the learning.

RESPONDING TO CHILDREN'S WORK

Using the steps described above, we can introduce the process of working with materials in a way that sets a tone for choice and discovery. We can carry forward this goal of thoughtfully supporting children's art making by being mindful of how we respond to their work during and after they are engaged in the process. In this section I will discuss ways of speaking to young makers to help develop confidence in their work and ownership over their creative process. Lacking positive models from our own experiences as young children, we may feel challenged by how to respond to children's work. In what follows, I will briefly describe and critique some ways we typically respond to children's work and then offer some more effective strategies for engaging with children about the things they make.

If you are like most people, you operate under the common misconception that the best way to respond to children's artwork is affirmatively, with a shout of "I love it!" or "It's beautiful!" While we should convey our deep interest in children's work, we need to develop more varied and specific strategies for responding to children's artwork. By responding with well-intentioned but vague compliments, we reduce children's capacity to learn and grow. Additionally we need to develop our skills in responding specifically and reflectively to what we see in the work and to cultivate children's capacity for self-assessment of their work.

At the beginning of each semester, my students read Robert Schirrmacher's 1986 article *Talking With Young Children About Their Art*. In this piece, Schirrmacher offers a pointed critique of the typical ways we respond to children's work. (e.g., "That's great!" "What is it?" "How lovely!"). Schirrmacher discourages the use of such responses, explaining that they reinforce the notion that children's work is only valuable when it is attractive to adults. Further, our questioning of content tells children they have not been successful in communicating what they wished to tell the viewer. Indeed, children's work need not be beautiful nor do we need to be able to understand what it represents for it to be important.

Schirrmacher (1986) follows his critique with an excellent set of recommendations for opening up a more constructive dialogue with children about their work. As an alternative, he suggests that we comment on the choices we see children making—noting line, shape, color, form and texture. Linda Louis modeled such descriptive language in her 1999 piece *In the Paint* on supporting children's work with an example of how she might respond to a child's painting of waves. "I see you have made a solid area with many layers of blues and greens and on top are brushy dancing lines" (1999, p. 62). Going beyond empty praise, this descriptive approach communicates to children that we are observing their work deeply and also supports them in seeing and assessing their own work. Done properly, this strategy conveys to children our deep interest in their work, even if, initially, we may not know what it represents. Additionally, responding reflectively opens up possibilities for the conversation about the work to continue.

While Schirrmacher's (1986) critiques and recommendations are critically important for my students to hear, their first response to the article is often to feel shut down themselves. They express guilt for all the times they, quite innocently, responded to children's work with vague praise or misguided questions. As we discuss the article they anticipate being stymied the next time a child brings them a piece of work to share. I explain that speaking reflectively, using a language of noticing that draws on the specific details of a child's work, may be the most difficult new skill they must master. Developing the skills to observe and describe children's work is like using a muscle that for most of us is weak from neglect. The only way to strengthen this muscle is by regularly exercising our capacity to observe and describe.

In order to expand our strategies for responding to children's work, I have my students break into small groups to describe an individual piece of children's work. We borrow from the Descriptive Inquiry Processes, developed by Patricia Carini and described in a 2002 handbook edited by Margaret Himley, to practice the art of observing and describing what we see. We take turns going around the circle, each taking a moment to hold the work in our hands, to look closely, and to describe one aspect of the work, including shape, line, color, pattern and texture.

In the first rounds we stick closely to description, though later we may speak more figuratively or poetically, identifying feelings that the work evokes in us. This process of close description is not about judging or evaluating the work but about seeing it deeply and appreciating the choices that the child has made in the process of working. Participating in this process helps my students to feel more adept at responding to children's work. As well, we develop a deeper appreciation of the complexity contained in even the smallest piece of work.

One final note on responding to children's work: though it is important that we as parents and teachers develop our capacity for observing and describing children's work, it is not necessary that the child be able to respond verbally or engage in conversation with us about what they have made. Though many children will take your observations about the shapes and textures they have created as an invitation to launch into an extensive narrative, others may prefer to let their visual work speak for itself. They may not have the spoken language to tell you more about the piece or they may not wish to share it in words. This is perfectly okay and you need not feel that your or their work is incomplete if you cannot elicit a narrative from a young maker.

In addition to developing our own skills in responding to children's work, we need to provide opportunities for them to experience others' work. Even at this young age, making art should go hand in hand with looking closely and responding to the works of others. In the next and final section I will describe some approaches to aesthetic education in early childhood and make some recommendations for providing children with meaningful experiences of important works of art.

AESTHETIC EDUCATION FOR YOUNG CHILDREN

It is clear that meaningful experiences of art making are absolutely essential in early childhood. Additionally, aesthetic education, which involves providing children with opportunities to observe and respond to works of art by other people, is an often overlooked but indispensable experience for young art makers. In his 1985 piece "Why Art in Education and Why Art Education," Elliot Eisner treats art education and aesthetic education as two critical sides to the same coin. Eisner and many others have argued we must provide children access to cultural institutions and their artistic heritage. Additionally, as educators we must foster children's knowledge of and appreciation for other cultures. Introducing children to varied examples of works of art provides them with tools for studying and responding to works of art, and helps them understand that there are many ways of seeing and interpreting the world.

Educators and scholars who address aesthetic education in early childhood encourage us to introduce this subject in much the same way we teach other concepts to young children, by offering multiple modes and opportunities for children to absorb and respond to new ideas. What follows are descriptions of several approaches to aesthetic education in which young children were introduced to works of art both on-site in the classroom and through field trips to museums and cultural centers.

Documenting a partnership between the Lincoln Center Initiative and the Early Childhood Center at Brooklyn College, Carol Korn-Bursztyn in 2002 described the ways in which the teaching artist incorporated movement, painting and literacy activities for young children responding to Van Gogh's Starry Night. Art educators in Cyprus, Eli Trimis and Andri Savva, in their 2004 article, recounted a project in which pre-service teachers introduced young children to the process of making art with found materials both before and after visiting a sculpture exhibit at a contemporary art center, while Angela Eckhoff, a teacher educator from Clemson University, offered a 2008 piece in which she studied the multiple verbal strategies used by a museum educator in Denver to engage young visitors to explore and respond to the museum's collections and the work that the children produced in response to their visits.

Though describing different circumstances and approaches to aesthetic education, each of these writers emphasized the importance of offering children multiple ways of observing and responding to works of art. Of equal importance is the understanding that aesthetic education should be offered repeatedly and over time. As children absorb new concepts and materials they need to live with them and revisit the work from many angles. Children also need experiences with a variety of works of art to understand the myriad ways that culture has been expressed and transmitted. This can be achieved through exposure to the work of artists from the long distant past on through to more contemporary work.

Parents and teachers who wish to foster experiences in aesthetic education can start by providing opportunities for children to look at important works of art—by searching for images on the computer, checking out books from the library, or purchasing reproductions at local museums. At-home and in-class explorations should be extended with visits to local galleries, museums and cultural institutions, many of which offer low-cost field trip options for school groups as well as family programs. If you do not have access to such locales, find out if a local artist would be willing to allow your class to visit her studio to hear her talk about her work. Understanding that the arts are a part of our culture and an integral aspect of our communities can be a vital experience for young children.

Once you have gotten over the hurdle of finding ways to access aesthetic experiences for young children, you may be wondering how to facilitate their experiences of works of art. For this you can draw on the skills you have developed in speaking reflectively with young children about their own work. Pose questions that support children in expressing what they notice in the works of art they are viewing. Have children identify and describe interesting shapes, colors, forms and textures. Wonder aloud with children about which materials the artist used and how they affixed, applied or constructed them. Ask the children to talk about the mood that the piece evokes, or to imagine the time of day or year the work was made.

Invite the class to work together to narrate the story they think the artist was trying to tell with his piece. Allow the children to respond to the work through movement, poetry or paint. Most importantly, let your young viewers know that there are no right answers in responding to work. A sculpture that gives one child a sense of strength might make another feel scared, while a painting that makes you feel melancholy might make another feel calm. Understanding of the nuance and the subjectivity contained in our responses to artwork is a vital lesson for young children and builds their appreciation of the complexity of human ideas and experiences.

CONCLUSION

As parents and teachers we strive to offer young children rich and varied educational experiences. It is clear that experiences in the visual arts are essential to young children's growth and development. However, many of us who have minimal experience with the visual arts or, worse yet, negative experiences of the arts may feel at a loss for how to begin in fostering meaningful experiences in the visual arts for young children. It is my hope that the ideas in this chapter will offer you a vision of the power of the visual arts for young learners. This chapter, as well as the readings found in my reference list, should offer you some starting points as you partner with the children in your life in exploring and growing through experiences in the visual arts. May you all discover and rediscover purple with as much delight as Max and I did together.

ACKNOWLEDGMENT

Special thanks to my colleagues at Brooklyn College, especially Linda Louis, Raina Elsner and Herman Jiesamfoek. Our ongoing conversations have deepened my thinking about the arts in education. And to David, Max and Zeke for the love and joy.

REFERENCES

Beal, N. (2001). *The art of teaching art to children: In school and at home.* New York, NY: Farrar, Straus & Giroux.

Carini, P. (2001). *Starting strong: A different look at children, schools and standards.* New York, NY: Teachers College Press.

Csikszentmihalyi, M. (1990). *Flow: The psychology of optimal experience.* New York, NY: Harper Collins Publishers.

Diamond, J. (2008). *Welcome to the aquarium: A teacher, her students and a year of learning.* New York, NY: The New Press.

Duckworth, E. (2006). *The having of wonderful ideas and other essays on teaching and learning*. New York, NY: Teachers College Press.

Eckhoff, A. (2008). The importance of art viewing experiences in early childhood visual arts: The exploration of a master art teacher's strategies for meaningful early arts experiences. *Early Childhood Education, 35*(5), 463–472.

Eisner, E. (1985). Why art in education and why art education. In the Getty Center for Education in the Arts, *Beyond creating: The place for art is America's schools* (pp. 64–69). Los Angeles, CA: Author.

Gallas, K. (1994). *The languages of learning: How children talk, write, dance, draw, and sing their understanding of the world*. New York, NY: Teachers College Press.

Gardner, H. (1983). *Frames of mind: The theory of multiple intelligences*. New York, NY: Basic Books.

Goldberg, M. (1997). *Arts and learning*. New York, NY: Longman Press.

Himley, M. (Ed.). (2002). *Prospect's descriptive processes: The child, the art of teaching and the classroom and school*. North Bennington, VT: The Prospect Center.

Kerlavage, M. (1997). Understanding the learner. In J. Simpson et al., *Creating meaning through art: Teacher as choice maker* (pp. 23–72). Upper Saddle River, NJ: Prentice Hall.

Korn, C. (1998). How young children make sense of their life stories. *Early Childhood Education Journal, 25*(4), 223–228.

Korn-Bursztyn, C. (2002). Scenes from a studio: Working with the arts in an early childhood classroom. *Early Childhood Education Journal, 30*(1), 39–46.

Louis, L. (1999). Tips for parents and teachers. In P. Ewing & L. Louis, *In the Paint* (pp. 56–62). New York, NY: Abbeville Kids.

Paley, V. G. (1998). *The girl with the brown crayon*. Boston, MA: Harvard University Press.

Schirrmacher, R. (1986). Talking with young children about their art. *Young Children, 41*(5), 3–7.

Smith, N. R. (1984). *Experience and art: Teaching children to paint*. New York, NY: Teachers College Press.

Trimis, E. & Savva, A. (2004). The in depth studio approach: Incorporating an art museum program into a pre-primary classroom. *Art Education, 57*(6), 20–34.

Vygotsky, L. S. (1978). *Mind in society: The development of higher psychological processes*. Cambridge, MA: Harvard University Press.

CHAPTER 6

MUSEUM VISITS WITH YOUNG CHILDREN

A Teaching Artist's Perspective

Judith Hill Bose
Longy School of Music of Bard College

Carol Korn-Bursztyn
Brooklyn College
and City University of New York

Barbara Ellmann
Painter/Teaching Artist

ABSTRACT

The following chapter is based on an interview with Barbara Ellmann, an encaustic painter, museum educator, and teaching artist. The interview takes up museum visits with children, from early childhood through the elementary school years. It poses a series of questions, leading the reader from the initial steps of considering a museum visit, to planning and preparing experiences that can enrich and deepen children's experiences. Additionally, the inter-

Young Children and the Arts, pages 91–102
Copyright © 2012 by Information Age Publishing
91

view addresses two intended audiences—teachers and parents—with ideas and suggestions offered to make museum visits with children valuable for both children and adults.

INTRODUCTION

The following chapter is based on an interview with Barbara Ellmann, an encaustic painter who lives and works in New York City. She is a working artist, who is also a museum educator at major NYC art museums, a consulting teaching artist for NYC-based cultural arts organizations, and a mother. This chapter is the result of ensemble work: the interview was conducted by Judith Hill Bose, while the chapter was prepared by Carol Korn-Bursztyn. Judith Hill Bose is currently the Director of Teacher Education at the Longy School of Music of Bard College in Cambridge, MA. Now an active soprano in the Boston area, Judith has also had a long career as a teaching artist in New York City. Carol Korn-Bursztyn is Professor of Education at Brooklyn College, and has collaborated with Judith and Barbara on projects related to the arts in education.

The interview takes up museum visits with children, from early childhood through the elementary school years. It poses a series of questions, leading the reader from the initial steps of considering a museum visit, to planning and preparing experiences that can enrich and deepen children's experiences. Additionally, the interview addresses two intended audiences—teachers and parents—with ideas and suggestions offered to make museum visits with children valuable for both children and adults.

WHY VISIT MUSEUMS WITH YOUNG CHILDREN?

First of all I would like to say that a lot of people are reluctant to take young children to museums. That's a shame. Because I think young children are extremely stimulated by art museums and very excited to be there.

The specter of young children making a dash for a Van Gogh can inhibit families from taking their young—and mobile—children to museums. Barbara observes that you can teach even very young children that there's going to be "no touching of the art objects." This dictum is readily understood by most children who already practiced not touching other children's art objects at home, during play dates, or in school. When using slides of art work in school settings, for example, Barbara follows what she calls, a "no touching the screen" rule. This rule serves the artistic purpose of teaching children that we describe with words and not by putting our hands on the art. For example, "At the very top I see . . . You don't have to touch the top—you just say 'at the top' or 'in the middle' as a way of drawing people's attention to the object."

Barbara doesn't use a pointer for the same reason—a pointer encourages touching. She observes that by the time you get to the museum, you are able to quickly reestablish all those rules you've practiced in the classroom or at home. Her advice about setting parameters for visiting museums will sound familiar to early childhood educators, who regularly set parameters for classroom behavior with young children. She observes, "Set this parameter: we are not going to touch the art objects. That's all."

Pace is another important variable to consider when planning a museum visit. Barbara's approach, which is oriented towards the child's needs, will sound familiar to early childhood educators, who work within a child-centered approach in which children's individual preferences and the pace at which they learn guide teachers in planning activities and in developing curriculum. It will also ring true to all parents who have ever tried to briskly and efficiently walk to a pre-determined destination with their young children, or conversely, have wanted to linger over a flower, while their child flies ahead. In considering the individual needs of children, Barbara turns to her experiences as a parent to inform her practice.

> When I think as a mom, instead of a teacher, another thing that can discourage children from museum going is when the pace is set by grown-ups. When I am taking my own child to the museum, I feel that the pace should be set by him. I never ask my son to go at my pace—I always go at his. It's faster than mine, and I'm trying to encourage his interest in being at the museum. So let the child be the leader.

Barbara clarifies that here, she's referring to individualized experiences, or even very small group visits. These are ideal ways of visiting museums with young children, as this approach permits the kind of individualized tailoring of experience that suits young children's varied interests and attention. Family visits to museums offer the possibility of both addressing individual children's attentional needs as well as their personal interests.

WHY PLAN?

Planning for a museum visit with young children can transform a class or family outing into an experience that lays down emotionally positive memories of interacting with art and with others in museum settings. Barbara comments on her process of working with classroom teachers to jointly plan visits to the museum. First, she begins by planning with individual teachers at the particular museums they plan to visit with their classes. At the museum planning session, she and the teacher will decide on the specific works of art that they would like to study with the children. Planning museum visits follows the same pedagogic principles that guide the development of early childhood curriculum and design of classroom activities. The children's interests—both developmental and particular to the group—should guide the selection of works of art as well as design of activities both within the classroom and the museum.

At the museum planning session, Barbara and the teacher engage in what she refers to as a brainstorming process, a free-associative process in which they notate all the ideas and reactions to each work of art under consideration. These might be personal associations, memories, observations or questions about the work of art. Barbara observes that "selecting a group of works often starts with getting interested by one piece, brainstorming around it and realizing—there are some juicy ideas here—lets see if there are other paintings that would fit in with this idea."

The next step is to identify a group of works that fit together. Barbara and the teacher will select several works of art, up to four or five. This takes some walking and looking through the galleries. Some classic themes that she and teachers have often settled on are paintings that have a common theme—for example, a group of paintings that all have animals, or a group of paintings that are all about people—these might be portraits or they might be people doing different jobs. Another popular theme Barbara observes is paintings that evoke narratives or that tell stories. Hot topics for young children, which correspond to early childhood social studies and science curricula, include "all about me; my family; my house; my neighborhood; animals."

However, in her teaching artist practice, Barbara leaves room for more abstract ways of considering connections between different works of art. She emphasizes that activities "need to have the aesthetic idea, or the theme, of the work embedded in them. It is the brainstorming of what is truly in the work of art—what is observable—that creates my initial activity ideas. From observing, from looking deeply at the group of objects, and from exploring thematic connections among them—from this careful noticing, the teachable ideas will emerge."

WHAT GOES INTO SELECTING WORKS OF ART?

Barbara observes that what children are drawn to is not always what their elders would choose for them. Sometimes children surprise with their choices, too. Barbara observes that children are often drawn to things that are scary and about which they are curious. She cites Bettleheim's ideas in his 1976 book, *The Uses of Enchantment: The Meaning and Importance of Fairy*

Tales, about children being able to work through and master their fears through fairy tales. She provides an example of a trip to an Aztec show at an art museum with a kindergarten class.

> Some kindergarteners and I confronted a clay figure in the Guggenheim Aztec show . . . you could see his internal organs and his ribcage. His hands were held up in front of him with these gigantic long fingernails, and he had a very scary look on his face. The object was displayed in a totally darkened room under a spotlight. And guess what—the kids loved this figure. Yes, they recognized that it was scary. They knew it was frightening. And when asked to make up what they thought this figure would say, they offered responses like, "I'm gonna eat you" or "Don't come closer" or "Stop." Lots of demanding and commanding remarks. They loved that.
>
> What the children were noticing was in the art work. To teach to the Aztec show and never discuss human sacrifice—and of course I *did not* discuss that in any way—well, that was really interesting. Sacrifice is such a strong piece of contextual information around the Aztec culture, and it definitely shows up in the art. So though it was impossible to remove what was threatening in the art work, it was possible for the children to find it very interesting. They were not genuinely scared—the fact that it is a work of art is significant. Not a real person, but a clay figure. They knew that it was old, that it was not going to come alive like the mummies do in the mummy movies!

When asked about whether she has looked at works that might be considered controversial with young children, Barbara observes that she would not pick a realistically nude figure. She notes that prior to high school, nude realistic sculpture is "too real—too close to an actual naked figure" though it's a major part of many art works in museums. Barbara was far more interested in exploring abstract art with young children—an unlikely choice for many teaching artists.

She observes that she introduces abstract art to young children by looking at what she calls action painters, among them Jackson Pollock, Franz Kline and Willem deKooning, and thinking in terms of actions. She might think with the children about all the different ways that one could propel a brush or she might investigate different kinds of actions with the children— "what it means to move our hands slow and smooth, and then what it means to make a mark that is slow and smooth."

Another approach she might use is reduction: starting with a very intricate form of a flower and then reducing it to its five essential lines. "Taking things away and taking things away until you had a very simple expression of a flower. This might occur in a way where the student artist knew it was still a flower, but maybe no one else recognized it as such. There are just many different ways to approach abstraction. Students can also read it in terms of its energy, as I mentioned—look at it in terms of color, its contrasts, where it is thick and where it is thin, where it is dense and where it is sparse—oppositions."

Barbara returns to a disciplined approach, to what she refers to as the "artistry of teaching." She observes that she decides first what the essential ideas are in the work of art that she can explore with children. She defines this as the larger ideas around that artwork. For example, she observes that if she is teaching a Jackson Pollock work, "I'm thinking not just what it means to be dripping and splashing paint—but what it means to have painting be a result of your physical action. This is the larger idea—there are many different physical actions that could propel a painting. When students have the opportunity to explore many ways, they are more prepared to be able to say, Jackson Pollock is doing this, this is where his actions seem to come from. Out of their process, they can begin to notice his particular choices."

WHAT'S THE PLACE OF CLASSROOM EXPERIENCE IN PLANNING A MUSEUM VISIT?

The museum visit itself occurs following exploratory work in the classroom, in which the children, teaching artist and their teachers explore the themes they have decided upon during their planning meetings based upon the children's interests and the class curriculum. Barbara describes an example, poignant for the historic moment in which it occurred. In early September 2001, she began a unit of study with three and four year olds at a university lab school.

> We explored the idea of stacking. By stacking, we meant one thing piled on top of another. In the classroom we did several stacking activities to prepare us to see the works. One was a kind of movement stacking—where you put one hand on top of the other, and then someone else puts a hand on top of yours—and then another. We made a stack of hands—a fluid stack of hands. Another thing we did was to stack blocks on top of blocks on top of blocks. After these, we looked at a series of paintings that involved stacking. We looked at Andy Warhol's "Coca Cola Bottles," where there are rows upon rows of Coke bottles, like you'd see in a grocery store refrigerator. The children practiced stacking with blocks and other familiar objects.

The activities need to be presented so that there is no one right way to do them. She notes that as many children as there are in the room, that many solutions to stacking will be created. After the activity, she recommends looking at all of the varieties of choices. Finally, Barbara notes that you might then see in the work of art, the particular stacking choices that Warhol made. She describes how the children created individual drawings on index cards, and displayed these on the door, one stacked upon the other.

Barbara observes, "Through all of these activities, the notion of stacking became quite physical and quite real for the children. I think that's a great example of taking an aesthetic concept in the works of art and exploring it in multiple ways."

As a teaching artist, Barbara is anticipating that she and the teacher will explore the ideas these works of art generate through developing classroom activities, and will be exploring these works in great detail during the subsequent museum visit, too. In this vignette, towards completion of the stacking theme, the terrorist attacks of 9/11 brought new images of destruction of buildings from home television screens into the classroom. The families of several of the children in the class were directly affected by the attacks; several children lost family members, while others had family members who narrowly escaped the devastation. Most of the children witnessed the towers burning and crashing on their home television screens.

The children spontaneously incorporated the art experiences they had with Barbara and their teachers into their attempts at mastery of this traumatic event. In their play, they repeatedly stacked blocks, and other objects into tall towers, which then came crashing down in heaped piles. These were, at times, referred to as "Twin Towers." Whereas the work with Barbara was directed towards construction, the children's play in the wake of 9/11 was, for many months, dominated by the theme of stacking and constructing, with the end result of destruction. The children were clearly working through their understanding of the terrorist attacks through their stacking and demolishing activities. They drew on the concepts of stacking they had explored in their sessions with Barbara, elaborating on these in order to work towards mastery of what for some was emotionally distressing, and for others, a traumatic event. It should also be noted that the children's classroom supported their explorations, and daily encouraged their expressiveness in play and in artistic media.

HOW CAN WE PREPARE CHILDREN FOR A MUSEUM VISIT?

In the classroom visit(s) prior to the trip to the museum, there is an active "making" part, in which the children work with materials, and there's a "looking" part, where the children look at what they've made and explore choices. This sequence prepares the children to look at the selected works of art in the museum. Structuring the "looking" part in the classroom is critical to teaching children how to look at and engage with works of art, their own as well as those of others. Asking good questions is a critical part of this process; it involves both the children's and the adults' careful observation of what they and the others have done.

Imagine that we've made several different constructions out of blocks; we might look at all of them and notice what these stacked constructions have in common. I might ask a question like, 'What do you notice that is the same in all these stacks?' Maybe it's that they all build up—or that they are taller than they are wide (if this is an observation that the children make). The students might notice that there are small pieces, as well as large things that have been stacked. So we might look at the general quality of all the projects. Then we might zoom in and take a closer view at particular stacking solutions. It's all done through the asking of questions—through asking what children notice, and through asking them to explain as specifically as they can about their noticing. Now this is incredibly difficult in the early childhood years because the kids have many more ideas than they are able to articulate.

Barbara observes that there is typically a lot of repetition in young children's talk about artwork. Sometimes, children will demonstrate rather than tell something they are noticing. She describes an encounter with a little boy, a recent arrival to the U.S., who was having great difficulty adjusting to the school and to learning in a new language. Every morning he wept when his grandmother left, but he joined the circle gathered around Barbara. A few sessions into her work with his class, she brought a slide of a painting by Paul Gauguin titled "Three Puppies." She describes the encounter.

(Three Puppies) has a tremendous tripling of objects—and given that the week before the students were counting all the Coca Cola bottles in the Warhol, I thought they would enjoy a whole painting that was based on numbers. In the middle of our discussion, this little boy went over to the bookshelf, got a copy of 'Clifford the Big Red Dog' and brought it right up to me. For me, this meant that he saw dogs in the picture, and he wanted me to know. I thought that was a big moment. He suddenly participated in a group discussion in a language he did not speak. He let me know—because he could speak my language—the language of image. He knew that I was all about showing pictures. He knew that I would understand his gesture, and I did. It was really, really beautiful.

Before going to the museum, Barbara advises that working in the medium that they are going to see is a great link to the specific medium. She qualifies this, however, and notes that "If you're going to be looking at clay objects and investigating how they have been made out of clay, then you're going to need to experience making something out of clay—playing with clay, exploring clay." She cautions though, that the materials connection is only one kind of connection, and is more important for some works than for others. She notes:

If you're going to be looking at complicated collage work—like the art of Romare Beardon—well you're going to have to make some collage to really understand what is extraordinary about his work. This way you are exploring some of the processes that he's engaged in his art making. And that makes a great entry point for children.

Sometimes, though, activities don't necessarily have to be in the visual arts. Barbara described that during work in the stacking theme, an "ah-ha!' moment for a three year old was in the dramatic play area, where she took slices of bread and slices of cheese and made an imaginary sandwich. She comments, "It need not be an art making activity where you end up with a product. I think that certain children are very happy working with art materials, but if your goal is to create an engagement with a work of art, then there might be other ways to reach some students that aren't so keen on drawing."

She explains how her approach to engagement with a work of art is at the heart of her work as a teaching artist.

> If a work of art is really terrific, it demands engagement in a variety of ways—and over time. You don't often have the full experience on your first time out. When you see that painting again on your next visit (to the museum), you realize that you could write about it this time—you didn't do that last time. I want to help students realize the richness embedded in the work of art. Honestly, that's a big part of what I'm trying to do. I want to build up the value of this engagement with work, to suggest that it's not one type of encounter, but a window into a variety of experiences and ongoing, lifelong love of looking and questioning.

WHAT HAPPENS AT THE MUSEUM?

"At the museum," Barbara observes, "I always sit the children on the floor." She does this when they will be talking about a work of art; when they are sitting, she notes, she doesn't have to worry about their getting too close to the painting or sculpture. Before the trip, she and the teacher visit the museum in advance of the class trip, to find out if there is enough room to sit down, or to make sure that the class will not be blocking a door. Also, she notes, she and the teacher(s) choose works that are large enough for everyone to see as a group. They also try to select works that are in quieter parts of the museum, and avoid special exhibitions that are likely to be crowded and loud.

So now the children have come to the museum and are seated in front of the work. Next is the conversation. Barbara usually asks students to talk about what they notice in the painting. She might ask, "What do you see?" She notes that when a student describes what she think it's a picture of, she asks her for evidence to back up what she thinks it is. She might do this by asking "Where do you see that? If she feels that there is ambiguity about the image, she might ask for other ideas, "Does anyone else see something different?" Barbara tries to keep the question "What do you see?" in the air for as long as possible, to get as many ideas about the work as possible.

Barbara observes that the ideas about the works of art the children often come up with are inspired by the classroom activities that preceded the museum visit. She might, for example, ask a group who had worked on stacking in the classroom, whether anyone saw stacking in the painting in front of which they were now seated. Eventually, she notes, she always asks students what the piece or work of art might mean. "How might they interpret it? What kind of title might they invent for it?" With older students she might ask, "If it was going to stand for something in their lives—what would that be?" The conversation shifts from description to analysis, to what Barbara refers to as a personal synthesis. In this interpretive turn, older students consider what the painting means to them, what the artist might be trying to express, and what it might tell us about the historic epoch in which it was created.

The purpose of conversation about a work of art is to open up meaning, rather than close it down by reaching for a consensus. To this end, Barbara employs documenting or sketching; often teachers take notes about new vocabulary the children are learning and documents what the children say for use back in the classroom. Sometimes, Barbara notes, she might ask the children who are seated in front of a painting, "How would you draw this line with your finger in the space in front of you?" Or she might have the children get up and ask, "How would you put your whole body in this shape?" She observes that creating movement with our bodies by looking at a painting is a natural response to children, especially young children. "Even in the museum" she notes, "I do often use other modalities—they are as important here (in the museum) as they are in the classroom, especially for young children."

In summary, in planning a museum trip the first step is for the adults planning the experience to go to the museum in advance of the visit, choose works of art to study, and themselves engage in looking carefully and deeply at the works. Then, the teaching artists, together with the teacher, decide on an essential idea or theme in the selected works on which to focus. Next Barbara and the teacher(s) invent classroom activities that explore the ideas or themes they have decided upon. These activities help to prepare the children to look more carefully at the selected works of art while they are visiting the museum. A great deal of thought is also given to giving shape to the conversation and activities that will happen at the museum, too. Barbara observes:

> It's important that all of these things make sense to the children as a whole process. The children should know that their museum discussion, the work of

art, the things they made or did—all are of a package—all fit together. I keep that in mind from the very beginning when I start looking at the works and thinking—what is it about the works that we want to investigate? What kinds of experiences and conversations do these art works require us to have?

WHAT ABOUT FAMILY TRIPS TO ART MUSEUMS?

When asked to consider how she might approach a museum visit as a mother and not as a teacher, Barbara advises choosing the exhibits carefully. She opts for either the permanent collection or an exhibition that might be especially interesting to young children. Art with energy is especially appealing to children. Then, she advises, "when you go to the museum, let your child set the pace." She compares the museum experience to visiting the library: "I don't feel the need to read every single book before I leave the library, and you do not need to feel an obligation to see every single painting in every single room in the museum." She advises selecting a few works of art, "You can go and look at five or six things, or four things—or even two things—and feel a great satisfaction in what you did at the museum that day. Above all, let your child set the pace and try not to do too much."

Fatigue can quickly set in during museum visits with young children. A sketch pad and pencil can help children rest. Drawing, Barbara advises, can help a child "take a little break" in the museum. If your child isn't saying too much about the art, she advises that parents try an open ended question, such as "What do you think this is?"

Before the visit and after, parents can research the on-line activities offered on museum web-sites. They, like teachers, can introduce children to a range of art materials and to combining materials, too. Barbara, suggests combining materials, such as painting and then drawing with a dark pencil or Sharpie on top of the paint. She suggests that it can be satisfying to bring in a level of detail to a painting. She suggests care in selecting materials, and cautions against popular arts and crafts materials.

> There are some materials that make everyone's work look individual and distinctive, and then there are materials that make everyone's work look the same. For instance, if you introduce googly-eyes—everyone's work is going to look the same. Or those little pom-poms. Suddenly all the work is the same— the material takes over and expression is consumed by the material. But if you simply give paint, all the paintings will look different. I think that the distinctive nature of early childhood drawing is so unbelievably great—I love to give children beautiful pencils and beautiful markers. The quality of the tool really matters—the material choices are key.
>
> Sometimes, I love to explore the difference between big paper and little paper. I sometimes give children something that is so small to work on—and

then something that is so large—and just see what happens. To make something the size of a postage stamp—and then to make something 18" × 24". What a contrast. How does that make you feel? Kids react so honestly to these materials and you can learn a lot about them.

Finally, Barbara leaves us with a parting thought about materials and building museum experiences with children. "So—the way this work with what we've been talking about is that the work of art you are going to study will lead you to which materials to use and which activities to do, if you are really attending to that work. That's really how I think about it."

REFERENCES

Bettelheim, B. (1976). *The uses of enchantment: The meaning and importance of fairy tales.* New York, NY: Knopf.

CHAPTER 7

ART-MAKING WITH YOUNG CHILDREN WITH DISABILITIES

Dana Freed
Brooklyn College, CUNY

Alberto M. Bursztyn
Brooklyn College and the Graduate Center, CUNY

ABSTRACT

This chapter explores art therapy concepts and approaches that may help children with special needs surmount emotional, behavioral, and social challenges in settings beyond the therapy room. The authors begin the chapter with two vignettes that illustrate the power of art-making for children with disabilities; subsequently they review contemporary research that informs how art therapy promotes positive change and psychic growth. The chapter introduces the benefits of introducing art to young children with emotional challenges since they benefit from creative and soothing activities; art-making also provides access to expression of their internalized and present conflicts. Children with autism spectrum disorder benefit from art activities that serve to strengthen their emerging capacity for self regulation and socially appropriate interaction. The chapter concludes with recommendations for adapting art therapy principles in various contexts.

Young Children and the Arts, pages 103–118
Copyright © 2012 by Information Age Publishing

INTRODUCTION

John Berger (1972) says, in *Ways of Seeing*, "We only see what we look at. To look is an act of choice. As a result of this act, what we see is brought within our reach—though not necessarily within arm's reach" (p. 8). Young children with special needs, depending on the impairment, see their surroundings, although often feeling powerless or vulnerable within. Teaching children how to consciously look at the world around them through various modalities offers a potential for greater sense of mastery, self control and engagement in their physical and social worlds.

This chapter explores art therapy concepts and approaches that may help children with special needs surmount emotional, behavioral, and social challenges. We begin with two vignettes that exemplify the power of art-making for children with disabilities and subsequently review contemporary research that informs how art therapy promotes positive change and psychic growth. We conclude with recommendations for adapting art therapy principles to various settings, including schools and other community venues.

VIGNETTES: SHANEA AND JESSE

Each Friday for the past eight years, the first author has facilitated an art workshop for children in foster care within the context of supervised visits with their biological parents. The following two vignettes describe how two young children with disabilities participating in this program express their inner turmoil and improve their capacity for self regulation while engaging in art-making activities.

Shanea

Visits between children and their biological parents are often fraught with emotional tension and ambivalence. The complexity of feelings on both sides is indescribable. I have witnessed how soothing painting, drawing, or playing with materials can be for a child (and a parent) during these difficult times. Toddlers and young children get momentarily lost in the flow of activity, easing the interaction by focusing on a shared creative experience.

Shanea, a seven-year African American girl diagnosed with attention deficit hyperactivity disorder (ADHD) and oppositional defiant disorder (ODD), was standing in the hallway with her arms folded staring at the floor, pouting. Shanea frequented the art room, so I knew her well. These types of behaviors were typical of Shanea and consistent with her diagnoses.

She was often challenging to authority figures; managing her behaviors in the art room was predictably difficult. She was diagnosed with ADHD in preschool, and ODD in first grade; her difficulties with self-regulation and self-control cause problems for her in school and at the foster care agency. Most interactions with peers and adults ended in conflict.

"Shanea, why don't you come make some art with me?" I asked. "No." She said under her breath while looking down at the floor, but as I walked she grudgingly followed a few steps behind me. When she entered the room she sat in the far left corner of the room and put her head on the table. "I'm not doing anything today. I'm mad." She mumbled. "Okay, you can do whatever you need to do. Just let me know if you change your mind. I'm here if you want to talk, too."

Less than a minute later she said, "I want to draw." I placed a stack of construction paper in front of her, markers, crayons, pastels, and materials for painting such as brushes, paints, and a paper plate for a palette. For child like Shanea, who has attention difficulties and poor social skills, it is important to be flexible and provide choices. Children with hyperactivity face difficulties remaining seated and they often need to switch from one art activity to another. Instead of facilitating multiple art projects, I often allow them different mediums for various versions of the same project. When children have options they feel more in control, which is not the usual experience for children with ADHD. In this instance, I chose not to have a structured project so Shanea could use the art-making process more therapeutically as a means of self-expression to explore what was bothering her at the time.

Shanea picked up one piece of construction paper and worked slowly at first. Then she picked up another and then another, feverishly drawing with markers and then filling in other areas with paint. When painting she mixed many of the colors together on the palette. She was unable to limit her mixing two colors at a time. "Why whenever I mix the colors they turn brown? I don't want brown. I'm trying to make purple!" "What colors make purple?" I asked. "Red and blue, but I want to use yellow, too." "You'll see what happens then; art is like science some times," I said.

She continued mixing with such ferocity she eventually made a hole in the paper plate and I quickly replaced it. She also needed constant reminders not to run around the room with a dirty paintbrush. "Why?" she asked. "Why do you think?" was my usual response. "Because you're mean and you're bossing me around." This was a typical answer. "Try again." "Because. Just because!" I praised her bountifully when she went back to her seat.

When she sat down again, she quickly created five very elaborate drawings and paintings, and her demeanor completely changed. "Let me tell you my story," she announced proudly. "This is the first picture. You have to follow me or you're never going to get it. This one is about a happy crayon and a sad marker. The happy crayon is standing on the island alone away from everyone. The sad marker is here." "Why is the marker sad?" I inquired. "It can't be alone," she said, "It has to be here," she pointed, "with the other children." I asked, "How did you show that the marker was sad?" She pointed to the frown and said, "He's blue." She held up the second picture. "This one here has only blind children. They watched too much television and lost themselves in the TV. Now they can't see anything."

In the third picture she explained, "The blind children are trying to get into the house even though they can't see where they are going. They want to go into the house, but they can't and there is no one to help them." "That must be really hard," I said. "They can handle it," she responded without hesitation. "They are very brave," I said. "This one," she said pointing to the fourth picture on the table "is still really wet. It's what the blind children will see inside." "Inside what?" I asked. "It's brown. They see brown, only brown, in the house." She paused for a brief second to show me the final picture without explaining. Instead she said abruptly, "What's next?" I'm bored."

Shanea was clearly accessing a difficult family circumstances in her narrative and I thought she was ready to imagine a better ending. I asked: "What if you were to change all of the colors in each picture? Do you think it would change the story? Why don't you try it?" With that encouragement, Shanea began the next phase of her series.

Comment

The class size, ages of participants and disabilities vary from week to week. Many of the children have similar challenges to Shanea, while others have more severe impairments. Because of the diversity of needs of the children in the class, my art rules for the sessions are consistent and general; when necessary I adapt them to work with children with different abilities. My rules of the room are quite simple and everybody knows them: (1) we speak kindly to each other; (2) we share; and (3) we think about color, line, and space. Most children know that a drawing is not complete until they can account for each part of the paper or canvas. These rules are easily transferable to home, school and community based settings.

The narrative quality of Shanea's pictures exemplifies that each part was considered. If it is blank, it is because leaving it blank was a choice. As artists we make choices even in the throes of creativity. We are in control of what we are doing. I teach that decision-making is part of making art. This is a basic philosophy behind my approach in this setting. Many of the children integrate this thinking into their work. However, many children who visit the class have more severe impairments. I have found that some general practices regarding art-making need to be adapted to better meet their needs. For children with lower levels of cognitive functioning or who have disorders that affect their understanding, I find alternate ways to engage them. In the vignette below, I describe the work, including the modifications to my art practice with a young child with autism.

Jesse

Jesse, an eight-year old Latino child first diagnosed with autism as a toddler, is someone whose special needs must be considered when he is in the art room. It is challenging to provide him with an enriching experience while also providing structure and setting boundaries. His enthusiasm, however, is undeterred when it comes to painting. "I want to paint! I want to paint!" he screams each time he sees me in the hallway or walks into the room.

He does not say hello or acknowledge me other than associating me with painting. I often vary the projects in the sessions so we do not always paint. On an occasion when he learned that I had not planned a painting activity he screamed and cried, "I hate you." The subsequent meltdown was characteristic of children with autism. He flung himself on the floor and wailed. I asked his mother to ignore the tantrum, which was a mistake because he soon began punching his younger brother. He cried inconsolably for a long time and eventually sought reassurance and comfort by hugging both his mother and brother, although he did not seem remorseful of his aggressive actions toward his brother.

In previous sessions when painting, Jesse would not follow instructions. Instead of applying paint to a canvas, Jesse painted the table around the canvas or compulsively mixed the colors until every color on the table was brown. Jesse poured paint directly onto the table and walked around the room, trying to take other children's paints and brushes. Jesse's behaviors created multiple challenges as the other students became angry and the setting can became chaotic.

Weary of his difficult-to-manage behavior, I decided to give Jesse painting sticks instead of a brush and water, explaining that the sticks were a special way to paint, more like painting and drawing at the same time. Jesse was not happy with the idea. "I don't want it! I want to paint! It's a crayon!" His response to the paint sticks was not surprising. Children with autism have a meta-representational deficit, meaning that they cannot hold two conflicting ideas at the same time. It was nearly impossible for Jesse to grasp that the paint was in a different form (i.e., the crayon).

Eventually, Jesse began to do what he always does with markers. He drew repetitive lines on a paper and wrote his name over and over again with the paint stick. "It's my name. Look at my name." He repeated with a big contagious smile. "It's a J. It's an E. It's an S." One strategy I have learned that works well for Jesse is asking the other students in the class to clap for Jesse when he is on task, sitting in his seat, or following the rules of the class. This was one of those times. "Let's clap for Jesse for doing such a fantastic job working with the special crayon and writing his name."

Jesse obsesses over each letter in his name and writing it is a source of pride. He exudes much happiness when he completes writing his name. Since he so enjoys working with letters, I put many cut out cardboard letters in front of him. He spread them around the table and rubbed his hands with the letters. Initially he just kept playing with the letters and never actually glued the letters to the paper. In subsequent sessions he searched for the letters of his name and continuously tried to spell his name.

I learned through painful experience that it is very important that there should be enough letters to spell his name more than once. If he is he is unable find the required letters, he becomes distraught and has tantrums. Guiding him in the process of gluing the letters onto the paper is the current challenge. As soon as Jesse squeezes the glue he is unable to stop himself and just squeezes the glue all over the page. Even when I give him glue sticks he finds a way to get the glue. This action is similar to his behavior while painting. At these times he becomes transfixed with the viscosity and flow of materials and impulsively drains the containers.

Comment

Both Jesse and Shanea exhibit special needs in the art classroom. Creating a safe environment where they can feel comfortable exploring materials and expressing themselves requires a differentiated approach to their unique needs. When they feel safe they engage freely in the art-making process and access aspects of the self that contribute to greater self-regulation and capacity to share with others. Getting to that place is different for each child; children with special needs may have greater challenges engaging in the creative process, but the rewards of doing so may be transformative.

Reflecting on the choice to give Jesse the paint stick and glue stick clearly made demands that shook his perseverative need for sameness and provoked anxious outbursts. Yet, without the newly imposed structure and materials, he was unable to create. He would not apply the paint to the canvas, and the art experience was limited to spilling paint—a sensory activity most commonly observed among much younger children. Given his developmental needs, working with Jesse is still less about product and more about process and discovery of the materials.

Providing structure and developing a new set of routines that are more age-appropriate allow Jesse to arrive at a sense of achievement, wonderment and surprise that art can give. Although his artwork is still limited in its symbolic representation, that may be his next potential breakthrough. Shanea, in contrast, used the art experience for self-expression and to visually communicate something emotionally painful. Both children were engaged in a positive process that reflected their individualized needs.

Art-making with young children with disabilities and emotional disorders, like Shanea and Jesse, require accommodations and sensitivity to their individual needs. Parents, educators, and others doing art with young children experiencing challenges may adapt art therapy concepts and techniques to help those children engage predictably in the creative process. In the following section we explore art therapy with children who have experienced emotional trauma, and with children who present with autism spectrum disorder.

ART AS THERAPY FOR YOUNG CHILDREN WITH DISABILITIES

Art-making has long been understood to have beneficial effects on self-awareness, cognitive development and on mental health. The preeminent American education philosopher and psychologist John Dewey (1934) emphasized the importance of providing art activities for children to encourage exploration and expression. In Dewey's view, art functions as experience. He conceptualized education as processes of inquiry, seeking and finding meanings that are transformative, and recognizing the moral dimensions of these new insights.

For Dewey, transformative experiences provoked greater perceptual understandings, which in turn opened paths for moral action. A transformative education experience is part of a process that increases the capacity of the learner for more experience, or "knowledge of something else" (Dewey, 1938, p. 12). His legacy has been the understanding of artistic experience as an impetus for cognitive and moral development, a foundational notion in progressive education.

The potential therapeutic benefits of art were described by Carl Jung (in Furth, 1988), who proposed that art could both alleviate feelings of anxiety and help to restore and heal those who had experienced trauma. Following Sigmund Freud's notion that emotional healing required bringing unconscious and suppressed conflicts into awareness, Jung (1959) explained that drawing, painting, and modeling can be instrumental in such purposes. He stated that "once a visual series has become dramatic, it can easily pass over into the auditive or linguistic sphere and give rise to dialogues and the like" (p. 190).

The influential British pediatrician and psychoanalyst Donald Winnicott (1971) understood that children's art could facilitate communication between therapist and child and empowered children emotional difficulties to be active participants in sessions. Winnicott recognized the value of drawing in helping children express their problems and worldviews. His work affirmed that drawings can be a catalyst for increased interaction and interchange, thus expanding the effectiveness and depth of the relationship between clinician and child.

In contemporary art therapy, visual arts activities are used as interventions with children who have experienced trauma or loss. While some practitioners propose that doing art is intrinsically a therapeutic activity, others consider art-making a process for developing a relationship and gaining access to the inner life of the child. We believe both to be true. Drawing facilitates communication for children, enhances rapport, and helps the process of recovery from trauma. Art-making can also serve as a therapeutic activity that lowers anxiety levels and enhances communicative abilities. This is particularly true for children with autism spectrum disorders, like Jesse, since these children often find art making as a soothing and pleasurable experience.

ART WITH CHILDREN WHO HAVE EXPERIENCED EMOTIONAL TRAUMA

Young children who have suffered trauma do not have the language and are not developmentally and cognitively ready to put their experiences and feelings into words. Art-making is known to be a viable approach for disclosing and resolving painful experiences since it entails tactile, kinesthetic, and visual activities (Malchiodi, 2001). The multi-sensory qualities can reduce stress, anxiety, and posttraumatic stress reactions in children while providing a way to communicate their narrative through a visual vocabulary. Drawing, an aspect of art-making that we will focus on in relation to young children who have experienced emotional traumas, is an effective therapeutic intervention that has become a treatment of choice for many mental health professionals. In order for children to successfully understand and find resolution to traumatic events they must relive the experience in a safe setting. According to Furth (1988), "We need to bring into consciousness what is submerged in our unconscious" (p. 15). Adults, for example, might be asked in therapy to write a letter or a story of the traumatic event. Working with children is very different, yet young patients have similar needs. Asking a child to draw what happened in great detail is one method of helping children to revisit traumatic experience (Malchiodi, 2001).

Patrice was a 1st grader who was "acting out" in class. The school psychologist was aware that Patrice had experienced a trauma prior to enrolling in the school. After developing a relationship with the psychologist, Patrice drew a picture of a house in great detail with all of the furniture on the lawn. Patrice explained while drawing that one day her mother came and took the furniture out of the house. The traumatic experience was that her mother had kidnapped her in the middle of the night from her father. The "furniture" was symbolic representation of Patrice being thrown out and feeling lost. Drawing provided a way for Patrice to figure out what happened.

This is an extremely delicate activity and can cause great discomfort for a child. Therapists need to provide an environment where the child feels safe to revisit a scary place. Other methods to alleviate the conscious and unconscious fear that the child is experiencing is to have her draw specific pictures of people involved in the traumatic event, starting with a self portrait and moving to other prominent people in the event. Spontaneous drawings, regardless of the different drawing procedures, reveal unconscious content (Furth, 1988). Some therapists have children complete a body outline by asking them to fill in areas based on their own or others' physiological responses to the event (Malchiodi, 2001). This method increases a child's physical awareness and knowledge of how bodies can communicate stress.

Malchiodi (2001) highlights five aspects to consider when using drawing in therapy to help children heal from traumatic events: (a) drawings do not need to be complex to communicate important information and help alleviate painful feelings; (b) therapists need to be curious about the drawings to make the child feel comfortable and enhance the interpretation; (c) always inquire about who or what is missing from the picture; (d) in order for the act of drawing to be truly effective, therapists need to ask questions related to the trauma; and (e) therapists need to familiarize themselves with these techniques and experience the activity prior to implementation.

Using art as a tool with vulnerable children has enormous benefits. It provides a way to work through the particular event while acting as a channel for the therapist to understand a child's experience. Subsequent drawings and play therapy need to focus on helping the child develop coping strategies, co-construct a more hopeful outlook, and practice approaches to relieve stress. Adaptations of art therapy to other art-making contexts with children with emotional challenges may offer opportunities for children to find better ways to channel their conflicts and engage in growth enhancing activity. A central concern in this work is to provide a safe and structured environment, where expectations are focused on art-making, rather than solely on self-disclosure and revisiting of traumatic events.

ART AND CHILDREN WITH AUTISM

During the 1980s, as autism's core characteristics became more widely recognized and diagnosed, educators, psychologists, and other mental health professionals began to report on the benefits of doing art with these children. Despite some challenges children with autism spectrum disorders (ASD) were observed to engage productively in art-making. Art seemed to promote more adaptive social skills and provide an avenue to relate appropriately with their peers.

Most significantly, researchers noted that while engaging in artistic activity, children with autism were able to gain some sense of control in typically anxiety producing situations and reduce their propensity for self stimulation activities (stimming). Art was also consistently described as a valuable tool for reducing anxiety among individuals of any age with autism spectrum disorder. Most published studies on art and autism have been descriptive in nature; researchers have observed closely the effect of art-making on individual children and have hypothesized reasons for its notable therapeutic effects. For example, David Pariser in 1981 provided a good example of case study research describing the artwork of Nadia, a nine-year-old girl diagnosed with autism spectrum disorder.

Nadia had begun drawing at an early age and her artwork was remarkably realistic. Pariser suggested that her productions were an indication of the literalness with which she read reality. He stated that the fact her work was so unschematic and literal revealed how little Nadia was organizing her visual world, in effect postulating that she was not analyzing what she saw but transcribing it unto paper. Subsequent therapeutic work with this child and her parents included art as a means to assess her capacities and deficits in perception. Despite her amazing drawings, she showed significant deficits in verbal conceptualization and in engaging with the social world.

As she grew older, Nadia began drawing more frequently and intently. Parisier relates that "art consumed her . . . and her behavior improved—she responded more to others, had fewer temper outbursts, and her spoken vocabulary became larger" (1981, p. 26). Parisier saw a causal the relationship between Nadia's art and her improved behavior. In this case study, art was understood as a critical activity that allowed her parents and therapists to support and encourage the child's emerging social competence, communication abilities, and capacity for self-regulation.

Julia Kellman (1998) in the late 1990s made a provocative association between individuals with autism approach to drawing and Ice Age artists. She contended that in both cases art functions a means to understand and organize reality. Kellman described nine-year-old Jamie's artwork as his effort to understand the world around him. She suggested that the boy, diagnosed earlier with autism spectrum disorder, drew images that he saw on books, CD covers, films, TV, and cartoons to organize his reality; art, for Jamie, was a frequent and necessary activity that increased his sense of control.

In a subsequent study, Kellman (1999) explored the relationship between art and autism following Peter, a young boy diagnosed with high-functioning autism. Kellman described how Peter's artwork facilitated his social, linguistic and emotional development. She identified Peter's art as a way for him to communicate with peers and avoid the uncontrollable social anxiety often experienced by children with autism. She stated, "... educators and parents of young artists with autism are afforded the insight that these young artists are also likely creating satisfying narrative meaning that may serve to structure both their individual and social experiences in various images they produce" (Kellman, 1999, p. 262).

Peter's fantasy narrative drawings helped him connect with his classmates. In the second grade, Peter became enthralled with *The Wizard of Oz*. With the teacher's support and encouragement, Peter's class produced and performed a version of *The Wizard of Oz*. Peter helped to shape the scenes of this play and was a central figure in the scenery production. He drew the images to be acted out and his drawings became the medium for his engagement with peers in the enactment of the play. Kellman noted that Peter's expressive language and social involvement improved in the context of his enthusiastic description of his drawings.

Beyond fantasy and scripted narratives, Peter also drew pictures that related to his own life experiences. When angry, frustrated or overwhelmed, he drew what his parents called "stress reliever art." These drawings were typically graphic and violent images, which reflected his anxious and vulnerable state. The drawings would give him a socially acceptable way for releasing stress and aggression.

Kellman's careful observation of the child and his artistic projects helped her identify another creative theme that she referred as "future drawings." These productions depicted wish fulfillment, or his desires for the future. One of these pictures was a self-portrait, depicting himself as a bookstore owner; another picture showed him with a cat. Kellman wrote that "Peter's various kinds of art seem to provide him a world he controls, a means of communication, a socially acceptable method for dealing with stress and anxiety, and a way to pull together the disparate parts of his experience into a whole that provides a future as well as a present" (1999, p. 271). Considering the role of art in Peter's experience and development, we recognize how artistic expression facilitates communication, serves as a stress releaser, and provides a conduit for imagining a more fulfilled and less stressful future. Although many children with autism may lack Peter's artistic inclination and substantial talent, his experiences point to art as a potentially effective intervention for a subset of children in the autism spectrum.

Taking an approach similar to Kellman's, Melinda Emery (2004) described her work with a six year old boy with autism over the course of seven months in individual therapy. Initially the boy presented as non-communicative. He had only begun speaking at age four; his speech was high pitched, mechanical, and repetitive—often lacking in meaningful intent.

When asked to draw a house, he wrote "house;" he also wrote "man" instead of drawing. He gravitated to a set of soft multicolored alphabet letters in the therapist's office and preferred to play with them instead of interacting. The therapist later found out that he had a similar set at home.

The comfort of sameness and routines is typical of children with ASD; therefore anxiety is bound to increase at the request to attempt new tasks in a strange environment. Understanding the challenge, the therapist worked first with play-doh, showing the boy how to make a ball. Later they engaged together in flattening the ball over paper and tracing the contours with a marker. The kinesthetic and repetitive quality of the experience was reassuring to the child and facilitated moving to more complex shapes, including the human figure.

Transitioning from play-doh to drawings on paper occurred easily as the child found it rewarding to depict objects and people in his environment. As he did so, his speech became more meaningful and less high pitched. Although the child still lagged in spontaneity and social engagement at the end of treatment, he had made remarkable progress through his exposure to and embrace of visual arts. Drawing offered a path for meaningful social interaction and may have served as a catalyst for organizing and mastering cognitive schemas.

It should be noted that for most children with ASD, spontaneous play does not develop easily and naturally. Many of these children will take a toy and make repetitive non-purposeful motions with it, suggesting minimal capacity for imaginative use of the object. In these circumstances, children need to be introduced to play in a safe and supportive way, since it may not emerge spontaneously. Art is a form of play and it may initially present as a challenge because of its unfamiliar script. In Emery's case presentation, the child's drawing progression mirrored that of children who are typically developing, but in a compressed time-frame. The sense of satisfaction that accompanied his growing competence suggests that contrary to popular beliefs, children with ASD may grow emotionally and cognitively through supportive interventions, rather than exclusively through behavioral rewards and controls.

Jan Osborne (2003) addressed the benefits of art therapy on children with autism in various settings, including school. Osborne suggests that art therapy is conducive to promoting interaction, since it emphasizes both verbal and non-verbal communication. Since children with ASD typically lack a pronounced desire to communicate, art therapy can serve as a process to support social interaction. Art therapy activities are particularly appropriate because the focus is not directly on face to face communication, something that is particularly challenging for many children with autism.

The use of art therapy approaches in schools, Osborne (2003) contends, offers promise but faces substantial obstacles. Schools generally lack the funding, time, and resources to support an art therapy program. Beyond limited training, teachers are often reluctant to implement the art therapy model because of the individualized attention it demands. Although studies support the effectiveness of art therapy as a promising intervention, it is rarely utilized in school environments because of the stated hurdles.

Addressing the challenge of art therapy in school, Kathleen Marie Epp (2008) recruited seventy-nine primary and secondary school children with autism spectrum disorders to participate in a quasi-experimental design study. She implemented a therapy model called "SuperKids," which adapts art therapies in a group setting to facilitate socially appropriate engagement for students with autism. Epp focused on a group therapy approach, rather than on individual therapy, hoping that her study's outcomes could be more appropriately generalized to the entire population of children with ASD.

Epp's study confirmed that the SuperKids model of therapy had a salutary effect; students with autism exhibited fewer problem behaviors (aggressive acts, poor-temper control, hyperactivity, and anxiety attacks) and demonstrated more socially appropriate behaviors (cooperation, assertion, self-control, and responsibility). Epp concluded that "the concrete, visual characteristics of art help these children [with autism], who often experience anxiety in social situations, to relax and enjoy themselves while they are learning social skills in the carefully controlled environment of the therapeutic group setting" (2008, p. 30).

A special educator working with children with Asperger's under the second author's supervision incorporated individualized art activities into the children's daily schedules in an inclusion setting. She found that each child's needs and approach to art-making differed significantly, yet all benefited. She observed that children with Asperger's in her care suffered from acute forms of anxiety under different circumstances.

She identified the stressful nature of academic demands, social interaction expectations, and emotional flooding as conditions that would typically provoke tantrums, stimming, shut-down, or flight in each of the children. All her students expressed feeling overwhelmed at least with one part of a regular school day. Art-making served different functions for each child, but in all cases it served to support self-regulation and curtail excessive emotional reactivity. A good example of how art helped a particular child is described in the following essay written by Kyle in class.

> I first started drawing when I was in first grade. Back then, my drawings were unrealistic and out of dimension. As time went by, I got better. My skills improved more and more with each year. Sometimes I feel stressed out at school, and I need to find a way to release that stress. For me, art is a release; art is a way to forget my problems and stress.

The reason I like to draw so much is because it lets me express my feelings in a way that I won't be punished for or hurt anything. I express my feelings appropriately through art. I once went to a camp where I did not enjoy myself. I recently drew a picture showing my desire for revenge against this camp. It depicts me and my friends annihilating the camp by different methods. This picture was a way for me to express my feelings without really hurting anyone.

My art takes me away from the stresses of the world. Art takes me to another world, like when I draw pictures of ships. I draw ships large and complex, and I try to picture myself on board them. When I picture myself on board these ships, I picture myself away from my stress. This makes me forget what I am stressed out about at that moment. It is a really good feeling to be away from this stress.

I often draw in class to relieve some of the stress I feel. Class can get difficult for me sometimes, so I draw to get myself away from the class while still being there. I listen while I draw, and many people do not understand this, so it appears as though I am not listening at all. I am actually listening. I love to draw because I feel at peace when I am making art. Art calms me down. It makes me feel confident and unique, which often makes me calmer. This is one reason that I do not like when people try to stop me from drawing. For example, in math sometimes I do not feel confident. When I draw in math, I feel more confident. This calms me down.

Art has helped me throughout school by giving me confidence so that I can do better, letting me express myself, and calming me down. One day I hope to become a better artist. I draw also to have fun and enjoy myself. I think art will always be a part of my life because I don't think I ever can really forget about it.

The tangible benefits of art activities for a child with ASD are eloquently described by Kyle; art soothes, engages the imagination, promotes confidence, and in some cases opens up channels for social engagement and vocational direction. Beyond the art-therapy setting, access to art-making in school, home and community based organizations offers children with autism access to a valuable tool for engaging with the world and cope with external and internal stressors.

CONCLUSION AND RECOMMENDATIONS

All children, regardless of their abilities and disabilities, benefit from art-making. However there are more challenges specific to children with special needs when it comes to art. Like Shanea, many children have difficulties with attention. Given that art rooms are unlike other familiar environments, it can be even more distracting. It is necessary to reframe the negative associations of hyperactivity and attention deficit and make these more amenable to art making, which can be tactile and kinesthetically engaging.

Children can make murals or action paintings like Jackson Pollock, rather than sitting for long periods. Children with autism or multiple disabilities may be more difficult to engage; in fact, some children with high functioning autism prefer to remain clean and not get their hands dirty. One remedy for this issue is to attach paintbrushes to long sticks, making it nearly impossible for these children to get paint on their hands.

With art, children have an opportunity to re-describe and process what they see and experience in their worlds through visual language. All children should have these creative opportunities, but children with disabilities stand to benefit the most because these children have fewer opportunities to exert control over their surroundings. Making art provides a space for children to be in control through the selection of materials, the limited rules of the experience, and the choices inherent in the process. These ideas are all important, yet none are as powerful as recognizing the essence of the relationship between children and art. Education for children with special needs should rely on the fact that children learn through play and art is a form of play.

Young children with varying degrees of emotional, behavioral, and social impairments can benefit from having opportunities to express themselves through the arts. Inherent in this work with children is the need to recognize and respect the capacity of this medium to give expression to inchoate feelings and life experiences. Art is a means to communication and opens up the possibility of a relationship with a hard-to-reach child. The act of making art has healing potential for the child who has experienced trauma. Similarly, art provides ways to make sense of a confusing and demanding social world for a child with autism. Integrating principles of art therapy in school, home and community settings may benefit all children, and particularly those who encounter the challenges in the social world.

REFERENCES

Berger, J. (1972). *Ways of seeing*. London: Penguin Group.

Dewey, J. (1934). *Art as experience*. New York: Minton.

Dewey, J. (1938). *Logic: The theory of inquiry*. New York: Holt.

Emery, M. J.(2004). Art therapy as an intervention for autism. *Art Therapy: Journal of the American Art Therapy Association, 21*(3), 143–147.

Epp, K. (2008). Outcome-based evaluation of a social skills program using art therapy and group therapy for children on the autism spectrum. *Children & Schools, 30,* 27–36.

Furth, G. (1988). *The secret world of drawings*. Boston: Sigo Press.

Jung, C. G. (1959). *The archetypes and the collective unconscious*. New York: Bollingen Foundation Inc.

Kellman, J. (1998). Ice age art, autism, and vision: how we see/how we draw. *Studies in Art Education, 39,* 117–131.

Kellman, J. (1999). Drawing with Peter: Autobiography, narrative, and the art of a child with autism. *Studies in Art Education, 40,* 258–274.

Malchiodi, C. (2001). Using drawing as intervention with traumatized children. *Trauma and Loss: Research and Interventions, 1.* Retrieved from http://www.tlcinst.org/drawingintervention.html

Osborne, J. (2003). Art and the child with autism: Therapy or education? *Early Child Development and Care, 174,* 411–423.

Pariser, D. (1981). Nadia's drawings: Theorizing about an autistic child's phenomenal ability. *Studies in Art Education, 22,* 20–31.

Winnicott, D. W. (1971). *Playing and reality.* London: Penguin Books.

CHAPTER 8

INTEGRATING THE THEATER ARTS

Creativity and Inclusion

Barbara E. O'Neill
Brooklyn College

ABSTRACT

This chapter presents adult-led storytelling and other forms of theater arts as activities that can be used to foster an inclusive, developmentally appropriate early childhood classroom environment. Examples from practice provide those working with young children—teachers, parents, and community artists—a window into what using the theater arts in early childhood settings can look like. Throughout the examples and discussion, emphasis is placed on how such activities can be inclusive in supporting children with a range of abilities, interests and needs, thereby fostering an inclusive classroom environment. These vignettes are offered to the reader not as a prescriptive how-to, but rather as inspiration and building blocks. The chapter aims to provide readers with the tools to create their own approaches to integrating the theater arts into work with all young children.

Young Children and the Arts, pages 119–140

VIGNETTE

We are centrally concerned with this method for early years work, as children bring skills in pretend play to school with them. If we do not use drama, we are ignoring a key way in which they teach themselves and make sense of the world from a very early age. (Toye & Prendiville, 2000, p. 1)

One day in Ms. Calella's (pseudonym) fours class there were some unexpected visitors. Several members of the nonprofit school's board of directors came in to see the center and take photos for an upcoming newsletter. The children in this inclusive preschool class had been cleaning up their snack and transitioning to the carpet for circle time when the visitors arrived. The energy level in the classroom started to rise as the strange adults wandered in with their photography equipment, asking questions of the teacher's aide, bending down to speak to some of the children.

Suddenly Ms. Calella asked in a loud confident voice, "Where are all my fishies? Fishies, stop what you are doing! We will clean later. Join me on the rug, quick, quick, swim over!" With that she herself puckered up her lips to make a fish face, put her hands together in a prayer position, fingers pointing straight ahead and used her hands to lead her in a swaying-fish-path to the rug. She stopped making a fish face for a moment and urged the children enthusiastically, "Hurry up! Over here! We will talk to our visitors later! Come on little fishies!" She resumed her swimming, fish-face sway-walk, and plopped down on the rug.

Each of the seventeen four-year-olds quickly followed suit, save one fishie-straggler whom the assistant teacher steered to the rug and pulled onto her lap. Ms. Calella continued, maneuvering her hands in front of her in the swimming motion as she spoke, "The fishies were swimming in the water. Oops, no talking! Don't talk under water because you will get water in your mouth! Lets just swim . . . oh, look at that, we are swimming past a big, big octopus . . ."

Within minutes the classroom had gone from bordering on chaos to the joyous group activity of pretending to explore the ocean together. Ms. Calella continued to lead, and took suggestions about what sea life they saw during their journey. Some children participated verbally, most participated physically, a few acted out their part as fish or shark with exuberance and a zeal for pretending, and one or two simply listened and watched.

INTRODUCTION

In the scenario described above, Ms. Calella used a simple imagination exercise to engage the children and to avert a potentially chaotic environment. Many early childhood teachers use and teach each other how to use teacher-led pretend scenarios such as the one provided in this example. Ms. Calella reports creating this exercise after being inspired by a resident storytelling teaching artist who came to work in her classroom. She explains, "I don't have a lot of tricks like Ms. Nora [the teaching artist]. I just make it up. Like, for physical education we pretend to go in a bubble. We blow bubbles and then go inside the bubble . . . Or, if I need to keep them quiet, I will use the one they already know: a fish going under the water, swimming."

Ms. Calella built on children's pretend play skills, and engaged the whole group in this inclusive preschool classroom in an interactive dramatic scenario. While her focus was on classroom management during an interruption by unexpected visitors, the children were given an opportunity to develop their literacy, motor and cognitive skills during the spontaneous activity she initiated. They used language, brainstormed ways to extend the pretend scenario, and used their bodies to move in the ways that fish move.

Prioritizing children's play and promoting inclusion have always grounded my teaching practice as an early childhood and special education teacher. My interest in the theater arts came later. I became interested in performance because I saw the power that it held for engaging shy, reluctant, difficult, and challenging children. When invited to participate in adult-led drama or theater improvisation games, children often surprised me. For example, one child who I previously taught, Yalith, seemed to behave in ways that were out of character for her—more sociable and assertive than she typically was. Rashan, on the other hand, showed increased compassion and restraint and worked collaboratively with others, whereas typically he was characterized as bossy. John jumped from speaking in two word utterances to twelve during theater improvisation (improv) activities after just a few weeks. In my experience, when engaging in drama, children often perform beyond themselves, just as Vygotsky (1933) explained that they do in play.

In the chapter that follows, I will explore adult-led storytelling, in addition to other forms of theater arts, and consider the ways that such activities can be used to create an inclusive, developmentally appropriate classroom environment. This chapter aims to provide those working with young children—teachers, parents, and community artists—a window into what using the theater arts in early childhood settings can look like. I will consider two ways to use the theater arts in working with young children. First, I will discuss ways that teachers can integrate elements of drama and storytelling across the curriculum and existing classroom activities. Second, I will give examples of different theater arts programs and how they can be enacted with young children of different ages and abilities. All of the examples that follow come from actual early childhood practice. These vignettes are offered to the reader not as a prescriptive how-to, but rather as inspiration and building blocks. It is my hope that each of you, with your own interests, experiences, and the particular children that you work and play with, will use the examples and discussion that follow to create your own approaches to integrating the theater arts into your work with young children.

INTEGRATING STORYTELLING AND DRAMA
THROUGHOUT THE CURRICULUM

While early childhood teachers may not be formally trained in how to implement drama and storytelling, a reliance on elements of drama and storytelling is part of the folk culture of many early childhood programs. Finger plays, puppets, imagination exercises, and oral storytelling weave their way into many a Head Start, child care or and nursery school even if they are not listed on the week's curriculum outline or covered in staff development programs. Every teacher worth his or her salt knows that when things get harried its time to sing *The Wheels on the Bus* or another class favorite, complete with acting out the motions and asking everyone to chime in to "ssh, ssh, ssh" and "sit on down."

Likewise, one must never underestimate the power of a circle time conversation with a beloved class puppet. Puppets have long been used by early childhood teachers to create a shared focal point, to engage the group in joyful and meaningful discussion, and to help the children to focus during circle time activities. These are just two examples of how elements of the theater arts can be found as part of the fabric of many early childhood classrooms. By using elements of drama and storytelling (puppets, acting out motions, pretending, taking on roles), early childhood educators capitalize on children's natural propensity for play and pretending. Integrating such elements can engage a wide array of learners who have a diversity of learning styles and ability levels by providing an array of avenues for participation. In the following section I will discuss several examples of how I and other teachers have incorporated such elements across the curriculum, often without any specific training in the theater arts.

Julie, a teacher I once worked with, taught me the power of storytelling in the early childhood classroom. Out on the lawn of Maple Valley Preschool, we sat for what seemed like hours one hot August morning. Julie, I, and eighteen three-year-olds waited for the announcement that the fire bell had indeed been just a bell and not a fire. We were toy-less, playground-less and plan-less. I would never have imagined how we would keep the children from running wild in this uncontained outdoor space for very long, let alone for the forty minutes that we ended up sitting there.

Julie, on the other hand, seemed nonplussed. "Do you want to hear about Booga Booga?" she asked the children. They all smiled and cheered and nodded their heads wildly. One child turned to me, smiled wide-eyed and exclaimed, "Booga Booga's gonna eat ice cream!" with delight. It quickly became clear that these children were well acquainted with Booga Booga. I, on the other hand, had just joined the class as the assistant teacher. I met Booga Booga, an imaginary monster friend of Julie's, for the first time during the forty minutes we spent on the lawn, on that unbearably hot August day. Below you can meet her, too.

> So, there I was with this monster baby, too little to speak, and I didn't know what to do with her. Every time I tried to feed her she screamed and cried like this, "waaaah!" Can you do that? "Waaaaah!" "Carrots" I asked her? "waaaaah!" "Cheese?" I asked. "waaaah!" "Potatoes?" "waaaaah!"

> Right, that's exactly what she sounded like. So I gave up. Then she made a different sound, a grunt, sort of: "hmmph." It did not sound like the word "yes," but I think that is what she was trying to tell me. She also seemed to be gesturing towards the freezer so I opened it up . . . each time I tried a freezer food: frozen broccoli, pizza, popsicles, "Waaaah!"

> Then, as my hand touched the ice cream she seemed to squeal with delight! Again, she went, "hmmph, hmmph, hmmph" but this time faster. But, when she tasted it she cried again! Now I was seriously confused. Sadly, I returned it to the freezer.

> But as I did so she made what I think was her happy-yes grunt again "hmmph, hmmph, hmmph." I tried to feed her the ice cream again: "waaah!" I tried to put the ice cream away: "hmmph, hmmph, hmmph." Over and over this happened! She seemed to be trying to tell me something, but I could not figure out what . . .

Julie's Booga Booga stories—of which there were many—were more than just a fire drill trick. The stories never failed to calm and center the children. It was a fairly diverse group of children in terms of their backgrounds, interests and needs. One child in the class, who had been diagnosed with Fetal Alcohol Syndrome, presented us with some behavior challenges that at times both Julie and I felt ill equipped to deal with, such as climbing up on the classroom table and dancing when we turned our heads. We also had three other children in the class who were receiving special education services; however, not all of them presented us with challenging behaviors. Without fail, Julie's stories seemed to focus the group and instantly put Julie and the children on the same page. At the same time the children were learning important literacy skills: sequencing, repetition, prediction. I noticed that certain children, in many cases the ones that seemed to constantly get redirected during the morning calendar meeting, though not only the children with diagnosed special needs, attended to these stories in ways that they didn't during other teacher-led activities.

I never dared to tell a Booga Booga story while I worked with Julie. I am sure she would have been supportive; it just never occurred to me. That was Julie's thing. I did tell stories at lunch, inspired by Julie's example. The stories I told were not of the monster sort, rather they were based on my own childhood experience. I told children the story of my first day of preschool. I did not remember that day in my life, but my own mother had told me the story.

> I wanted to bring my bottle of milk, or "baba" as I called it, to Alphabetland Preschool. I was three years old, just like some of you, and at home I still drank from my baba. On that first day of school I was waiting for the little yellow bus to pick me up. My mother had told me it would come for me and I was *very* excited to go to school! I was holding my bottle and suddenly my mom told me to put it in the refrigerator. I was very confused. Why on earth would I do that? It was coming with me, of course! My mother told me, "Okay, put it in your school bag, and when the other children take out their babas you take out yours."

> So, when I got to school I put my baba, still in my school bag in my cubby. It was playtime. I looked around. No babas. The other children had not taken out their babas, so I knew it was not time for babas yet. During the clean up song I looked around again. No babas. Okay, probably during snack. So, after we washed our hands, I sat down at the big blue table and looked around. Snack time is a great time to drink babas! But, guess what? That's right: No babas. Just little plastic cups of juice.

> This is a funny place. When do they drink their babas?! I started to get worried. Then they said storytime was next. Okay, while listening to a story, that's a really great time to drink from a baba! But, how did you know? That's right: No babas! I went home that day with my baba still in my school bag, untouched.

One of the children asked, "Then what happened?" I explained that I handed the bottle to my mother when I got off the little yellow bus and proclaimed, "no more baba." In future renditions of the story I incorporated the answer to that question as the ending, explaining that I did not drink from a bottle again after that first day of school. In that way the children helped me create the telling of the story over time. During the first and many subsequent tellings of the baba story the children often asked, "What about playground time?" Or, "What about nap time?" In this way they indicated to me that they understood the repetitive aspect of the story, waiting to see at each transition if that would be the time to drink from the bottle.

The children helped me tell the story and showed me how they used their own experiences of school demands and routines to understand the story. In later retellings, I added playground time and naptime to extend the sequence. I embellished, added sound effects and told it with repetition, pausing for the children to help me out by filling in the predictable parts. It was both similar and different from the version my mother had told me. For many of us, when we stop to think about it, we realize that we have stories handed down to us by our parents, grandparents or other adults in our life. While it may not occur to everyone to share these with young children, I have found that they are enchanted by an array of such tales.

CHILDREN AS STORYTELLERS

Children are natural storytellers. All of us who have worked with young children can think of times when children have told elaborate tales of birthdays, vacations, or simply what happened at bedtime on the previous night. Sometimes adults become concerned when the facts do not seem to add up. In the worst case scenario we get into a discussion of truth versus lies. But stories are not about telling the truth. Stories are a way to share our experience of the world, use our imagination, and share with the listener. By telling my first day of preschool story, I am sharing a story that the children can relate to, and I judiciously weave in details and elaborate in ways that to varying degrees are grounded in my memories. By telling our stories we give children a model and license to go further in sharing and extending their own stories.

By telling children stories—real or imagined—and by inviting children to participate by asking questions, making sounds, making suggestions, repeating phrases, and filling in the blank, we create pretend scenarios with them. Children can become part of the story and participate in collectively creating it through their words and movements. Whether an individual child contributes much or little to the story, the group is having the experience of entering and creating a shared world with a trusted adult. Whereas in play the child initiates the collectively created pretend experience, in teacher-led storytelling, storytelling is initiated by the teacher, yet builds on children's propensity for play. Each child can contribute in his or her own way, thus storytelling can be inclusive of children who have a wide spectrum of abilities and needs.

While storytelling can be seen as a type of theater arts experience, and there is certainly merit in training teachers in the art of storytelling as well as in drama, I argue that no specialized training is needed to begin telling stories. While some families and cultural groups may have more developed practices and norms of storytelling, most of us tell each other stories every day. It is part of the human condition. We tell stories of our trip to the store, our struggles with family members and coworkers, stories of our bad day, good day, or something we saw along our day's journey.

As soon as I took a position at a new school and stopped working with Julie, I found that the Booga Booga stories simply flew out of my mouth. I didn't practice or have a precise plan. I just began one day, and they came. I did not tell the story quite the same way as Julie did. I borrowed heavily, relied on what I remembered the most, modified, added, and embellished. I also continued telling my first day of school stories to the children at lunchtime. Just like the children at Maple Valley Preschool, the children at University Early Childhood Center loved both my baba story and the Booga Booga stories. "More more! Again again!" They would request the stories repeatedly. What was the allure?

At the time I did not give it much thought. The children's requests and rapt attention made me feel that I was a good teacher, and that was enough at first. They sat quietly and intently as I told the familiar story of the monster, Booga Booga, being left in my car, how I took care of her, and how I finally figured out through her grunts of glee and displeasure that the only food she ate was French fry ice cream. The children chimed in to sequence and recite the repetitive parts of my story, coached me in stirring the French fries and ice cream together to make French fry ice cream, mimicked grunts of glee and displeasure, together with other sound effects. They never got enough. They requested that I tell the stories over again the second they were over.

In this new school I worked with a teacher named Yokiko. She told stories, too. Yet, she had a different storytelling approach. Yokiko used a doll, Minako, at circle time and told stories about the trial and tribulations of Minako's life. She did this in order to address classroom safety, conflicts, or to spark conversation about issues in the children's lives. During the first week of school, Yokiko introduced Minako to the children. She explained that Minako was scared because she was at a new school. Most of the children could relate to this and had a lot to say in response. Yet, they also listened quietly as Yokiko relayed in detail what the experience of the first weeks of school and making friends were like for Minako. The children advised the doll and elaborated on her story when Yokiko invited them to do so. In the weeks that followed, Minako dealt with everything from having a new baby in her house to scissor safety.

During the course of the school year we also met Minako's friend, Peace, a purple pelican puppet who had apparently flown all the way from Japan to follow Minako to our school. Peace had many adventures. She often dispensed advice and sometimes needed to be coached in conflict resolution. Yokiko's storytelling with the doll, Minako, and puppet, Peace, was one of the most brilliant examples of classroom engagement and management I had ever seen.

Years later, this time in another preschool, I acquired a purple bird puppet who embodied many aspects of both Yokiko's Minako and Peace. I used my purple bird puppet to tell stories borrowed, adapted and new, naming her Minako in honor of all that I had learned from Yokiko. The puppets provided a physical presence for the main character of the stories. Using puppets created an opportunity for something that I had never seen in the case of the original Booga Booga stories. During playtime the children would talk to Minako as she sat out of reach on a high shelf. Sometimes they would ask me to take her down; sometimes they would simply project what they thought Minako was saying or feeling.

In these moments my teacher-directed activity of storytelling with a puppet and child-initiated pretend play intersected. The children used what I offered during story time in their play, and in turn I often built on these initiatives in subsequent circle times. Thus, teacher-led pretend activity and child-initiated pretend play were both an integral part of classroom life and were in relationship with one another. Each of these activities provided opportunities for both children and adults to play the roles of initiator and responder as they collectively created a storytelling classroom culture. Both teacher-led storytelling and the children's play created opportunities for teachers and children alike to continue to develop their pretend play skills as well as their abilities to develop ideas and extend pretend scenarios.

Ms. Calella, the teacher whom we met at the beginning of this chapter, engaged her class not only in imagination exercises like the fish swimming activity, but also integrated other elements of drama throughout the curriculum, through the use of puppets and story enactment. After using puppets at circle time to help the children express themselves or act out a story, she left the puppets or props on the classroom shelves, thus encouraging the children to integrate them into their play. At the same time, she chose books to act out or scenarios to explore based on her observations of children's interests or important issues. While Yokiko, Julie, Ms. Calella and I all created our own approach to integrating elements of drama and storytelling into circle time and other areas of the curriculum, in each scenario the teacher is building on the children's propensity for pretend play, while creating engaging activities that can further their development.

CURRICULAR APPROACHES TO DRAMA AND STORYTELLING

While many early childhood teachers may be familiar and comfortable with using elements of drama within circle time or other curriculum areas, most early childhood teachers have not been explicitly trained in the use of drama. Therefore, they might justifiably feel intimidated by the thought of enacting an ongoing storytelling or drama curriculum. Likewise, many artists trained in theater who work with young children may not have knowledge of early childhood development and may feel ill-prepared to create or adapt curriculum for young children. What is critical in enacting theater arts experiences with this age group is that it needs to focus on the group's process. The particular theater approach or method that is used is of far less importance than following the children's own group process. Different teachers and teaching artists have developed unique curricular approaches that are based on their own experience, interests and expertise. I will describe several of these approaches later in this discussion. When used most successfully, each approach is then further refined and adapted based on the particular groups and individuals who are participating. There is no one right way to do theater arts with young children.

Drama in the early childhood classroom, however, is not synonymous with putting on a play. In creating and enacting early childhood theater arts experience, the emphasis should be on the process not the product. In early childhood, theater arts activities should not focus on getting children to do any particular thing or act in any particular way. Rather, in enacting theater arts activities with young children, whatever their initial way and level of participation, it should be accepted. And, there should be a long-term goal of enabling all participants to become more proficient at working together and learning the art form.

For example, if one is teaching children to tell stories, then one sentence or one word or even a gesture, or an observation is an acceptable starting point. With this philosophy, from the moment the activity begins all children are considered participants who can be expected to advance, albeit at their own pace. This attitude is, in part, what lends the performing arts their inclusive nature, dovetailing with a developmentally appropriate approach to early childhood curriculum. Teaching artists and classroom teachers can work with children to create an environment where a wide range of learners can develop and where everyone is provided opportunities to perform beyond themselves, while simultaneously being accepted for who they are and what they can do. In my experience, when provided with this kind of environment, children will rise to the occasion, and often the entire group will advance in unexpected ways.

There are certain key elements that may guide teachers and teaching artists alike in creating theater arts programs for young children that are inclusive. These follow:

1. An encouraging environment that accepts a range of abilities/behaviors
2. Participation via multiple modalities—listening, observing speaking, moving
3. Use of a consistent structure
4. Improvising by building on children's ideas, interests and initiations

5. Behavioral expectations/directions are embedded within the activities
6. Adults play and pretend with children and collaborate with one another

In order to understand what these elements look like in practice, the reader is invited to take an in-depth look at the approaches to storytelling and creative drama that follow. These examples are highlighted in order to provide a sense of the array of theater arts approaches that exist and how programs might vary to account for the child age and developmental level.

GROUP STORYTELLING

In order to better understand what the theater arts look like with young children, I invite the reader to step back into Ms. Calella's Fours classroom and participate in a storytelling session with Ms. Nora, a storytelling teaching artist. Each week Ms. Nora tells the children an interactive story, inviting them to participate by listening, speaking, pretending and moving. She also leads the children in an array of imagination exercises and drama warms ups, and they each are given an opportunity to tell their own short story. She accepts each child's ability and willingness to participate, simultaneously creating an expectation and environment where each child will advance throughout the course of her residency.

The twelve children present in "The Fours" class are each seated on one of the colored squares on the big oval rug that covers the floor in the sometimes-block-area-sometimes-circle-time-area. The blocks have just been placed neatly back on their shelves, along with the other toys throughout the classroom that were stacked and sorted and stored by the children and the teachers. Ms. Calella has just finished leading the children in song. Suddenly, one of the children calls out, "Ms. Nora!" Most of the children turn their gaze to the door as Ms. Nora walks in. This is Ms. Nora's first visit of the year.

Ms. Calella rises to her feet and exclaims, "Ah, Ms. Nora's here! Look everyone, say, 'Hello, Ms. Nora.'" The children chime in, "Hello Ms. Nora!" in that singsong way that children repeat what a teacher or parent has just asked them to say. Ms. Nora, the storyteller, smiles widely as she puts her coat and backpack on the child-sized table in the center of the room. She pauses at the table, looking at the group of children still seated on the rug, and says, "Hi! It is so good to see you all!"

Ms. Nora pulls a child-sized chair from the table and places it on the edge of the carpet. She leaves her belongings on the table behind her. When she sits down, she turns behind her to adjust a tiny, dark blue vinyl shopping bag with a picture of Peter Rabbit on the outside. The bag is on top of her belongings and is within arms' reach.

"I have a story for you today," begins Ms. Nora, "but first, do you remember my secret signal?" Ms. Nora has been working at this school for many years, and this is her third year working with the Fours, some of whom have been at this school since they were in the Twos. Some of the children nod or say yes; others look around at one another or stare ahead. She goes on to explain that when she says "secret signal," everyone needs to look at her, and put their hands to their ears. Then, she shows them how to put their fingers to their lips and finally put their hands in their laps. They walk through the three motions together twice, each time prompted by Ms. Nora happily exclaiming, "secret signal!"

After reviewing the secret signal, Ms. Nora begins to tell this week's story: "The Gingerbread Man." She invites the children to copy her motions. Sometimes there is a sound that goes with the motion, such as a squeak when she pretends to open the oven door. The children are encouraged to join in by making these sound effects and copying her motions. On occasion she makes these directions explicit by asking, for example, "Can you put your cow ears on?" just before she puts her own hands to her head. Another example is when she says, "Let's say, 'Yum. Yum!'" At other times, the direction to copy her is implied. As she tells the story many children do copy her motions, and some imitate the sound effects. Some children move in and out of copying, repeating her words and sounds, simply listening, or in some cases looking off in the distance. Ms. Nora accepts all of this, occasionally prompting individuals or the group to refocus their participation or reminding them to copy her.

Ms. Nora invites the children to participate verbally. She does this in two ways during the Gingerbread Man story. First, as she tells the story, the Gingerbread Man character sings, "You can't catch me . . ." retelling each character in the series he passes along the way. As the Gingerbread Man lists the characters, Ms. Nora pauses, allowing the children to remember the order of the characters and fill in the blank. The children call out the answers, and as soon as one or several of the children call out the correct answer, Ms. Nora continues to tell the next part of the story.

The second way the children can participate verbally is when Ms. Nora asks them to use their imaginations to think up some new characters for the story. She asks the children to raise their hands and they are given an individual opportunity to share their ideas with the group. The story continues, repeating the sequence each time the Gingerbread Man encounters a new character. On the first day of storytelling, the children struggle to come up with new characters and repeatedly go back to "lady," "woman," and "man." While Ms. Nora does eventually accept the suggestion of "man," for the most part, she encourages them to use their imaginations and try to think of who else could be in the story on this first day. This does not appear to be an easy task for this group. Toward the end of the story, one child comes up with "cowboy," and Ms. Nora exclaims, "A cowboy! Now you are really using your imagination!" Taking suggestions and then putting them into action with a gesture is one of the many moments that Ms. Nora has planned for, but that is improvised.

Another child suggests "cat." Interestingly, she does not say "cat" when Ms. Nora calls on her; rather, she picks up on the use of gesture and motion as a means of communication and makes a gesture of cat whiskers when she is called on. Ms. Nora replies, "Great! What is this?" copying the whisker-gesture as she asks. The child replies, "cat," and then they use the cat character with the whisker gesture in this story. Here it becomes evident that communicating nonverbally is acceptable not just when Ms. Nora suggests it, but when the child initiates as well. This is one of the many ways that Ms. Nora continually sends the message that varied forms of participation are acceptable and in this way creates a supportive and encouraging environment.

After the Gingerbread Man story is finished, Ms. Nora calmly says, "Let's wiggle our heads, how about our shoulders, elbows, ribs." As she says each body part, she herself wiggles or moves that part of her body, and most of the children copy her motions. Then she says, as she is still wiggling her ribs, "...Ready here we go...wiggle wiggle up!" As she says this, she stands up from the little wooden chair that she has been perched on. She leads the "wiggle up" activity by shaking her hips and bouncing her fists alongside her body. She smiles and looks around at the group as she stands.

The children push themselves up from their purple, orange, blue, red, green, and yellow spots on the carpet and meet Ms. Nora in a standing position. Most of them copy the wiggle up procedure. A few stragglers are still seated or are resting on their knees. Ms. Nora urges enthusiastically that everyone "Wiggle wiggle up!" and Ms. Callela supports her by calling some of the children by name and saying, "Come on, stand up!" Without further ado Ms. Nora begins to chant:

> Now clap your hands
> just like me, clap your hands
> stomp your feet, stomp your feet
> touch your tummies...
> heads, shoulders, tummies
> knees, tummies, shoulders,
> heads (almost whispering now), nose, shoulders
> tummies, knees.

Ms. Nora continues this rhythmic chant, tapping each body part as she says it. As I watch the videotapes of the storytelling sessions, I notice that there are no directions given prior to or separate from these activities. Rather, the instructions are embedded in the chants/activities just as they are in the game Simon Says or in a follow-the-leader activity such as a teacher leading children on a bear hunt ("run up the mountain, now run down the mountain").

The transition to the next segment also happened in the blink of an eye, even though nothing throughout the session feels rushed. Still using her body as a model for the children to copy, Ms. Nora introduced an activity that she calls an "imagination warm up":

> Now, quietly, get out your favorite piece of bubble gum
> Don't talk about it
> Open up your bubble gum, put it in your mouth
> Hum and chew
> Hmmmmmmmmmmmmmmmm...
> Keep doing that, let me hear a little more humming...
> Very good, take a little bit and stretch it really far...

As she recites the words that guide the children through the imaginary bubble gum activity, she acts out each part of what she is saying. First, she holds her hands in front of her, using her fingers to pretend that she is holding, and then unwrapping, her favorite piece of bubble gum. After pantomiming the unwrapping of the gum and putting it in her mouth, she hums and pretends to chew while leaning forward, taking an exaggerated look at how everyone is chewing. Then, when she asks them to stretch out their gum, she pretends to take the gum from her mouth and stretches her right hand way out to the side. She makes what can only be described as a gum-stretching sound, a high-pitched sound that goes up as the arm swings out and back down as she brings her hand back to her mouth.

They repeat this sound and gesture together twice. She returns to humming and chewing, and most of the children follow along. Then she says, "Lets blow a big bubble, ready here we go..." and uses her hands at her mouth to gesture how the bubble goes from being just an inch or two wide to way out as far as the arms will stretch. Then she says, "and pop it!" The children pop their bubbles by clapping one big, loud clap with Ms. Nora. The activity continues with Ms. Nora leading them in gesturing and making sounds, humming, chewing, clapping, blowing bubbles, and eventually throwing the gum in an imaginary garbage can.

There are no behavioral directions given at the beginning of the activity. Just as in the other segments of the session she does not wait for everyone to stand still and quiet down. She smiles and enthusiastically gives the directive, "Get out your favorite piece of bubble gum." This manner of embedding behavioral expectations within the ongoing pretend or game-like activity is repeated throughout the sessions. "Now clap your hands, just like me, clap your hands." In this way she teaches the children that their job in the activity is to observe, listen and copy her. At times the directions are implicit, at other times she reminds them, ". . .just like me . . ." Indeed, most of the children imitate Ms. Nora's actions and sounds to varying degrees.

She does not address the children who are not copying her by name, or do anything about the fact that they are not copying her during these warm-ups. In future sessions, I will see her address children by name on occasion. It seems that in this first session she takes another approach. She moves from one warm-up activity to the next, continuously giving the directions, "just like me." She thereby encourages the children to join in and reminds them of how these games are played. Yet, she also is comfortable with vary-ing levels of participation.

In the next segment of the 23-minute storytelling session, each child is given an individual opportunity to use his or her "storyteller's voice." Ms. Nora reaches into the tiny blue vinyl Peter Rabbit bag and takes out an egg shaker. She says nothing as she retrieves it from her little bag. She reaches for it with an animated flair and holds it in her fingers and then the palms of her hand as if it is one of her most precious possessions. The mood seems to shift, and there seems to be a great focus and anticipation in the room. The exuberant activities of blowing bubbles and chasing gingerbread men have quieted the group and the children have their attention on Ms. Nora and this very small egg.

In a quiet, but audible, voice, Ms. Nora says, "When you have the egg shaker, it's your turn to talk, and when you don't have the egg shaker, it's your turn to _____." Some children chime in and say "listen" when Ms. Nora pauses. "OK, Ms. Nora's going to go first, ready? Ms. Nor-a." As she says her name, she shakes the egg three times. She says the syllables of her name in time with the shakes of the egg. She passes the egg to the child on her right stating firmly, "We're going to go this way. . . ." They pass the egg around the circle to one another. Most children take a turn. Some children shake the egg in unison without saying the syllables of their name. Others shake more or fewer times than their names warrant. One child shakes and passes without saying anything.

Marisol neither shakes, nor speaks, nor passes, and instead stares at the rug in front of her with her chin in her hands as the child next to her holds out the egg. Both Ms. Nora and Ms. Calella encourage Marisol to give it a try. No verbal or physical response. Then, Ms. Nora asks, "Marisol, you don't want to take a turn?" seemingly putting words to Marisol's embodied performance of "No." In response, Marisol shakes her head vigorously side to side. "Okay, then just pass the egg," says Ms. Nora. Again, no response.

"Juan, just pass the egg, then," suggests Ms. Nora, indicating that Juan should pass it to the child who is sitting on the other side of Marisol. He does. The activity continues with the last few children. Both teachers sitting in the circle also take a turn when the egg comes to them; they collaborate with Ms. Nora in this way and send the message to the children that the storytelling session is one that is valuable and worthy of their participation, but that they may also choose not to participate. When the egg has made its way back to Ms. Nora, she tucks it securely back into the Peter Rabbit bag.

Throughout the session, and perhaps most vividly in the example of Marisol, we see Ms. Nora simultaneously accept children's participation while urging them to perform in new ways. Within six weeks of taking this approach Marisol took the shaker, and by the end of fifteen weeks she was telling her own three-part story when it was her turn to do so.

PARTICIPATORY THEATER PROGRAM

Oily Cart is a children's theater company in the UK, with 25 years of experience working with both young children and people with profound and multiple learning disabilities. Young (2004) conducted a case study of Oily Cart's participatory theater work with children under two-years-old and their caregivers. The participatory theater program took place in an inflatable dome. Following some music and movement led by the actors, the caregivers and children sat on the carpet in a circle. The actors guided the performance. They were in costume and used puppets and props to engage the children as they enacted a series of events that were playful and narrative, without relying on a narrative structure.

While theirs is a very different approach than that taken by Ms. Nora, the Oily Cart actors also seem centrally concerned with creating an encouraging environment, offering participation via multiple modes, allowing for improvisation within an intentional structure, embedding directions within the activity, and collaboration between adults. Young (2004) noted that the actors' ability to notice and improvise with children's initiations and to create with such playful exchanges became central. For example, one toddler became interested in a feather. She looked at it intently and then picked it up neatly with finger and thumb. One of the actors watched carefully and then pinched his finger and thumb together imitating the child's motion. The toddler and actor then took part in a series of finger and thumb gestures.

Here we see how the adult within the context of enacting a performance with a specified structure allows for improvisation as he mirrors a child's activity. This is one of many examples that shows the ways that the adults pause to follow the child's lead, improvising and creating together, and thereby creating a positive and supportive atmosphere. Young (2004) also stresses the importance of allowing children to participate via multiple modalities, calling this a "distinctive feature of improvised theater" (p. 19). She emphasized that the improvised exchange is not just verbal, but multi-modal, including sounds, facial expressions, gesture, and the use of puppets and props. The actors allowed for a wide range of behaviors, sometimes struggling to know how much leeway was appropriate, and working to decide this based on the particular children and the relationship with their caregivers. Given the age range of the child participants, from six months to two years, this was especially important. Some children used spoken language and were up on their feet, while others crawled, or watched wide-eyed from their caregivers' laps.

In order to collaborate and communicate with the children's caregivers, the actors worked to embed behavioral expectations and directions within the performance itself, just as Ms. Nora embedded directions by saying "Copy me" or by prompting the children to move or pretend with her. While those working with older children would do well to embed messages to the children, for very young, preverbal children teachers should, however, keep talking to the children, while conveying messages about behavior and participation to the other adults in the room, which also furthers collaboration between actors, teachers and/or caregivers.

An accepting and supportive atmosphere allows children to go beyond their initial ways of participating and encourages participation.

TEACHER IN ROLE

Toye and Prendiville (2000) offer examples of another approach to drama with young children in England. They present an approach to drama and story-acting that relies heavily on Heathcote's concept of Teacher in Role (TiR) (Heathcote & Bolton, 1995). The children play the role of the "expert," directing the activity and offering suggestions as invited to do so by the teacher. In their book they discuss the benefits of this approach and offer the reader step-by-step directions for enacting twelve different dramas with young children. Each drama follows a clear structure, and there is consistency in structure and method across the dramas; however, there is also ample room and suggestions for improvised activity.

One noticeable aspect to their writing about their work is the success they have had in engaging children with special needs, and creating an environment within the drama curriculum where children perform in new ways. In their chapter on children with special needs, they assert, "One of the most appealing aspects of using drama is its capacity to engage children across the ability range. The dramas we offer in this book will work for children of all abilities" (Toye & Prendiville, 2000, p. 105). It is clear that these authors have both a commitment to and success with using the drama activities with children of many ability levels.

One example of how this manifested in practice took place in a classroom that included a child, Paul, who had learning difficulties that were primarily language-related. The authors describe a scenario where a teacher led a group of children in a discussion of what helping people means. The authors explain that while Paul contributed to the early discussion of helping, they could not understand what he was saying and that what he contributed was "difficult to relate" (Toye & Prendiville, 2000, p. 106). The teacher then led the class in creating role-play scenarios centered on the theme of helping (child needs help finding a teddy bear, child needs help because he got in trouble with his mother, etc.). In this second activity, the teacher adopted the practice of teacher in role (TiR), staying in character throughout the activity, even when giving group direction.

During the pretend search for the lost teddy bear, Paul pointed to the bear, seemingly frustrated with the pretend nature of the scenario. Toye and Prendiville (2000) report that at times he seemed not to be tuned in and his attention wandered. At other times, he is described as looking, commenting, and attending. They go on to describe what they saw as Paul's "most notable involvement and contribution" (Toye & Prendiville, 2000, p. 106) by sharing dialogue between Paul and the Teacher in Role (TiR):

> He sat fascinated when I came in as the boy and showed how grumpy and unhappy I was, which was all done non-verbally. Paul paid closest attention as they advised the boy how to apologize to his mother if he wanted to be allowed to watch television. Suddenly he said to TiR, *And you must not stamp your foot.*
>
> TiR as boy, *What?*
>
> Paul, *You stamped your foot.*
>
> TiR as Boy, *When?*
>
> Paul, *When you came in.*
>
> TiR as Boy, *What do you mean?*
>
> Paul, *Like this.* He got up and stood crossly with arms folded, his face grumpy, as I had when I first came in as the boy, and then he very deliberately stamped his foot as I had done.
>
> TiR as Boy, *Oh did I?*
>
> Paul, *Yes, and she won't like it if you do that! And, she won't let you watch telly!*
>
> The rest of the children sat and watched carefully through this and supported Paul very strongly, something I suspect did not happen in this way very often.

In this scenario, we are given a powerful depiction of a child with language-based difficulties engaging in passionate communication that crossed nine conversational turns.

Another example offered in this book described Melanie, a child with severe learning difficulties, who was able to participate in a teacher-led drama game with support from a teacher. One teacher led the children in a drama where they were pretending to be in a giant's castle. The class was given the task of trying to get Jack out of the dungeon. The teacher suggested that the children try in pairs to get the key that was next to the giant (an adult who was pretending to be asleep). After three volunteer pairs were unsuccessful due to not being quiet enough, Melanie and another child were given a chance to try. At this point, the other teacher, still in the role of the giant, let Melanie and her partner succeed in obtaining the key.

While Melanie was reportedly not very interested in the rest of the drama during that session, she kept repeating the act of taking the key. She acted out the event over and over, at times by fetching the key from a peer and at other times miming the event or speaking about it to other students. Toye and Prendiville (2000) conclude by stating that in the examples of both Paul and Melanie, "the main element in the involvement of these two children is the power of the non-verbal, a way of communicating that is always available in drama although not often utilized in other classroom activities" (p. 107). Toye and Prendiville (2000) also reference other examples of young children with special needs being allowed to observe, at first, if that is what they want to do. In all examples, these children then became increasingly engaged in the drama.

CREATIVE DRAMA

In Bethesda Academy theater arts, Bailey (1993) offers compelling accounts of the use of drama with young children. Bailey describes her work as the Special Needs Director at Bethesda Academy, a nonprofit organization that provides creative drama classes both at Bethesda Academy and at nearby public schools through in-school residencies. Based on several decades of experience in the theater and at Bethesda Academy, Bailey details the array of skills that she believes can be developed through drama. These include listening, eye contact, awareness of body in space, physical coordination, physical expressiveness, verbal expressiveness, focus and concentration, flexibility and problem solving, social interaction, and the development of self-esteem. Moreover, she asserts that drama activities can be particularly helpful to children with special needs and with inclusive groups.

> If an individual can experience success, be valued for her ideas, and have her feelings validated, her self-confidence and self-esteem begin to grow. When attitudes about the self change, obstacles become surmountable. Choices multiply. Life becomes filled with excitement and joy. Making friends and sharing experiences creates a sense of belonging to community, of having a right to exist and enjoy life alongside everyone else. To be acknowledged

for artistic creations leads to the decision to contribute more—to the self, to friends, to family, and community. (Bailey, 1993, p. 18)

Indeed, the anecdotes Bailey shares from the classrooms at Bethesda Academy suggest that many students with special needs grew to contribute to the group performances over time, and many of their parents reported that their children had an increased sense of self-esteem or pride. She describes her work with Angela, who presented with autistic features. Angela did not like to sit and participate in circle-time activities and had difficulty acting out stories with the other students. She could, however, act out characters from a story on her own and draw pictures, though her drawings were limited. According to Bailey, she drew the same cat over and over again. When asked to draw anything else she said, "You draw it, you draw it!" (Bailey, 1993, p. 85) and would become upset if the other person did not draw it.

Because she did not like to sit with the group, Bailey let her leave the group and draw her cat pictures at a table. One week, a change occurred that showed that Angela had indeed been listening to the stories while she was drawing each week. One day Angela came to class and asked Bailey to draw *Goldilocks and the Three Bears* for her. This was the story that the class had performed the previous week. Bailey decided not to draw it for her and asked her to draw it herself. To avoid a conflict about this, Bailey quickly started class with the other children. Angela stayed at the table and drew. Later, when Bailey went over to Angela, she was surprised to find that "she was drawing a very complex and detailed rendition of Goldilocks and the three Bears' chairs" (Bailey, 1993, p. 86). This was the first time Angela had ever drawn anything other than a cat, and from then on she stopped asking others to draw for her. Each week she would come to class excitedly talking about the story from the week before and draw a picture about it while Bailey worked with the rest of the class on a new story.

This anecdote, as well as others in the book, suggests that there is something about creative drama that can have a positive impact on children with varying degrees of comfort in interacting and participating with others. What stands out here and in the Teacher in Role (TiR) approach (Toye and Prendiville, 2000) is that the adult leading the drama activities accepts whatever level of performance each child is able to give. Everyone is invited to participate fully, but both in Bailey's (1993) and Toye and Prendiville's (2000) descriptions, no one is forced to participate. The adult works to make use of whatever the child is able to contribute, continues to invite them to do what the group is doing, and as was evident in the case of Angela, looks for opportunities to challenge the child to try something new. This acceptance of each child's participation and preferences seems to be an essential factor that makes creative drama, by its very nature, an inclusive activity.

CONCLUSION: STORYTELLING, THEATER AND PLAY

Storytelling, theater and play all rely on our human capacities to pretend and imagine; they all share many elements. Therefore, by introducing aspects of storytelling and theater into the early childhood classrooms, teachers can build on children's natural proclivity for pretend play, can create an environment where children and teachers are engaged in joint activity, and can use storytelling and play in ways that are inclusive of all children—children who may have a wide range of abilities, needs and interests. Readers are urged to use elements identified and examples offered within this chapter to creatively build their own approaches to drama and to weave its elements into their existing curriculum.

In creating stories and theater arts experiences for young children, teachers are encouraged to adopt a posture of acceptance and inclusivity. While of course firm limits have to be set with regard to safety and other concerns, teachers can follow Ms. Nora's and others' examples in creating an environment where children can participate based on their individual abilities and proclivities. Children should be permitted to participate as they choose, while encouraged to participate in continuously new ways. Based on the examples from practice described above, it seems that the best way to do this is not to focus on outcomes. In creating theater arts experiences with young children the focus should be on teaching the method. Whatever the specific approach is, the teacher's focus is on how the group is working together and on conveying the message, "this is how we tell stories, join me and try it," and by urging the children to advance their storytelling skills by developing more imaginative, linguistically rich stories.

When leading drama activities or weaving elements of drama into the curriculum, teachers are advised to steadfastly observe and respond to children's initiations. Paley (1990), in reflecting on a pretend play scenario from her classroom, explains that it is the teacher's job to observe and build on pretend initiations. One child says, "The monster is coming! He's almost here!" Another responds, "Get the magic belt! When you put it on, he gets froze!" Paley concludes, "New conflicts arise everywhere; it is our business to find the magic belt if we can" (Paley, 1990, p. 18). Like play, drama holds the potential for getting the magic belt. When adults lead children in drama, they constantly run the risk of inserting logic, accuracy and truth into the children's stories. These have no place in the world of play or in the early childhood theater arts curriculum. The adult's emphasis should be on creativity and collectivity—on helping the group of children work together to dream of and create the magic belts of the world.

REFERENCES

Bailey, S. D. (1993). *Wings to fly: Bringing theatre arts to students with special needs.* Rockville, MD: Woodbine House.

Heathcote, D., & Bolton, G. (1995). *Drama for learning: Dorothy Heathcote's Mantle of the Expert approach to education.* Portsmouth, NH: Heinemann.

Paley, V. (1990). *The boy who would be a helicopter.* Cambridge, MA: Harvard University Press.

Toye, N., & Prendiville, F. (2000). *Drama and traditional story for the early years.* New York: Routledge.

Vygotsky, L. (1933). Play and its role in the mental development of the child. *Soviet Psychology, 12*(6), 62–76.

Young, S. (2004). It's a bit like flying: developing participatory theater with the under-twos: a case study of Oily Cart. *Research in Drama Education, 9*(1), 13–28.

CHAPTER 9

PLAYWORLDS AND EARLY LITERARY ARTS EDUCATION

Beth Ferholt
Brooklyn College
City University of New York

ABSTRACT

Engagement of young children with the literary arts in activities that value the full potential of play is rare. Why? This chapter answers this question through a discussion of a unique pedagogy that combines play and the literary arts, specifically the reading and exploring of children's literature through adult–child joint play. This pedagogy, called "playworlds," embodies what is described in this chapter as a "post-modern" form of play, in which children and adults engage in adult–child joint play for the purpose of promoting the development and quality of life of both adults and children. Playworlds are based on L. S. Vygotsky's theories of play, art, imagination and creativity (1967/2004, 1971, 1976, 1978, 1986), which allow us to appreciate the full potential of children to be creative humans.

There is a widespread opinion that creativity is the province of a select few...This is not true. If we understand creativity in its true psychological sense as the creation of something new, then this implies that creation is the

Young Children and the Arts, pages 141–154
Copyright © 2012 by Information Age Publishing

141

province of everyone to one degree or another—that it is a normal and constant companion in childhood. (Vygotsky, 1967/2004, p. 33)

VIGNETTE

Engagement of young children with the literary arts in activities that value the full potential of play is rare. Why? I will answer this question through a discussion of a unique pedagogy that combines play and the literary arts, specifically the reading and exploring of children's literature through adult–child joint play.

I will begin with a description of a pivotal moment (excerpted, slightly modified, from Ferholt, 2009) in a particular classroom's adaptation of this pedagogy. The students are members of a kindergarten-first grade class in a public elementary school on a military base in the United State,s and the classroom discussion that I will describe below took place near the start of this century. (Many weeks after the discussion the children did, indeed, prepare and perform a play for their families based on the conclusions they reach in this discussion.)

After lunch the children gather for the meeting in which they will write a play based on a work of children's literature. However, the list of characters soon includes a monkey, a parrot, and baby fauns, and Pearl says that she does not like these "extra characters" (characters who were not in the novel from which the children are working). Nancy responds by saying that "this is our play," so that "extra characters" are welcome.

Michael, the teacher, states that this issue must be decided before the class can continue writing of the play, and he suggests that people who agree with Pearl move to one side of the meeting circle, while those who agree with Nancy move to the other side. He splits the class fairly evenly and then a heated and impressive debate begins. Although Michael's splitting of the class could be critiqued, it serves as a catalyst for several surprising events. To start with, Nancy and Pearl, particularly, pit their arguments and rhetoric against each other like professionals.

After approximately half an hour, when the floor is covered with the bodies of the younger children, heads in arms, Michael finally stops the conversation. He intervenes and tells the children that they just want two different things, and so they will have to choose between the two options instead of trying to find a resolution. No one is changing his or her mind despite the great talking, he says. Michael then turns to me (the participant researcher who is filming these events), commenting that he had not anticipated this dilemma, and asks if I can think of a metaphor to help him explain to the children that there is no compromise to be found. I suggest that Michael use a metaphor that he had used just the day before, and he says that this is a great idea. He tells the children that they enjoy anticipating opening gifts, and also enjoy gifts themselves, but that they cannot possibly enjoy both of these things at once.

Pearl is not yet sure of her response to Michael's intervention but she begins to take charge immediately. She is sitting on a low table and uses many head and hand gestures as she speaks. She observes that everyone on the other side of the room is crowded around Nancy and asks why. She points out that her younger sister, Andrea, a kindergartener in the class, has something to say, and she asks why no one else on her side of the room is talking, motivating some of her followers to speak up. She is a rousing and eloquent speaker.

Someone then suggests that the class should split into two groups and do two different plays. Pearl says, simply, "No." Her face is so honest and expressive as she speaks this one word that we all are all brought to attention, waiting for what will come next. Michael gazes at Pearl as she speaks. The children who had become tired and were lying on the floor, picking at their noses and shoelaces, sit up straight and still their hands. And then Pearl delivers a speech in which she tells the class that that they are all her best friends and that she does not want two separate plays. She says, "Everyone (in this class) is my best friend."

After this speech, the most unexpected thing happens. As if they have been physically lifted by Pearl's words, several of the children on the other side of the room simply stand up and walk over to Pearl's side of the room. Then the most outspoken advocate for the opposing camp, Nancy, silently stands up, walks across the circle, sits down on the floor next to Pearl and rests her head on Pearl's knee. There is a still in the room, a static, as the rest of us pause and wonder what has just happened, and if we can believe our eyes.

It seems, now, that we have no solution, no possible direction to go from here. Then Alice says, "We can do two plays, one each way, each with all of us." Pearl asks her to explain this again, and she does, and then Pearl smiles the very biggest smile. Everyone is practically cheering. Then Nancy raises her hand and retells Michael his own metaphor as a story, ingeniously changing the meaning by adding time:

> Because you know how you said that gift thing? Like first you have breakfast, then you go downstairs . . . then first you see you see what's under the Christmas tree . . . Then the first part is like, we, the first part we do it our way, with, like, it's our play with no, with . . . and then you're going to open the gift, so that's their part.

In other words: we anticipate opening our gifts as we walk towards the tree, then open our gifts, and in this way we have both the anticipation and the gifts—just as we have both the two casts of characters and the community of "best friends" intact. Michael takes everyone outside for a run.

Outside, in the field, the children do not all race to the end of the field and back as they usually do. Instead, many of the children weave from side to side as they run, some of them waving their arms. They look like they are flying, or swimming, and Michael tells me that in all of his fifteen years in the classroom he has never witnessed a class discussion as amazing as this one.

BACKGROUND

Michael and his class are working from the classic novel by C.S. Lewis, *The Lion, the Witch and the Wardrobe* (1950), to make their play. Lewis gives us a complex tale of greed and loyalty, friendship and bravery, fear and anticipation, and the conversation between Michael and his students, in which the students work with Michael to overcome those "teacherly" actions of his that threaten their unity, explores these themes fully, beautifully and at many levels of abstraction simultaneously. It is a discussion that embodies as well as contains these literary themes, and this class of best friends displays a grace of thought and intelligence that is impressive by any standards.

John Dewey, the American philosopher, tells us that education is "a process of living and not a preparation for future living" (1897, p. 78). This discussion stands out for Michael and for myself, the researcher participating in and observing his pedagogy, as one of the most amazing we have ever seen in part because it is true education in this sense. Even from the above brief description, it is clear that these children and their teacher are very much engaged in a process of living literature for the here and now, of solving an immediate and pressing problem, and are not going through rote activities in order to be able to write or read literature "at a higher level" in a possible future.

The above discussion took place in a contemporary U.S. public elementary school, but the reasons that this kind of conversation—a conversation in which children passionately and thoughtfully engage with the literary arts, each other and their teacher—is so rare here and now will require us to look at young children and the literary arts quite broadly. I will begin this chapter with a discussion and description of Michael's pedagogy, situating this pedagogy in a historical and geographical context, and end with a tentative answer to the question of why such engagement of young children with the literary arts is rare. Throughout, I will be guided by Dewey's present-focused definition of education. I will also be following the conclusion reached by the Russian psychologist, L. S. Vygotsky, that "a child's greatest achievements are possible in play" (1978, p. 100).

PLAYWORLDS IN CONTEXT

Many of the ways that westerners think about childhood and children today have been shaped in part by the great change in our understanding of age that took place during the Enlightenment (Fass, 2007; Wolff, 1998). Philosophers such as Jean-Jaques Rousseau and John Locke, whose work was very influential on political discourse, also told us how to think about children and childhood, and their ideas combined with various social events to change both our definitions and awareness of these categories. Our modern western ideal of childhood, with its emphasis on the innocence and malleability of children (Aries, 1962; Fass, 2007), is, therefore, both relatively recent and just one of many, competing understandings of childhood.

For example, as Fass (2007) explains, in the United States there existed a contradiction between the ideals of equal treatment for all and individual self-realization, and the reality of slavery. This contradiction came to wide spread public awareness in the 1840s, and one response was an effort to shape the American future through the careful design of children's lives. Literature and institutions—which drew heavily on the work of Rousseau and Locke, among others—were then produced or adapted for this purpose of ensuring democracy through properly created and effectively reformed childhood: *Uncle Tom's Cabin, The Adventures of Huckleberry Finn* and *Little Women;* schools, orphanages, reformatories and juvenile courts; the invention of the ideal women "devoted to home, chastity, fidelity, and selflessness" (Fass, 2007, p. 247).

The ways that we engage with children's play are shaped in great part by our ideas of children and childhood. Therefore, if we accept that ideas of children and childhood change across place and time, we would expect to find different models of play have been most prevalent and powerful in certain places and at certain times. Elsewhere (Ferholt, 2009) I suggest the following description of various forms of adult engagement with children's play. (Here I propose, not an argument in support of a narrative of enlightenment or progress, but rather a description intended to help us to think critically about those forms of adult engagement with children's play that we may accept as "given.")

We can describe a form of pre-modern children's play, in which children's play is sometimes integrated with adult activities, and sometimes conducted apart from adults, but is neither directed, protected nor jointly created and exploited by adults. Goncu and Gaskins challenge the assumption that the origins, frequency and development of children's play follow the same general patterns all over the world (Gaskins, 1999, 2000; Gaskins & Goncu, 1992; Goncu, 1999; Goncu, Tuermer, Jain, & Johnson, 1999). For instance, in a case study of young Yucatec Mayan children's engagement in their world, Gaskins (1999) explains that Mayan children constantly interweave maintenance activities, social orientation activities, work and play, and provides a detailed description of an 18 month old child mixing all four activities while moving silently among her mother and siblings.

We can then describe a modern condition, in which children's play is isolated from adult activities, and then either directed towards adult-determined goals or protected from adult interference. This is what we see in most of our preschools and elementary schools today. This is a clear manifestation of our understanding of children as innocent and malleable: We set up the play corner with child-size blocks, props and costumes, and then leave the play to the children, *or* we try to make various kinds of learning "fun" by harnessing the appeal of play.

A third type of play would be post-modern play, in which children and adults engage in adult–child joint play for the purpose of promoting the development and quality of life of both adults and children. Here the Enlightenment understanding of age is challenged. Children's play becomes something that adults wish to engage with for purposes that are solely their own, as well as for the purpose of helping children to develop. Or, as Henry Jenkins explains such play, it "seeks to provide children with the tools to realize their own political agendas or to participate in the production of their own culture" (1998, p. 30). Jenkins asks us to "embrace the approaches to teaching and social policy that acknowledge children's cultural productivity and that provide them with the materials and skills they need to critique their place in the world" (1998, p. 31).

The yearlong classroom activity that generated the above discussion among Michael and his students was such a form of teaching. In this discussion, we can see Michael support his students as they produce the means and metaphors which move the discussion, and the discussion shows that Michael must have provided his students—over the course of the past year—with the necessary materials and skills to critique their teacher's literal and figurative placement of their bodies and minds. (See Ferholt and Lecusay, 2010 for an in-depth analysis of this discussion—but also feel free to reread the discussion with these points in mind.) These qualities are also clearly manifest in the activity that generated this discussion: a relatively recently emerging form of adult engagement with children's play, an adult–child joint play-art (or play-science) activity, called playworlds.

Vygotsky argues, in his lesser-known work on creativity and imagination in childhood, that, "the creative processes are already fully manifest in earliest childhood" (1967/2004, p. 6). Furthermore, Vygotsky tells us that, "we can identify creative processes in children at the very earliest ages, especially in their play . . . all these children at play represent examples of the most authentic, truest creativity" (1967/2004, p. 6). From this understanding of childhood, and the role of play in early creative processes, it is possible to conclude that it is not always best to direct or protect children in their play.

Instead, we may want to interact with children in play as we interact with other creative human beings (adults). We may want to learn from children in play. Learning from one another is, after all, a great part of how we nurture the arts, literary and otherwise, among our adult selves in our adult art activities and discourses.

While this work of Vygotsky's was not translated into English until 2004, it was read in Sweden, Finland and the former Yugoslavia in the last century. In these countries this work, along with the work of many others, has inspired educational researchers, educators and artists to create and study playworlds for several decades. In Japan the famous Japanese pedagogue, Saitou's Kyouzai–Kaishaku or "interpreting the teaching material" approach, in which successful teaching depends on the teacher's reinterpretation of and renewed personal engagement with the curriculum, has been fruitfully combined with Vygtosky's (1971) psychology of art to create and study playworlds for almost a decade.

PLAYWORLDS

The understanding of play and art that lie in the root of playworlds originated in Vygotsky's theory of play and imagination and his psychology of art (Vygotsky, 1971, 1976, 1978, 1967/2004). Other theoretical foundations of playworlds include Wartofsky's (1979) philosophical writings on art and education, Bakhtin's writing on dialogue as the basic form of human engagement with others (Bakhtin, 1984; Bakhtin & Holquist, 1981), and Lindqvist's (1995) aesthetic theory of play. The pedagogical practice that Linqvist called "playworlds" was based on her radical reading of Vygotsky (Lindqvist, 1995). Marjanovic-Shane's study of metaphor in child development (Marjanovic-Shane, 1989a, 1989b), Hakkarainen's educational experiments in narrative learning in Finland (Hakkarainen, 2004, 2006, 2008), as well as Japanese pedagogue Saitou's notions of Kyouzai–Kaishaku (Miyazaki, 2008, 2009a, 2009b, 2010) also provide theoretical foundations of playworlds. (See Marjanovic-Shane et al., 2011, for more details on the playworlds of Sweden, Finland, Serbia and Japan, and their theoretical underpinnings.)

Michael is one of the first practitioners of playworlds in the United States, and his methods are informed by international playworld practices as well as by the theoretical underpinnings of playworld work. As occurs in all playworlds, in Michael's playworld adult–child joint play was made possible through the creation of a common fiction, a space in which both children and adults are creatively engaged. As in Swedish playworlds (Lindqvist, 1995), in Michael's playworld the researchers and his students worked together "to bring (a classic piece of) literature to life" (Lindqvist, 1995,

p. 72) through joint scripted and improvisational acting and the creation of stage sets. As in many of the playworlds of Belgrade (Marjanovic-Shane et al., forthcoming), Michael's playworld also included several researchers, all of who engaged in the playworld as fellow actors.

In all playworlds the arts and sciences, including the language arts, are viewed as activities in which adults are imagining and creating. Following Vygotsky (1967/2004), children's play is understood to be the medium in which children are best able to imagine and create. When adults engage with children in a joint activity that combines language arts and play, both adults and children benefit from the other participants' creative processes and products.

Playworlds are a truly hybrid play-art intergenerational activity, in which adults learn to play while children learn to engage with literature, because they create the possibility for children to strongly encourage adults to participate with children in play at the same time as adults are strongly encouraging children to participate in art and science (Ferholt, 2009). In playworlds adults are engaged (through rich literature, for instance) in the study of epistemological and ethical dilemmas of great interest to people in a variety of life stages. Adults might be interested in the playworld as a tool for furthering their own understanding of a topic, for example, such as fear. And adult participants appreciate that these dilemmas are such that it is the combination of different perspectives, rather than skills or experience that come with age, that produces solutions to these dilemmas. These dilemmas might include such dilemmas as "What is real?" or "What to do if someone you love is doing something harmful to themselves and others" (Hakkarainen, as cited in Ferholt & Lecusay, 2010). Adults in playworlds therefore accept and pay close attention to instruction in play from children who are play "experts." (See Ferholt, 2009 for a detailed discussion of this process.)

Michael explains why he finds performance in a playworld useful, in the following words:

> I (when not in a playworld) imagine the things I cannot be. I do not *be* the things I cannot be. In the PW (playworld) I can *be* a witch. A kid has to act because he cannot imagine. I have to act like the things that I know that I cannot actually be . . .

> A PW (is) kids and adults *having* to act. Adults (are) acting things they cannot be. Kids (are) act(ing) things they cannot internally imagine. (As quoted in Ferholt, 2009)

The children are playing because they cannot yet imagine without play. And the adults are not joining in play only to promote and guide the development of the children. They are also joining in play because this allows them to experience things they are not able to experience through imagination alone—things which appear too far from the possible to be experienced through imagination without play.

What follows is a description (excerpted, slightly modified, from Ferholt, 2010) of how the playworld, which led to the discussion above, manifested itself in Michael's classroom.

The first half of *The Lion, The Witch and the Wardrobe* was read aloud to the children over the first half of a single academic year. The second half of the novel was never read to the children. Instead, the children became more and more active participants in the acting of the story, until they collectively wrote and directed their own resolution to the novel's central conflicts. Playworld sessions occurred weekly on Fridays, lasted approximately two hours, and included reflection upon the enactments in the form of discussion and then free play or art activities. Every Friday, over the course of the year, four researcher-actors playing the four child heroes entered Michael's K–1 classroom and performed another scene from C. S. Lewis's novel.

Every Monday the students in this class found a few of the words from the book, words concerning the novel's imaginary world of Narnia, on the floor of their classroom, such as trees, cave, beaver dam, castle, table, sewing machine, cage, and created these set pieces or props out of cardboard and paint over the course of the week. As the weeks went by, the classroom became covered in the colorful, delicately-wrought trappings of the world of Narnia until, eventually, Michael stopped moving the cardboard structures for his other classroom activities, and, instead, moved these activities into Narnia.

As the Friday sessions came and went, the back came off the wardrobe so that the actors and the class could move through this portal into the world of Narnia. The ice in Narnia was real ice chips, cold on bare feet. The eggs and tea that everyone ate and drank in the cave of the faun, Mr. Tumnus, was real food and drink, tasty and filling. And the children's often asked question, "Who is the White Witch?!" was answered when Michael entered the play in a white fur coat and long white gloves.

The children soon followed the actors and their teacher into this other world. Once arrived, they designed and carried out a plot to save Mr. Tumnus from the evil White Witch, and to make the White Witch "good." The children then moved their playful relationship with Michael out of Narnia and into their classroom meeting area, where they guided Michael in the design and rehearsal of a wild play, containing only child actors, of their adult–child joint playworld, for their families.

In this final play of the playworld, many of the characters were played by several children simultaneously, some dialogue was improvised and some was memorized, and set pieces and props were a mixture of originals from the playworld and replicas—the wooden wardrobe painstakingly reproduced in one half size with cardboard and duct tape. The play for the families was very long and the audience, men and women in fatigues and armed with video cameras, had neither separate space nor seats. The families watched their children's performance while standing in Narnia themselves, sandwiched between the wooden and cardboard wardrobes, in the shadow of the White Witch's castle and at the entrance to Mr. Tumnus's cave.

DISCUSSION

The type of engagement of young children with the literary arts that took place in Michael and his students' playworld is rare. I suggest two main reasons why this may be so, and both of my tentative answers are related to my contextualization of playworlds in relation to modern western children's play. First, the literary arts, defined as the creation and appreciation of literature, are usually reduced in early childhood education to what is referred to as "literacy," not an artistic process nor a process of aesthetic appreciation, but instead the ability to decode and comprehend texts of all genres. This reduction takes place for several reasons. The most obvious reasons are that early childhood educators are often not prepared to work with a variety of literature creatively, and that the emphasis on accountability and the proliferation of testing has reduced teachers' ability to practice creatively in all areas of the curriculum.

My second response concerns the limitations we impose on play with our modern western dichotomization of play. We often see adults playing with young children in an effort to teach them something about academic subjects such as reading, writing, history, math or science, or about social interactions, regulating emotions or real-life skills. The great market for toys for young children that have numbers and letters on them is a testament to this trend.

As an alternative to this mode of adult engagement with children's play, we see adults creating spaces for children in which these children are free to play with little adult intervention. These spaces may even be equipped with toys that have been selected because they appear to the adults designing these spaces as more suited to the natural innocence of childhood. For instance, toys that have been created with materials, and created in the image of objects, with ostensibly less human adult intervention are often favored. Replicas of technologies from another time, such as wooden trains, may be favored over, for instance, a disconnected computer keyboard.

The direction of children's play towards adult-determined school readiness goals leaves us open to question, "Is there a better way to teach children competencies in literacy, math and social-emotional development?" If we think the answer to this question is "yes," then we no longer have a defensible interest in preserving play. While oriented towards such goals, we are not primarily concerned with those activities that help young children to grow now. We are instead concerned with what, of those things we adults have already mastered, these children will be able to do in the future.

If, however, we seek to protect children's play from adults, we are driven to argue that, as early education does not involve adult engagement with children, then early education does not involve adults sharing their adult knowledge with children. This argument leads easily to the conclusion that early education does not require professional teachers, but instead competent caregivers (usually women who are planning to be, are or have been mothers). And this argument also leads easily to the conclusion that early literacy and math teaching are not useful, which we know to be wrong (Office of Planning, Research and Evaluation, Administration for Children and Families, U.S. Department of Health and Human Services, 2010). It thus de-legitimizes its own corollary that play should be maintained in early childhood education, albeit in this protected form.

Faced with these two most prevalent forms of adult engagement with children's play, not only is engagement of young children with the literary arts in activities which value the full potential of play rare, but it becomes possible to argue convincingly for the reduction of playtime in classes for young children. We are left defenseless in the face of the current crisis in early childhood education, in which young children are being given less and less time to play. Unfortunately the scope of this move and its possible consequences cannot be overestimated.

Many preschool directors, elementary school principals and teachers of young children in the United States are no longer defending their students' right to play. They are not following the ubiquitous research and practical experience that tells us that early childhood education should be play-based, and they have abandoned their responsibility to educate parents about the importance of play. Vivian Paley, a renowned teacher, teacher-educator and scholar/story-teller of young children, describes our behavior by delivering the following dire warning: "What we are in danger of doing is de-legitimatizing man-kind's oldest and best-used learning tool" (2004, p. 8).

However, if we challenge our understanding of childhood, and hence these forms of adult engagement with children's play, we undermine the two options described above. Instead of emphasizing innocence or malleability of children, we can foster an appreciation of children's creativity. This move allows both for the integration of play and art through activities such as playworlds in early childhood classrooms, and for the weakening of the two arguments outlined above, which are frequently used to support the position that playtime for young children is expendable in early education.

CONCLUSION

In the example of a year-long curriculum that generated the above discussion among Michael and his students, the first dilemma confronting
successful engagement with the literary arts in early childhood, that early
childhood teachers do not engage their students in the creation and appreciation of literature, was solved because Michael was working from a book he
knew and loved particularly well and because he kept the playworld activity
entirely separate from all test-preparation activities. The second dilemma,
the segregation of play and art, was solved with the playworld adult–child
joint play-art activity. It was the playworlds activity that allowed Michael to
see his students' play as a relative of the literary arts, and therefore gave him
the freedom to bring his appreciation of literature, and his creative abilities
in relation to literature, fully into his early childhood classroom.

Playworlds, and the play theory upon which playworlds are built, also give
us two excellent reasons why play *must* remain the central activity of every
day for all young children. If "creation is the province of everyone to one degree or another; . . . (and thus) a normal and constant companion in childhood" (Vygotsky, 1967/2004, p. 33), and if "a child's greatest achievements
are possible in play" (Vygotsky, 1978, p. 100), then decreasing playtime in
early childhood education is decreasing that time in which young children
are practicing the same activities of imagining and creating that constitute
the literary arts (and all the other arts, math and science). And, if children
can create something new in play, then children have something to teach
adults through play. To take away children's playtime is to take away not just
students', but also their teacher's learning time. Michael actually read *The
Lion, the Witch and the Wardrobe* with his students, played the novel with his
students, and merged reading with play in his classroom, so that he could
learn more about this particular novel, the art of creating a novel, and himself. I would suggest that it was this motivation and the engagement of his
whole self in his teaching that allowed Michael to create, with his students,
early childhood education that was truly "a process of living" (Dewey, 1897).

REFERENCES

Aries, P. (1962). *Centuries of childhood.* New York, NY: Alfred A. Knopf.
Bakhtin, M. M. (1984). *Problems of Dostoevsky's poetics.* Minneapolis, MN: University
    of Minnesota Press.
Bakhtin, M. M., & Holquist, M. (1981). *The dialogic imagination: Four essays.* Austin,
    TX: University of Texas Press.
Dewey, J. (1897). My pedagogical creed. *School Journal, 54,* 77–80.
Fass, P. (2007). *Children of a new world.* New York, NY: New York University Press.

Ferholt, B. (2009). Adult and child development in adult–child joint play: The Development of cognition, emotion, imagination and creativity in Playworlds. Unpublished doctoral dissertation, University of California San Diego, San Diego.

Ferholt, B. (2010). A multiperspectival analysis of creative imagining: Applying Vygotsky's method of literary analysis to a playworld. In C. Connery, V. John-Steiner & A. Marjanovic-Shane (Eds.), *Vygotsky and Creativity: A Cultural-Historical Approach to Play, Meaning-Making and the Arts* (pp. 163–179). New York, NY: Peter Lang.

Ferholt, B., & Lecusay, R. (2010). Adult and child development in the zone of proximal development: Socratic dialogue in a Playworld. *Mind Culture and Activity, 17*(1), 59–83.

Gaskins, S. (1999). Children's daily lives in a Mayan village: A case study of culturally constructed roles and activities. In G. Goncu (Ed.), *Children's engagement in the world: Sociocultural perspectives* (pp. 25–61). New York, NY: Cambridge University Press.

Gaskins, S. (2000). Children's daily activities in a Mayan village: A culturally grounded description. *Cross-Cultural Research: The Journal of Comparative Social Science, Special Issue in Honor of Ruth H. Munroe: Part 1, 34*(4), 375–389.

Gaskins, S., & Goncu, A. (1992). Cultural variation in play: A challenge to Piaget and Vygotsky. *The Quarterly Newsletter of the Laboratory of Comparative Human Cognition, 14*, 31–35.

Goncu, A. (1999). Children's and researchers' engagement in the world. In A. Goncu (Ed.), *Children's engagement in the world: Sociocultural perspectives* (pp. 3–24). New York, NY: Cambridge University Press.

Goncu, A., Tuermer, U., Jain, J., & Johnson, D. (1999). Children's play as cultural activity. In A. Goncu (Ed.), *Children's engagement in the world: Sociocultural perspectives* (pp. 148–172). New York, NY: Cambridge University Press.

Hakkarainen, P. (2004). Narrative learning in the Kajaani Fifth Dimension. Paper presented at the American Educational Research Association 2004 Annual Meeting, San Diego.

Hakkarainen, P. (2006). Learning and development in play. In J. Einarsdottir & J. T. Wagner (Eds.), *Nordic childhoods and early education* (pp. 183–222). Greenwich, CT: Information Age Publishing, Inc.

Hakkarainen, P. (2008). The challenges and possibilities of narrative learning approach in the Finnish early childhood education system. *International Journal of Educational Research, 47*(5), 292–300.

Jenkins, H. (Ed.). (1998). *The children's culture reader.* New York, NY: New York University Press.

Lewis, C. S. (1950). *The lion, the witch and the wardrobe.* New York, NY: Macmillan Publishing Co.

Lindqvist, G. (1995). The aesthetics of play: A didactic study of play and culture in preschools. Doctoral dissertation, Uppsala, Sweden, Uppsala University.

Marjanovic-Shane, A. (1989a). *Metaphor beyond play: Development of metaphor in children.* Unpublished PhD Thesis, University of Pennsylvania, Philadelphia, PA.

Marjanovic-Shane, A. (1989b). "You are a pig": For real or just pretend?—Different orientations in play and metaphor. *Play & Culture, 2*(3), 225–234.

Marjanovic-Shane, A., Ferholt, B., Nilsson, M., Rainio, A. P., Miyazaki, K., Hakkarainen, P. (2011). Playworlds: An art of development. In C. Lobman & B. O'Neill, (Eds.), *Play and culture* (pp. 3–32). Lanham, MD: University Press of America.

Miyazaki, K. (2008, July). *Imagination as collaborative exploration: Art education in Saitou pedagogy.* Paper presented at the 3nd Annual Research Symposium on Imagination and Education. Vancouver.

Miyazaki, K. (2009a). *Kodomo no manabi kyoushi no manabi: Saitou Kihaku to Vygotsky— ha kyouikugaku.* [Children learn, teachers learn: Kihaku Saitou and Vygotskian pedagogy]. Tokyo: Ikkei Shobou.

Miyazaki, K. (2009b, June). *Teacher as the author of polyphonic novel: Bakhtinian analysis of a Japanese view on dialogic education.* Paper presented at the 2nd International Interdisciplinary Conference on Perspectives and Limits of Dialogism in Mikhail Bakhtin. Stockholm.

Miyazaki, K. (2010). Teacher as the imaginative learner: Egan, Saitou and Bakhtin. In K. Egan, & K. Madej (Eds.), *Engaging imagination and developing creativity in education.* Newcastle upon Tyne: Cambridge Scholars Publishing.

Office of Planning, Research and Evaluation, Administration for Children and Families, U.S. Department of Health and Human Services. (2010). Head Start Impact Study. Available at: http://www.acf.hhs.gov/programs/opre/hs/impact_study/index.html

Paley, V. (2004). *A child's work: The importance of fantasy play.* Chicago: University of Chicago Press.

Vygotsky, L. S. (1971). *The psychology of art.* Cambridge, MA: MIT Press.

Vygotsky, L. S. (1976). Play and its role in the mental development of the child. In J. S. Bruner, A. Jolly & K. Sylva (Eds.), *Play—its role in development and evolution* (pp. 537–554). New York, NY: Penguin Books, Ltd.

Vygotsky, L. S. (1978). *Mind in society: The development of higher psychological processes.* Cambridge: Harvard University Press.

Vygotsky, L. S. (1986). *Thought and language.* A. Kozulin (Trans.). Cambridge, MA: MIT Press. (Original work published 1934)

Vygotsky, L. S. (2004). Imagination and creativity in childhood. *Journal of Russian and Eastern European Psychology, 42*(1), 7–97. (Original work published 1967)

Wartofsky, M. W. (1979). *Models: Representations and the scientific understanding.* Dortrecht: Reidl.

Wolff, L. (1998). When I imagine a child: The idea of childhood and the philosophy of memory in the enlightenment. *Eighteenth Century Studies, 31,* 377–401.

CHAPTER 10

A JOURNEY OF MUSICAL COLLABORATION

Judith Hill Bose
Longy School of Music of Bard College

ABSTRACT

This chapter describes a collaborative journey into the study of music with young children in which the author explores live musical performances through a case study of children's own music making and reflection-in-action. A close description of the collaborative process in which activities and experiences were co-designed with early childhood teachers is described. The author contextualizes her work within a model of aesthetic inquiry, based on the philosophies of John Dewey and Maxine Greene.

INTRODUCTION

This chapter traces the shape and findings of a collaborative journey into the study of music with young children. It draws on my work as a consulting teaching artist with a university lab school for preschool children. In my work as a teaching artist, I work within a model of aesthetic inquiry process based on the philosophies of educational thinkers that include John Dewey and Maxine Greene. Each aesthetic unit of study centers on a specific live

Young Children and the Arts, pages 155–171
Copyright © 2012 by Information Age Publishing

performance—rather than on general arts principles or on music as a discipline. I believe that attending to the specific details of a particular work of art leads to personal, meaningful engagement with that work—and ultimately to the larger world as it connects to elements in the work. Greene puts it well, and also begins to account for how the approach may at first seem controversial.

> Aesthetic experiences require conscious participation in a work, a going out of energy, an ability to notice what is there to be noticed in the play, the poem, the quartet. Knowing "about," even in the most formal academic manner, is entirely different from constituting a fictive world imaginatively and entering it perceptually, affectively, and cognitively. To introduce students to the manner of such engagement is to strike a delicate balance between helping learners to pay heed—to attend to shapes, patterns, sounds, rhythms, figures of speech, contours, and lines—and helping liberate them to achieve particular works as meaningful. And it is perhaps the refusal to control what is discovered as meaningful that strikes traditional educators as at odds with their conception of norms or their notions of appropriate cultural literacy. (Greene, 1995, p. 125)

What Greene describes as "conscious participation" is at the heart of my practice. Together with classroom teachers I create a unique unit for each group of students. This unit consists of a set of experiential activities that engage children in exploring musical performances by making the kinds of artistic choices that are related to the kinds of choices the musicians under study have made. Additionally, we create opportunities for students to reflect upon all their experiences, and guide the students to see more, hear more, and "wake up" to the world of a particular work of art. Through their new window of perceived possibilities, students may become personally present, authentically participatory, and able to make their own meaning with the work—and ultimately with the world around them. They are freed to bring themselves and their own lives to interact with specific musical performances.

Greene further provokes our thinking by asking if, in the end, education shouldn't aim *primarily* to prepare participatory, articulate people.

> Aesthetic education engages you precisely with what is right around you. You are aware of yourself in relation to the work. You begin to see the world like that—and the social implications are tremendous. (Greene, 1995, p. 178)

Greene adds that it is this kind of interaction that will begin to guide students to participate not only in a musical performance, but also in the larger world—to act and to question, rather than to passively receive, or worse, tune out.

THE COLLABORATION

At the lab school, the arts formed a core component of the curriculum and were emphasized as ways for young children to explore their own expressive capacities. The teachers thought about how they could strengthen the connections between music and early childhood experience, including curriculum, especially in the area of literacy. Together, the teachers at the lab school and I created connections to ongoing classroom activities and other curriculum initiatives. I visited each of two preschool classrooms several times during each of two units (with some visits occurring before the performance and some afterwards), while the teachers continued to explore the music and the curricular connections in the days in-between my visits.

Working within an action-research tradition, we met regularly to talk about and plan activities in the classroom. At these meetings we shared documentation of research data (such as classroom observations, children's portfolios of artwork and journal writing, video and audio recordings) and posed questions that arose from the work. The following chapter will share some of the questions and observations as these relate specifically to the works of music under study.

Two live musical performances were explored in our musical studies: *L'histoire du Babar* for orchestra and narrated by Francis Poulenc, and *The Art of the Toy Piano*, a solo program featuring pianist Margaret Leng Tan. *The Art of the Toy Piano* included transcriptions of works originally written for the concert piano (such as *Moonlight Sonata* of Beethoven and *Gymnopédie No. 3* of Eric Satie), transcriptions of some works written for other media (such as *Eleanor Rigby* of the Beatles), as well as original compositions for the toy piano (including pieces by Toby Twining and Stephen Montague).

CURRICULUM DESIGN

The teachers and I came to the planning table already familiar with the performances and began by considering out loud the points that interested and engaged us. These points served as "entry points" that guided the development of exploratory activities for the children, and that helped to establish a framework for structuring the unit. My approach to aesthetic education differs from traditional arts education in that it is not associated with any specific sequential learning program. There may be *multiple* possible points of entry to any given work of art, rather than a learning agenda that studies music from a set beginning point and follows in a simple to complex sequence.

Different methods of music study, of course, have varying approaches. Some begin with learning about melody, rhythm and harmony, for example; others start with rhythm via kinesthetic movement and move forward from this point. But, whether in the general music classroom or in more specific instrumental or choral study, there is most often an explicit structure of sequential building blocks. The approach to aesthetic education that guided my work here allowed for equally rigorous and provoking musical exploration, while focusing on the processes of listening, perceiving, understanding, and meaning-making. It may, perhaps, be described as a web-like unit of study—rather than a linear, sequential one. The musical performances provided a rich resource of many possible "ways in."

The teachers and I selected several entry points and then began to construct pathways of study around these points. Led by a process of inquiry and exploration, and guided by the children's own discoveries and perceptions, the paths fanned out to encompass myriad connections and unexpected explorations. The teachers devoted much energy and planning time to tracking the individual needs and interests of their students. Their guiding philosophy was child-centered and progressive. The children's developmental, social and emotional needs, as well as their genuine interests, became the foundation for most curriculum decisions. Therefore, in our collaboration we jointly developed a hybrid model that took into consideration both my own music education practice and the early childhood progressive education approach that the lab school endorsed. The collaboration relied on performances that were performed on the university campus, and that the children were invited to attend.

Musical Works and Entry Points

L'histoire du Babar was the first work under study. It is a small gem of an orchestral piece in which Poulenc has alternated narration of the classic *The Story of Babar* (De Brunhoff, 1960) with short musical vignettes. Poulenc uses some surprising juxtapositions of sound to illustrate the different characters and situations in the story. Many times extreme tempi are set next to each other, orchestration and articulation switch from heavy to light with great frequency, some of the sections have surprising abrupt endings while others have a more constant flow, and the dynamic range is broad, with many extremes of forte and piano set next to each other.

Thus we chose, as an initial point of entry to the piece, an exploration of opposites: fast/slow, heavy/light, stop/go, long/short, and loud/soft. We first experienced these opposites in movement alone, then movement combined with listening to music, and finally by actually making our own sounds and music within the parameters of these opposites. Throughout the unit, children learned to manipulate musical opposites to express affect (much easier and more accessible for the four year olds), to illustrate animal characters like those encountered in the Babar stories (more accessible for the three year olds), to add "orchestration" with simple classroom instruments to stories their teachers were reading to them, and to tell their own stories with music and narration. In the main, they created their musical opposites with an "orchestra" of classroom rhythm instruments.

Within this course of study, we also explored musical concepts such as "ensemble"—what it takes to play together and coordinate, and "leader and follower" —focusing on the role of a conductor. We explored "rhythm" in the following ways: how rhythm enables us to stay together, what a tempo is, and the presence of silence in music—"stops" or rests—rhythm as patterns of both sound *and* silence. The topic of ensemble and leader/follower came up organically from the children. Our attempts to play together, like an orchestra, led to musing about how we might be more effective group music-story tellers. The children came up with ideas about how a conductor might facilitate this, and of course, they were very inspired directly from observing the conductor at the performance.

Conducting became an engaging activity instantly and spontaneously. As they all took turns conducting their orchestra of classmates playing instruments, they began to distinguish when they were leading and when they were following. Not only was this a sophisticated study in the skills and processes of a musical ensemble, but it also began to permeate their view of classroom organization. They began to rethink the classroom dynamic of teacher and student, and the teachers reported a marked impact on students' social behavior. Their play began to include acting the part of teacher/leader and a growing fascination with experiencing both the roles of leader and follower.

In *The Art of the Toy Piano*, artist Margaret Leng Tan played the grand piano, as well as several toy pianos and other assorted toy instruments. For this performance, our initial point of entry was to look at things that were the same and different between big pianos and toy pianos—with a special emphasis on the difference/sameness in sound and playing technique. We looked, listened, and played both kinds of pianos. The notes on the piano itself inspired us to explore "steps, leaps and repeated notes," as did the discovery that Margaret's pieces featured prominent repeated chords. Again, our explorations could always be traced back to their roots in the specific performance, and in the children's authentic interest, rather than in the necessity to cover certain musical concepts. Because we could look at the piano and hear the difference, we talked and sang about high notes and low notes.

Margaret played a piece by Jerome Kitzke entitled "The Animist Child," which used vocal sounds, percussive sounds and toy piano to express, as Leng Tan stated at the performance, "the temper tantrum I never was allowed to have as a child." The children immediately gravitated to this piece, and perhaps understood it in a visceral way that no adult could truly access. This led us to explore making feelings of anger first in rhythmic words and them into patterns of rhythm sounds (modeled on techniques used in the piece). The toy piano has a completely different timbre from the grand piano; its inner workings are really like a metallic xylophone—so we also embarked on a very creative exploration of timbre differences in musical instruments, with special emphasis on distinguishing the unique timbre of instruments made of metal.

The children soon began to spontaneously expand this musical experience to an exploration of the timbres and sounds of other instruments, as well as of other objects in the world around them. Teachers noticed the children tapping on rocks and sticks and other items in the play-yard in order to see what kinds of sounds these items made. Finally, we made some short inquiries into the idea of stage presence at a performance—exploring the idea of beginning and ending a piece, a soloist's attitude, and even the use of bowing as a possible way to end a performance. These ideas were inspired by Leng Tan's unique, theatrical stage presence.

Music Skills

A list of musical concepts introduced in the two units of study might include: dynamics, ensemble playing, conducting, instruments (rhythm instruments, piano, toy piano, toy accordion), some piano techniques (including glissando and steps/leaps/repeated notes), rhythm (tempo, rests, a beat), timbre, high and low pitches, and the idea of stage presence at a musical performance. However, it must be emphasized again that we were not trying to teach the children "how to do anything" or even "about" any of these concepts in isolation. Our action research did not involve singing songs for the sake of learning about melody or voice production. It was not about the correct way to play percussion instruments or about creating specific rhythmic patterns. All of which is not to say that we didn't sing, play instruments, and explore rhythms. Rather, we started from the two works of music under study and thought about how we could give children active experiences that would illuminate those works. In the process, we consciously encountered and explored many musical elements that are covered in other sequential music education approaches.

Our practice differs from other skills based approaches in how, when and why particular musical concepts are studied. They are discovered and explored rather than explained. They are often internalized through fantasy and play. And they are encountered as a web of connections that reaches out to the context of the broader world, rather than as a linear, or sequential curriculum. They are also explored as ways for children to actively engage with a specific work of art and art form, rather than as drills to master a set of skills or a concept.

This approach allows important structural elements of music to be encountered within the context of perception and aesthetic understanding of a particular piece, and with rich connection to other aspects of learning and living. In the cases of both musical works of art described here, the children spontaneously built upon their classroom experiences as well as on their experiences of attending the performances in remarkably creative and expressive ways—sometimes musically and sometimes in another modality. Nevertheless, it is very interesting to compare some of the methods and practices used in our classes to some of the processes and ideas encountered in other forms of music education. In the sections that follow, I will describe the music vocabulary that the children gained in studying these musical works of art, and differentiate between the approach to aesthetic education that I describe here, and other approaches to music education.

Music Vocabulary

In most methods of music study, students engage in acquiring and understanding musical vocabulary. Our classes were no exception, and they included many basic words, such as "orchestra, piano, conductor, tempo, rhythm, steps, leaps, repeated notes, and glissando." In the main, the children encountered these words by hearing either me or the teachers (deliberately) using them in context, rather than through introduction of definitions. More importantly, they experienced ownership of these words and concepts by active music making. In our classes they were encouraged to use made up words like "ting" and "dub" to describe the tone color of certain sounds around them (though they were not necessarily required to attach the musical term "timbre" to these discoveries). Also, familiar words were experienced in a fuller way. They learned that some words that they already knew, such as "fast" and "slow," could also apply to something in music called the tempo. Their bodies could move at different tempos and similarly, musical instruments could be played at different tempos—they could even listen to hear different tempos in music. In a sense, they were acquiring an embodied literacy.

The children began to develop a sense of specific musical words, used them at times in the context of other activities and environments, and gained confidence in using all kinds of vocabulary, including specific musical terminology, to speak about their musical experiences. Often, early language and vocabulary acquisition are taught solely through visual images of pictures, words, and letters. Through musical activities, the children were experiencing a deep language understanding that included kinesthetic and rich aural learning as well. This kind of important learning in multiple modalities has, by now, been well documented by Howard Gardner, in his theory of multiple intelligences (Gardner, 1993).

They began to acquire a vocabulary for making music, but also for talking *about* music; they began to articulate their own experiences—an especially crucial point at this age of emergent literacy. The music of Poulenc and of Margaret Leng Tan awakened the *desire* to communicate in many of the children. Because language is such a powerful means of personal expression and communication, huge strides were observed as children were emboldened to stretch their emerging literacy skills. This manifested in the forms of narrative, made-up music dramas, and discussion centered on listening to music.

Other Music Education Methods: Similarities and Differences

In American musical education, the post World War II era saw numerous systems of music from abroad gain popularity in this country; for example the Kodaly method from Hungary, the Orff method from Germany, and the Suzuki method of violin playing. Though our research project in no way involved the study of, or intentional borrowing from, any of these popular traditions, it is interesting to note that it bore some significant similarities to at least one of these methods. Carl Orff's approach to music teaching supposes that feeling precedes intellectual understanding. According to Orff, rhythm is the device through which the child can be led to explore music because rhythm is related to the child's own speech and movement. Music is built by beginning with the rhythmic pattern of a word, then two words, and finally phrases (Efland, 1979).

One of our activities exploring the "The Animist Child" piece played by Margaret Leng Tan involved a discussion of angry feelings, finding words to express those feelings, and then finding the rhythm of those words. A final step was to make instrumental rhythm sounds (based on the word rhythms) combined with vocal ones to create unique musical expressions. Also, in our study of *Babar*, we created some instrumental music accompaniment to rhythmic chants ("We're going for a walk in the forest") and movement. As in the Orff method, we discovered that the innate rhythm of words and movement can be building blocks for creating purely musical rhythms and phrases.

Non-Western Musical Ideas

We can also look beyond traditional western music methods for parallels with our classroom practices.

Knowledge exists and learning occurs in specific contexts. Music education in traditional societies is more explicitly linked to the continuity of students' life experiences; music is not something that they learn in school, it
is something that they do as part of a community. This, in turn, engenders
an entirely different attitude towards the music-learning process; it is not
a top-down, imposed activity, but a natural function of human interaction.
As we consider non-western approaches to music, it is important for us to
recognize the prevalence of adult modeling that occurs in authentic musical
performances. Children see and hear their elders making music in time-
honored ways; they are aware that their own futures hold these sounds too.
(Senders & Davidson, 2000, p. 22)

Our project allowed the children to have musical experiences that placed
a live performance, their own music making, and the bigger world around
them into meaningful relationship. By singing, by playing different kinds
of pianos, exploring how their own breathing related to a toy accordion,
storytelling with ensemble instrument playing, experimenting with sound
colors, conducting, and by improvising their own pieces, the children experienced a wide variety of musical activities. But they also learned to relate
these experiences to the world of music in which adults participate. They
learned that what they do is related to the world in which Beethoven, Poulenc, the Beatles, and other musicians make music. Although it was not
necessarily part of our approach for this age group of children to "learn"
those names, they certainly *heard* these names and implicitly learned that
lots of different kinds of people are involved in meaningful music making.

Of course, our process does not begin to approximate a traditional culture's community, but it does establish a more organic idea of classroom as
a community of learners where people do musical things. This approach
may go a long way towards dispelling the traditional separation of certain
activities into "music class." We also established an important model of collaboration and community for the children to absorb. Such an integrated
place of musical learning may come closer to the way music is experienced
in non-western cultures—music as a "natural function of human interaction"—rather than as a separate music class.

Active and Creative Listening

Many methods of music education emphasize the important skills of listening. But John Paynter makes some important distinctions about the way
listening is used by different musical practitioners. First, he points out that
music is both a creative and re-creative art:

...contrasting on the one hand the inventiveness of composers and impro-
visers with—at the other end of the spectrum—the passivity of the receiving
listeners. In the middle are the re-creators—the performers—clearly contributing something of themselves, but by and large serving the interests of the
composers in order to give pleasure to the listeners. (Paynter, 1992, p. 11)

He suggests that though this may paint the unfortunate picture of much
of today's music business, it is not necessarily the way to experience music most richly, nor does it suggest that such a picture should not be challenged. In fact, he believes that through certain types of musical education
there is realistic reason to expect to see a growth in active, creative, involvement with music. Active listening is a special feature of the musical experience not only for composers and performers, but also for audience.

That too, demands a commitment of imagination through which, as it were,
the composer's sound world is re-made within the individual. It may be a different kind of creativity from that of the composer but it is, nevertheless, a
creative act. The listener participates ('If I could have made this music, this is
exactly how it would be.') and the experience becomes an adventure which
provides both a sense of self-sufficiency and the recognition of a driving force
beyond us. (Paynter, 1992, p. 12)

Certainly this view is consistent with contemporary progressive constructivist views of education. Gone are the days when the mind was seen as absorb-
ing or reflecting the world. Today, in contrast, it is widely accepted that
through experience, we actively contribute to the process of understanding. Dewey reminds us, though, that mere experience is not enough.

The belief that all genuine education comes about through experience does
not mean that all experiences are genuinely or equally educative...Every-
thing depends upon the *quality* of the experience which is had...Just as no
man lives or dies to himself, so no experience lives and dies to itself. Wholly
independent of desire or intent, every experience lives on in further experiences. Hence the central problem of an education based on experience is
to select the kind of present experiences that live fruitfully and creatively in
subsequent experiences. (Dewey, 1938, pp. 25–28)

The question that concerns Paynter and Dewey is the same question that
guided our aesthetic approach—"How then, can we begin to design meaningful experiences that teach such creative listening?"

Children playing toy pianos, trying out the moves that they observed Leng
Tan make, beating rhythms with her at the concert, building a classroom orchestra to create music for stories—aren't they participating in exactly what
Paynter imagines? ('I am now making this music and this is exactly how it
should go.') Their music making experiences are not only for the making

itself (although that is important), but also for learning to perceive music—learning to creatively and actively listen. Because the unit is oriented around a performance, students are empowered to *live* Margaret Leng Tan's playing, and thus hear passionately, because they know in their bodies what it feels like to have fingers on a big piano and fingers on a toy piano.

They are wrapped in the moment of the Poulenc orchestral performance because they themselves know what it is to be a conductor and an ensemble and to have to stop and start together. The end result is that they listen differently. Their ears are not explicitly told what to listen for, but through experiential learning, they are attuned to a bigger world of possibilities that can be heard. At the end of a lesson, I once had the children hold out their hands, into which I placed imaginary "new ears." We fastened them on and kept them for the week to listen at home and in the classroom for the musical ideas we had been exploring. But in a sense, we kept them on permanently, as the entire aesthetic approach is about attaching new ears and eyes. Our imaginative listening allows us to explore how music might connect to us not only in the performance at hand, but beyond in the world around us.

Eric Booth, in his book *The Everyday Work of Art* (1997), talks about the ability "to attend well" as an important perceptive, artistic skill. Students learn this skill as a direct result of the aesthetic approach to arts education. And in the case of music, it strongly and specifically impacts their capacity to attend as a listener. How full our world is of background sound—some noise, some music—but to most of which we do not *attend*. I would even venture to say that a majority of any given audience is not truly *attending* a performance they have paid to hear. Active listening and engaging is not equal to being physically present. Even if children do not ever embark on the technical study of a musical instrument, vocal or music theory studies, we can give them powerful, rigorous, and experiential ways to perceive and understand the art form.

We cannot possibly underestimate the value of engaging children in the true process of attending at an early age, but also as a continuing and vital part of their education. Booth, who is interested in etymology, says that the word "attend" means to stretch out of the self. He remarks that investment—or reaching out—of the spirit is a skill best learned in the arts, though it rewards one in every field (Booth, 1997). Though no statistics yet exist to document this hypothesis, we might imagine that a child who has steadily learned to attend to musical performances throughout her education would hear and listen to the entire world around herself rather differently than a child who had not benefited from these experiences.

One very exciting finding in our research was that teachers felt they were "attending" to their students differently as a direct result of our musical sessions. In fact, they were connecting their own new discoveries in imaginative and engaged musical listening to the very way in which they experienced and listened to their students. This speaks powerfully for the ability of aesthetic education to connect us meaningfully, and change the very quality of our connections with the world around us.

Extra-Musical Skills

It was clear in our research that musical experiences have benefits that extend beyond the purely musical. Playing instruments and conducting expand on the motor skills that early childhood students are in the process of developing. Cognitive and problem solving skills are employed to figure out how to stay together in an ensemble, or how to be an effective leader or follower. Associative skills are put into play as a child translates the idea of "stop and go" from body movement, to making sound, to hearing sound, or as he makes his feeling of anger into a rhythm pattern. And important socializing skills are put into play as a child learns what it takes to collaborate, cooperate, and organize music in a large or small group situation.

Our aim was never to explicitly enhance students' academic performance, or to use musical explorations as handmaiden to other subjects. Winner and Hetland (2000) remind us that we need to be careful about the claims we make about academic links to art experiences. We established an environment that offered a nurturing place for children to explore new musical territory, rather than one that espoused right and wrong ways to do things, or used music to teach other subjects. Yet when these new ideas began to take hold in other areas, the teachers encouraged and expanded on the children's own discoveries. Participation and imaginative reaching are important skills for this age group that may have academic resonance as well, but they do not necessarily need to be justified by such correlation.

These skills are vital in the realm of artistic creation, as artistic choices do not develop fully under the tyranny of right and wrong. But developmentally it is also important for children of this age group to feel the pride and joy of making an artistic choice, following it through and reflecting on the results. It has been documented in several studies of arts education that children gain far more benefits in self-esteem and empowerment from experiencing success rooted in their own creativity and choice making, rather than from success achieved by correctly repeating or replicating a given concept.

> . . . my own research has shown, when students are involved in art and music, the quality of their experience improves very significantly above their average levels. By contrast, the quality of experience while engaged in "academic" subjects like math and science is accompanied by a very significant decrease in the quality of experience. Even highly talented math and science students, when doing math and science tend to feel less happy, less strong, less motivated than they do while doing other things. (Csikszentmihaly, 1997, p. 22)

There is a freedom in an approach that nurtures an authentic, personal response rather than a prescribed or expected response. Using the elements of music in improvisations, for example, as a way to discover piano techniques, can be a powerful experience. Rules, parameters, techniques, and concepts are important things to learn, without a doubt, but our approach replaced the traditional order of learning. In other words, first engagement and exploration; techniques and explanations second—and only when relevant to the students' own explorations.

PROCESS SKILLS

Translation

Our students used certain "process" skills that did, in fact, extend broadly to other domains, as well as to many of the challenges of daily living. These skills are more unique to the aesthetic approach. They may or may not occur in other music methods, but they are particularly encouraged in aesthetic inquiry. Our work demonstrated that the children spontaneously tried out musical ideas in multiple modalities. During the study of *Babar*, for example, one child completed his first painting, which he clearly described as illustrating light and dark—his reinterpretation of the musical exploration of opposites.

Learning connections, seeing how one concept inter-relates in various fields, disciplines and art forms, is a sophisticated and important skill for school, for most careers, and for life. Especially in an age when the amount of information available is vast, making connections between bits of information and concepts is a vital process. Studying music from an aesthetic approach invites and encourages connections in a way that skills based training might not. The lens of perception is somewhat broader than the finely focused lens necessary for acquiring a specific skill. Again, this is not an argument that one approach should replace the other or is ultimately more important. They are, of course, both vital.

Translating concepts from one modality to another, as our student's painting, is one of the first steps in a chain of higher order thinking, as laid out in Bloom's *Taxonomy* (Bloom, Krathwohl & Masia, 1964). The process skill of translation is not limited to art. Yet, the artistic world opens especially rich and limitless doorways into the possibilities for application.

Connecting Musical Experiences to the Surrounding World

Eric Booth (1999) speaks to the idea of connections, about education in the arts as a way to explore the wide palette of ways to make connections both to ourselves and to our world. He points out politely that schooling so often over-emphasizes logical connections: if we are studying Africa, let's listen to African music. But the arts afford us such wonderful opportunities for emotional connections, visceral and associative connections, narrative and intuitive. In this research project, we began to ask a big question: How does living in a utilitarian, standardized, "back to basics" educational culture shape our expectations? Does it in some—maybe not so indirect—way cause what Booth calls the "overemphasis of the logical" connection? Such logical connections are certainly what get emphasized as students enter primary school. Yet what we discovered in this musical exploration in the early childhood setting was that the children's rich and varied spontaneous connections were so original and deep that they almost defied any kind of categorizing; they were often personal, intuitive, emotional and visceral, rather than what we might term "logical."

One child was inspired to completely new narrative heights about grocery bags, by looking at the shape of a gourd rhythm instrument (covered with a beaded net that resembles a woven shopping bag). There were several spontaneous performances that were staged in the dramatic play area of the classroom—some organized around sound and music, some organized around concepts of opposites, and a puppet show based on timbre and sound colors of voices. At one point a group of students made up a jungle story, while others manipulated plastic jungle animals to show the action, another group played instruments and another group "took notes" furiously as they listened and watched. This last group was fascinating to observe; they produced passionate scribbles—their emerging writing, and they had internalized very deeply this idea of attending to the performance in an important way—almost as journalists. This activity most surely was partially inspired by the adult observations and note taking going on in their classroom, but regardless of the exact source, it was the individual connection that came out of them in the moment.

The children regularly tried out different tempos and qualities of movement as they played. And a new world of sonic possibility was opened with the idea of different timbres. They frequently explored classroom objects, and I even ran into a mother who said her child was stopping her at home to listen to all kinds of sounds and attempting to categorize them, while also experimenting with the sounds of pots, pans and other kitchen objects. The children's explorations became wildly alive with the many connections that sprang, uniquely and imaginatively, out of our musical explorations.

During the study of *Babar*, I spent one morning playing many different types of music (on cassette) for small groups of children, or in some cases individuals. We talked about what kinds of things we heard (based on the concepts we had been studying), and then I began to encourage narrative that might accompany the music (like the narration that occurs in the piece). One child in particular had what his teachers thought of as a break-through experience. He demanded to hear again and again a Bach organ passacaglia because he was creating an elaborate story to go with it. The story turned out to be a dramatic and verbal tour de force from a child who had previously exhibited narrow vocabulary and a predictable source of narrative material, consisting almost exclusively of guns and bad guys. This was a creative flowering that was, in some unnamable way, directly connected to his experience of a particular piece. Logical? Certainly not. Important and meaningful? Certainly.

THE SHAPE OF REFLECTION IN EARLY CHILDHOOD

It was John Dewey (1964/1933) who in 1933 said that education is essentially meaningless without the ability to reflect upon your experiences. We have learned in aesthetic education that including reflective moments provides ways for students to better grasp and understand what they have seen, heard and perceived. Aesthetic education practice typically incorporates reflective practice, including journal writing, note-taking, peer interviews, and discussions where students step out of "activity" to think reflectively about their "doing." There is typically an overlap, even a blur between "regular activity" and "reflection," in that many activities have a reflection component built in, or require a certain amount of reflection to execute. But our project in early childhood education seemed to show that with this age group, the boundary between the two was not just blurred, but had actually vanished.

In other words, when working with small children whose language abilities are still emerging, designing an activity where they can actively conduct an orchestra of their peers helps them reflect on the performance in which they were audience. Activity and doing *are* reflection for them. The way that they approached the piano after the Margaret Leng Tan performance reflected their absorption of her artistry. The way they chose to sit at the toy piano, the way they vocalized in accompaniment with their playing (as they had seen her do in "Animist Child") were both their own authentic responses and simultaneously, their own reflections on the performance.

With older children, we often try to take a step out of the active "doing" and give them a moment to articulate or organize information in a quieter, reflective way. But this seemed artificial with three and four year olds; everything is more organically wrapped up together—the doing, the reflecting, the organizing of information and the meaning making. This is consistent with some of Lev Vygotsky's findings about the importance of make-believe play. Play is what helps children separate thought and meaning making from actions and objects, while language is also greatly enriched by play experiences (Berk, 1994). Howard Gardner's (1989) studies with Project Zero and ARTS PROPEL also support these ideas. He noted the following.

1. In most areas of development, children simply improve with age. In several artistic spheres, however, evidence suggests a surprisingly high level of competence in young children, followed by a possible decline during the years of middle childhood. This jagged or "U" shaped curve in development is particularly evident in certain areas of artistic production, though it can perhaps be manifest as well in *selective areas of perception.*
2. Notwithstanding certain deficiencies in their performance, pre-school children acquire a tremendous amount of knowledge about and competence in the arts. As is the case with natural language, this acquisition can occur without explicit tutelage on the part of parents or teachers. The evolution of children's drawings constitutes a particularly vivid example of this self-generated learning and development. In this respect artistic learning stand in sharp contrast to most traditional school subjects.
3. In nearly every area, an individual's perceptual or comprehension capacities develop well in advance of productive capacities. Once again, however, the picture in the arts proves far more complex, and at least in some domains, comprehension actually appears to lag behind *performance of production capacities. This finding underscores the importance of giving young children ample opportunity to learn by performing, making, or "doing"* (Gardner, 1989, p. 73).

CONCLUSION: FINALLY . . .

All involved in the research were struck by how music seemed to inspire the children to enter new territory, and even to confront some of their deepest fears. Our students' narratives often provided dramatic examples, too. When listening to the CD of *Babar* with his teacher for the first time, one three year old became frightened of the music where Babar's mother gets chased and killed by a hunter and visibly cowered and became teary-eyed. But after he was actively engaged in creating scary music by playing a drum, he had a markedly different reaction at the live performance. Music helped him sort out the elements of fantasy and reality. Music did not necessarily solely lead him to these discoveries, nor was this piece written to assist children in such a process. But his profound experience, which appeared to be directly linked to this performance, begs the question—what is different when such early childhood developmental experiences are steeped in the arts, occur within an art-rich environment and in a place where teachers can nurture such important awakenings?

Investing energy in an art work is to invest in a complex thing. By virtue of this fact alone, students' experiences are being shaped in a sophisticated, multi-layered way. The orchestral performance is layered with many intricate connections: story to music, players to instruments, instrument sounds to each other, conductor to ensemble, character and situation to music, and emotion to music. Such fertile ground invites students to make equally layered and sophisticated meanings out of their experiences. The three-year-old child described above was able to experience the distinction between reality and fiction/art in an incredibly rich and layered environment. Might not a musical work like *Babar* represent the complexities and layers of life more fully than nursery rhymes?

The two musical performances in our study opened up a complex world and invited these young learners to bring their own unique young lives, bubbling with developing literacy and social learning, to two musical performances and to their own musical explorations—with the main agenda of making their own meaning with and out of these experiences.

REFERENCES

Berk, L. (1994). Vygotsky's theory: The importance of make-believe play. *Young Children: 50*, 30–39.

Bloom, B., Krathwohl, D. & Masia, B. (1964). *Taxonomy of educational objectives: The classification of educational goals.* New York: Longman.

Booth, E. (1997). *The everyday work of art.* Naperville, IL: Sourcebooks, Inc.

Csikszentmihalyi, M. (1997). Assessing aesthetic education: Measuring the ability to ward off chaos. *Arts Education Policy Review, 99*(1), 33–38.

De Brunhoff, J. (1960). *The story of Babar the little elephant.* New York: Random House.

Dewey, J. (1964). *John Dewey on Education.* Chicago, IL: University of Chicago Press. (Original work published 1933)

Dewey, J. (1938). *Experience and education.* New York: Collier Books.

Efland, A. (1979). Conceptions of teaching in art education. *Art Education, 32*, 21–33.

Gardner, H. (1993). *Multiple intelligences: The theory in practice.* New York: Basic Books.

Gardner, H. (1989). Zero-based arts education: An introduction to ARTS PROPEL. *Studies in Art Education, 30*, 71–83.

Greene, M. (1995). *Releasing the imagination.* San Francisco: Jossey-Bass Publishers.

Paynter, J. (1992). *Sound and structure.* Cambridge, MA: Cambridge University Press.

Senders, W., & Davidson, L. (2000). Music and multiculturalism: Dimensions, difficulties, and delights. *New England Conservatory Journal for Learning through Music, Spring, 2000*, 18–27.

Winner, E. & Hetland, L. (2000, September 27). Does studying the arts enhance academic achievement? *Education Week, 64*, 46, 64.

CHAPTER 11

MUSIC-MAKING WITH YOUNG CHILDREN

African Orff and Rhythmic Intelligence

Andrew Aprile
Graduate Center, CUNY

ABSTRACT

In this chapter, I discuss creative approaches to African music education for young children. Using recent research in the field of neuroscience that shows a unique and profound connection among speech, rhythm, movement, and music, I propose that African music is an especially promising starting point for the development of children's rhythm and musicality. In addition to outlining some of the activities and practices that I implement with my own students, I elaborate on the compatibility between African music and Orff approaches to music education. Furthermore, I explicate some of the tensions and possibilities inherent in progressive and creative approaches to multicultural music education.

Young Children and the Arts, pages 173–193

VIGNETTE

The djembe rhythm has changed, and one by one, the kindergarteners' eyes start to perk up. They are searching for the next dance step. Some of them continue with the movement prescribed by the previous rhythm, and others stop to try to sound out the musical patterns. A few have caught on. One student, so impressed by her own discovery and confidence, shouts out the answer to the musical clue: "Climb that rope and wave your hands in the air." The peers that hear her begin the short choreography. Following the three loud djembe slaps which correspond to the words "climb that rope," the students pump their vertical fists downwards, then let go to wave their hands by their ears.

For one of the students who didn't hear the answer, I ask "Which rhythm is this?" His distraction turns to curiosity and he looks up to the ceiling, trying to latch on to the beat and simultaneously pronounce the words encoded in the rhythm. After one more repetition, he is able to coordinate the phrase and the drum pattern. I continue with this rhythm until everyone is entrained, dancing with, in, and to the groove. Consciously or not, all these kindergartners have identified and internalized the constellation of music, movement, and mnemonics, brought together through a game of freeze dance whose goal is to unify their mind, body, and spirit in a fun way.

I play the break, a common djembe rhythm that the students have learned as the phrase "Everybody look here! Freeze dance." They jump and clap emphatically with the last two notes of the rhythm as they transform themselves into statues, popsicles, ninjas, and animals. Frozen, I ask if anyone would like to raise their hand and teach us a new dance move. My most challenging student, seemingly incapable of sitting still at times, eagerly raises her hand. I call on her and she begins to chant "Rock your head, Rock your head," while nodding and moving around. I join the chant with my drum—Ba-da-Boom, Ba-da-boom—and before I know it, the whole class is rocking out.

INTRODUCTION

When I embarked upon a career in music education three years ago, I had an intuitive sense that world percussion would prove to be a most worthy and appealing venture for the toddlers, pre-kindergarteners, and elementary school children with whom I work. Perhaps it was the lingering exuberance I felt from a course of study in college that led me to musical styles from around the world. Or perhaps it was the knowledge that I gained and felt so compelled to share from my excursions to Ghana and Madagascar in search of the elusive African triplet. One need not defend a music curriculum based on world rhythm beyond its enriching and humanistic potential. But I remain convinced of and committed to the social and cognitive benefits conferred by musical learning that takes place outside the conventional western canon of children's music. What's more, percussion and communal, groove-based musicking[1] constitute a profound opportunity to learn by doing in a collaborative and cooperative framework centered on fun and imaginative explorations of rhythm.

From the outset of my teaching career, I have placed myself in a position at once promising and perilous. Having shirked the conventional path of teacher certification, I have continuously searched for curriculum materials that might facilitate the formulation of my own unique pedagogy. But in those first two years, I found myself grappling with profound issues in childhood development. Though I maintain that every single human is musical, and that every child can learn music, I had to ask myself why certain children were so much more musically adept and motivated towards creativity, and how I might reach and encourage others whose potential talent and imagination remained unfulfilled.

Slowly, my classes began to take shape. I recognized early on that songs were best learned in conjunction with movement, and that it was wise to introduce rhythms through language. From a creative standpoint, I made explorations on musical instruments the cornerstone of my practice. For toddlers, this meant building on an extant enthusiasm for percussion and guiding their natural inclination towards noisemaking.

All of my early childhood classes begin with a hello song in which a small percussion instrument is passed around to each child. For example, instead of "He's Got the Whole World in His Hands," I might sing, "Hello to ____ over there, s/he's got the shaker in her/his hands." Some children will play the rhythmic pattern of the hello song, others will find the downbeat, but most will explore the rhythmic and timbral possibilities of the instrument while they have it. For some songs, we will imagine playing an invisible instrument, or we will use sticks to simulate violins or trumpets. I still introduce real instruments as though they are the coolest toys in the world, hiding a new type of shaker and asking the children to guess what I'm concealing, or dazzling with some of the musical possibilities on different drums. With pre-kindergarteners and elementary school students, I use their proficiency with steady beats as a scaffold for explorations of phrasing, musical meter, and new rhythmic patterns.

My experiences with and observations of young children confirmed two suspicions that I held about the nature of musical development. First, the process of enculturation was already well underway by the time children began to express themselves musically. Secondly, many children were entirely capable of some of the more complex rhythmic tasks, such as syncopation and execution of compound meter, that are often deemed too intricate for young ages. Their natural affinity for call-and-response phrases, their propensity towards gesture, and their intuitive sense of the flow of language and rhythm allowed for creativity and explorations of culture that might prove more difficult for older students already accustomed to certain cultural norms. Moreover, the teaching and learning that has taken place in my classrooms suggest the need for a more nuanced view of musical cognition—one that identifies the areas of cognitive overlap between the domains of sound, speech, and movement.

The first two sections of the following chapter deal with the psychological dimensions of musical cognition and present recent research in neurobiology that confirms a profound and intricate connection among music, movement, and speech. In the following sections, I propose that African idioms are well suited for a progressive music curriculum that builds upon the integration of speech, sound, and movement. These sections also outline some of the tensions inherent in such an endeavor and make the case that explorations of the imaginative possibilities in world percussion can promote social justice and a more musically beautiful world.

LINGUISTIC INTELLIGENCE, MUSICAL MNEMONICS, AND SHARED LEARNING MECHANISMS

Music is an especially powerful shaping force, for listening to and especially playing it engages many different areas of the brain, all of which must work in tandem: from reading musical notation and coordinating fine muscle movements in the hands, to evaluating and expressing rhythm and pitch, to associating music with memories and emotion. (Sacks, 2011, p. A19)

One of the most startling discoveries that has emerged through brain imaging is the ability of anatomists to identify the brain of a musician. As yet, there is no other vocation that necessarily affects the shape, structure, and content of a brain image in way that is recognizable to neuroscientists. Music, from a neurobiological standpoint, is thus unlike any other human activity. This phenomenon is a result of an enlarged corpus callosum (which connects the two hemispheres), an enlarged and asymmetric auditory cortex, and increased volumes of gray matter in the cerebellum as well as the motor, auditory, and visuospatial areas of the cortex (Sacks, 2010). These neurobiological manifestations of musicality provide evidence for the host of networks (approximately one dozen), scattered throughout the brain, which are deployed in a process of "using, or recruiting, or co-opting brain systems that have already developed for other purposes" (Sacks, 2010, p. xi). Indeed, "musicality comprises a great range of skills and receptivities...that [are] in principle...dissociable from one another" (Sacks,

2011, p. 104). This dissociability, the overlap of musical processing and other forms of cognition, and the lack of a specific music center make it clear that music processing is unique among all forms of cognition.

Such distinction has compelled many theorists to make the case for a separate "musical intelligence." Most notable among these theorists is Gardner (1999), who describes a distinct type of processing—musical intelligence—that encompasses pitch, rhythm, timbre, and harmony. Though Gardner's theory of multiple intelligences lends much promise to studies in musical cognition, his hypothesis fails to account for the dissociability of musical abilities and the overlap of what he might deem to be separate intelligences. Neurological research on music perception and performance (Levitin, 2006; Patel, 2008) points to the expansive ways in which music processing is inseparably linked to other brain functions, particularly the acquisition and development of language skills. Though positing the independent existence of linguistic and musical intelligence, Gardner acknowledges their parallel structure in the following passage:

> Musical intelligence entails skill in the performance, composition, and appreciation of musical patterns. In this view, musical intelligence is almost parallel structurally to linguistic intelligence, and it makes neither scientific nor logical sense to call one (usually linguistic) an intelligence and the other (usually musical) a talent. (1999, p. 42)

Gardner's (1999) initial conclusions reflected nascent inquiries in the field of neuroscience and the "amazing, counterintuitive patterns of spared or lost capacities resulting from [brain] damage" (p. 29); for example, "human singing and human language are different faculties, that can be independently damaged or spared" (p. 30). Thus, the fact that aphasia (inability to use or understand language) and amusia (inability to comprehend or respond to music) can exist independently of each other compelled Gardner to declare linguistic and musical intelligences distinct from each other. But this theoretical tenet misses a potentially crucial point to which Patel (2008) alludes: that learning mechanisms involved in developmental processes may begin as shared and segment over time. Patel (2008) postulates a "shared sound category learning mechanism hypothesis... [in which] a clear conceptual distinction must be made between the end *products* of development, which may be domain specific, and developmental *processes*, which may be domain general" (p. 72). Such insight is of profound import to educators who seek to develop children's capacities in ways appropriate for the early childhood. Even more remarkable, Patel's understanding of the connection between music and language sheds light on the evolutionary genesis of music, which may in fact be more closely tied to a communicative function than an artistic one.

It is believed by some that the origins of music lie in the proto-communication region of the brain. One need not stretch the imagination too far to conceive of our ancestral predecessors using pitch- and rhythm-coded messages to convey information. Nor can we ignore the affinity between tonal languages and the presence of perfect pitch. In many African and Asian cultures where languages are tonal (i.e., intonation or accent express word meaning), children have shown an increased capacity to sing specific notes with precision and identify their attendant names without any initial reference. The pedagogical implications of this harmonious relationship between language and music are especially critical before the age of ten, when neural networks and synapses begin to cement. Levitin (2006), citing Chomsky's work in the field of linguistics, remarks that our developmental predisposition to language learning "shapes, builds, and then ultimately prunes a complicated and interconnected network of neural circuits" (p. 109).

Oran Etkin, world/jazz musician and creator of the inventive and inspiring Timbalooloo music classes, points out that if music is to be regarded as a language, instruction should be geared towards the natural way in which children acquire language in their formative years. Etkin (2011) asks us to consider the awkward way in which students learn foreign languages, conjugating verbs and attending to grammatical rules without the experience of communication and conversation. Much like language, music must be learned through immersion, not imposed, formulaic structures. Indeed, children become acquainted and gain fluency with language and music through a combination of exposure, active listening, mimesis, gesture (which I will elaborate on in the next section on movement), and experimentation with syntactic structures. As such, echoes (repeating the musical phrase of the leader), call-and-response, and embedded musical cues are integral to the songs and music that I teach. These strategies also provide ample opportunity for creativity. For example, students can invent rhythms for the rest of the class to echo, or partners can compose a call-and-response (or question-and-answer) phrase.

The convergence between music and language is one that has appealed to educators since the inception of the common school, when teachers would use rhymes and song to facilitate rote memorization. Though this practice has been deemed archaic and insufficient for a complete learning experience, Campabello, De Carlo, O'Neil and Vacek (2002) have shown that song is a useful mnemonic device to aid in the memory of new facts, skills, or concepts. In fact, many current curricular materials make use of musical mnemonics. Hip-hop-inspired educational resources created by Flocabulary use rap music to teach vocabulary, reading, math, science, as well as other academic content. From the time of Homer to the griots of West Africa, music has proved indispensable to the art of recollection, helping storytellers recount epic poems and oral histories for millennia. Equally impressive is the fact that the converse also holds true: words can just as easily help students remember a musical phrase or rhythm.

As a percussion teacher, I am consistently awed by the fact that simple sentences can be my best teaching tool when trying to get students to execute a rhythm. A djembe break that seemed impossible for many of my sixth grade students was executed effortlessly once I introduced words to match the rhythm. Because this learning mechanism holds so much promise, I teach musical and cultural concepts as rhythms, building both word and rhythmic vocabularies by allowing the mutually reinforcing mnemonic aspects of speech and song to emerge from a systemized connection between vocables (spoken syllables) and literacy instruction.

Spoken syllables are a centerpiece of African drumming pedagogy as well as host of other musical traditions from around the world. Locke (1998) advocates first becoming adept at vocalizing rhythms, because, as Ewe drummers say, "Beat the drum with your mouth" (p. 15). Vocalization allows a useful means to remember and practice, and in addition offers the prospect of immediate participation, unmediated by the demands of percussion technique. However, rather than solely incorporate arbitrary syllables or vocable components of a specific ethnic style, my teaching model builds on the approaches of Calla Isaak (2006) and Abraham Adzenyah, my former teacher. Like both teachers, I teach rhythms that employ words and their syllabic constituents as a mnemonic memory device.

Unlike Isaak and Adzenyah, I provide phrases that teach words meanings—for example "Per-cus-sion: Bang a drum;" "What is tempo? How fast or how slow;" "Syncopation: Between the beat;" "Recreational means having fun;" or "Diversity, New York City: Shapes and sizes, colors, hair styles." Thus, percussion offers a mutually reinforcing means to mnemonically remember both rhythms and word meanings. The word meanings in the examples provided are primarily concerned with musical concepts, but they also touch on cultural issues. Most importantly, this model of practice allows teachers and students to apply drumming mnemonics to any word or phrase, thereby tapping into creativity in the verbal realm.[2] Though I do not establish and rules for student compositions, the children in my classes often feel compelled to match their musical ideas with spoken counterparts. While this practice can inhibit musical creativity at points, it is more importantly a crucial learning support for students whose musical memories are not yet well developed. And how inspiring it is to see pedagogy reflected in student behavior.

MUSIC, MOVEMENT, AND THE JUNGLE JAM DANCE

The vignette that opened this chapter dovetails with the musical mnemonic teaching approach and adds the element of movement. In the activity, which I developed for kindergarten afterschool drumming clubs and now use with four year olds as well, children must identify a drum rhythm and execute a specific dance move that goes along with the rhythm. Surely, dancing is an integral component of musical practices from around the world. But the extent to which western cultures have allowed music to become a spectator activity is significant. Once inseparable, "the ties between musical sound and human movement have been minimized" (Levitin, 2006, p. 257). Whereas some cultures make no semantic distinction between music and dance, ours tends to specialize musical performance, and in doing so, social dancing has declined. Nevertheless, "virtually every culture and civilization considers movement to be an integral part of music making and listening" (Levitin, 2006, p. 57).

For those who play an instrument, it should be clear that our bodies maintain responsibility for the execution of rhythm. Sacks (2008) goes so far as to call musicians "athletes of the small muscles." Indeed, any performative task that involves rhythm necessarily involves the body. A startling discovery, however, has been the extent to which the mere act of thinking rhythm strikes at areas of the brain known to be associated with motor function. The cerebellum, responsible for timing and coordinating movement, essentially acts as our beat tracker and internal clock, revealing similarities between music perception and motor action planning (Levitin, 2006). Iyer (2002) argues that an "essential component of [cultural] disparities is the status of the body and physical movement in the act of making music" (p. 388). Thus, rhythm is inherently mental *and* physical; when we are tapping along, we are also tapping into something.

Most early childhood educators know that movement must necessarily play an important role in music instruction. Classic songs like "Itsy Bitsy Spider" and "Open and Shut Them" would probably not hold as much prominence if they were not accompanied by motions that followed the lyrics of the song. I love to build on students' extant knowledge of this repertoire by replacing lyrics in classic songs with instructions for rhythm instruments (i.e., "the sticks on the bus go tap-tap-tap;" see Connors & Wright, 2004). Over the past year, my younger students have been enthralled by renditions of K'Naan's popular "Wavin' Flag," in which we get "older" (putting our hands high in the air), "stronger" (making muscles), and "wave" our flags of freedom back and forth.

For drum rhythms, I often have students play an "invisible drum" before applying their technique to an instrument. Beyond the gestures, inventions of movement are an integral component of Orff approaches to musical pedagogy. Orff Schulwerk involves informal, child-centered strategies for musical learning that stress play, the natural acquisition of music as language, and discovery-based explorations of instruments. After learning a song by rote with the Orff method, students are to apply small movements (clapping, patting laps, heads, or shoulders) that fit melodic phrases. Once students can repeat these movements in harmony with each other, percussion instruments are introduced for polyrhythmic exercises, then melodic instruments for the students to perform in harmony.

Our principal duty as educators is to engage students. Though informed by theories of cognition and pedagogy to a great extent, my own teaching intentions and instructional objectives would be nothing without those aspects of the class that facilitate motivation—that crucial, quirky, nebulous, and fleeting characteristic—and participation. Surely, my passions for the subject matter and the music I teach convey a certain level of excitement that students often find appealing. But it is curiosity and openness that teachers and families must cultivate to truly motivate children to participate and be creative. I am not intently concerned with the perseverance required of children for many of the stricter forms of music education; I am more concerned with sustaining their curiosity and enthusiasm for music. Connecting music with positive experiences engages dopamine and serotonin receptors that, by their very nature, stimulate the desire to learn and sustain interest. Provoking interest demands a hook, an imaginational spark.

One can think of no other primary fascination more compelling to young children than the mere fact of diverse animal species scattered about this remarkable planet. In order to take advantage of younger students' fascination with animals, we play many games in which students invent, perform, and/or dance to rhythms that are connected to animal noises and movement.

I knew, almost as instinctively as a child knows boredom, that the canon of animals—those ferocious lions, terrifying tigers, lumbering elephants, clever bunny rabbits, elegant birds, flitting butterflies, hopping frogs, snapping turtles, thumping gorillas, hooting monkeys, howling wolves, sly foxes, quick and quiet cheetahs, and slithering snakes—would inherently spark their interest and would provide the perfect foundation for explorations in movement and music. In addition to original songs about "Rocky the Rooster," who wakes us up, and "Ellie the Elephant" who is shy but plays the saxophone when she is alone, I established a catalog of rhythms that students would play in concert and have to identify during games of "Jungle Jam Dance," in which I would play an animal rhythm that the students would have to identify in order to dance like that animal.[3]

Those early tendencies, still very much a part of my teaching practice and identity as an educator, have given way to a more generative approach and a more challenging issue: what to do once a child's imagination is engaged. My own rhythmic inventions for animal sounds and movements were logical and generally provocative, but I also had to consider asking students for their thoughts and ideas. Similar to the way I will ask beginning drum students to explore potential sounds on an instrument before teaching them about basses and tones (the first two notes that we learn to play on the djembe), I have found it so important to ask, "What do you think that animal sounds like?"

Eliciting students' competing ideas can be challenging during storytelling or playing, but imagining possibilities is a quintessential aspect of promoting musical creativity. Children's picture books written with anthropomorphized animal characters are an especially useful resource. When a new animal is introduced, students are asked to consider the possible sounds. In many cases, these books have short onomatopoeia phrases and rhythms built into the stories, which the children can echo on their instruments. Many of these books also give insight into specific forms of cultural heritage outside the western canon.

VENTURING OUTSIDE THE WEST: CRITICAL MULTICULTURALISM

Though I am wont to offer opportunities for students to compose rhythms, choreograph dances, conduct and direct dynamics, express their opinions musically, and set parameters for musical games, I know that my responsibility as a teacher involves a very discriminate selection of content and repertoire. For a number of reasons, not the least of which is my own fascination and passion, I am committed to music that falls outside the western canon. My students are consistently fascinated by the musical journeys that we take after boarding our imaginary airplanes, but cultural tourism demands a critical element. A critical multicultural approach, according to Kincheloe and Steinberg, "exposes and challenges the socio-cultural politics of systemic oppression while affirming cultural differences and the contingency of identity" (cited in Morton, 2001, p. 36).

My approach, which has as its starting point a sampling of music traditions from Africa and the African diaspora, is necessarily concerned with issues of social justice and social change. The extent to which musical practices reflect dominant forms influenced and perpetuated by mass media and educational institutions raises the specter that oppression might be found in precisely the music that is so easily omitted from research; that is, the stories and musics that are or have been silenced. Beyond the mere fact of their inclusion, African musics contain a history woven into the fabric of our culture. It is imperative that we pose this history to our youth in order that they form the habit of mind to ask questions about fairness and challenge forms of oppression. This is more so the case because African cultures remain underrepresented in most subject matters and curricula. Repertoire, choice of musical content, and methods of instruction are thus integral to the process music curriculum development. If, as Barrett, Mc-Coy and Veblen suggest, we "reinforce the integrity of musical meaning by emphasizing the importance of cultural and historical studies" (cited in Morton, 2001, p. 38) through dialogue and conversation, then we can ensure the socio-cultural and humanistic benefits of multicultural music education are conferred alongside critical consciousness.

From a purely aesthetic standpoint, though, African idioms present a refined and compelling alternative to the development of rhythm, musicality, and musicianship. For young children lacking a musical vocabulary with which to express their creativity, why not try to expand cultural horizons in ways that might not otherwise be available? Early music pedagogues like Rousseau and Pestalozzi insisted that "music had to be introduced in manageable pieces" (Benedict, 2010, p. 147). They supported the idea that musical activities "could be broken from the complex into discrete subskills" (Benedict, 2010, p. 149). The premium placed on simplicity and the resistance to expressivity in this model has no doubt had an indelible impact on the genre that we have come to know as children's music. Children who are exposed to only this type of music are to a large extent precluded from engaging in different ways of thinking musically.

One of the musical ways of knowing that I am principally concerned with in my own classes is African polyrhythm, which privileges syncopation and suggests the possibility of different meters and varying conceptions of "the one," or first downbeat. Unfortunately, this type of musicality is not entirely compatible with prevailing notions of music pedagogy. Music educators are all too often compelled to establish objectives that are characterized by a narrow definition of musicianship, one that is principally concerned with musical literacy as defined by the ability to read and write in European staff notation. To a large extent, marginalized musics are representative of folk traditions and cultures that are also marginalized in school curricula. Sadly, the preoccupation with musical notation has other unfortunate consequences. Not only is the cognitive complexity of reading music discouraging to many young children who would otherwise engage in music-making, but the task of reading music requires a repertoire simple enough to read.

Thus, songs are introduced that will easily allow for instruction in the reading of musical notation. This is not to say that musical notation isn't a great learning or memory tool, but that its prominence in music pedagogy often forces out content that is less amenable to its constraints (i.e., a strict conception of meter and a definitive first downbeat). Such is the case even in many early childhood music programs, where music is largely taught by rote, but where the standard repertoire reflects the simplicity and lack of affect to which Rousseau and Pestalozzi alluded. Though "Twinkle, Twinkle

Little Star" and "Row, Row, Row Your Boat" are important components of my toddler sing-along and preschool classes, I find it important to pair this repertoire with African idioms.

PEDAGOGIC SYNCRETISM: AFRICAN ORFF AND AFRICAN MODELS OF MUSIC INSTRUCTION

In many African music cultures, there is no distinction between music for adults and music for children. With the exception of childhood music games, which I will briefly touch on in the following section, younger generations acculturate to the idioms and performance practices that exist for adults. Nzewi (1999) posits a three-stage template for "systematic life-music education" that is representative of "most African cultures" (p. 75). The first stage inculcates sense of pulse from birth to childhood through passive sensitization as the child is attached to his or her mother in the act of dance, chores or other rhythmic activities. The second stage inculcates sense of rhythm through active participation in communal musical events. The third and final stage of "general musicianship" can begin as early as age eight and lasts the remainder of one's life.

This stage involves explicit instruction on an instrument towards fluency in musical idioms. Here, Nzewi recommends assigning newcomers with a "crucial ensemble responsibility" in order to inculcate a "keen listening habit" and instill confidence (1999, p. 75). He proposes a curriculum made up of the following sequence of modules:

1. Concept of rhythm—music as patterned movement of sound in time.
2. Concept of pitch and melody—how music moves up and down in space and time.
3. Investigating sources of music sound.
4. Necessity, organization and presentation of music in society.
5. Ensemble practice.

For Nzewi, African music begins with rhythm and is embedded within a particular sociocultural context that maintains a specific code of practice, which lends itself to rhythmic and musical development. Insofar as rhythm is integral to our ability to communicate with each other and synchronize with nature, it behooves us to explore the first component of Nzewi's sequence and consider those crucial first two stages of musical childhood, when children are meant to have acquired this all-important (yet so taken for granted) capacity: finding the groove—the steady, underlying beat upon which rhythm, melody, and harmony are expressed. The implications are especially profound for early childhood schooling contexts, when the onus for "communal musical events" falls almost exclusively on the shoulders of music teachers.

Perhaps the most important feature of African polyrhythm (and groove-based music in general) is the facilitation of engagement and entrainment, allowing listeners and participants the opportunity to experience community through the vehicle of music. At the heart of this project is a reconceptualization of our ways of thinking and knowing, both musically and socially. To appreciate the "3-with-2ness" in more complex West African polyrhythms, as described by Locke (2011), and to participate in the solidarity of social dancing constitute approaches to music and life that can only expand our cultural horizons and range of perception.

This review of an example of African music curriculum development should not imply that we on the other side of the Atlantic are capable of adopting African pedagogies in full force. However, it is important to note that traditional oral-aural methods in African musical acculturation are didactic. Though our aim must be a democratic classroom in which students can actively contribute to the structure and content of their education, it is imperative that we not discount the apprenticeship model and the nature of teaching African musics, whereby teachers take the role of cultural bearers charged with memorizing a vast repertoire of music and instilling this repertoire in students by rote. We must also acknowledge that this mode of instruction relies on the complementary experiences of children playing music games, improvising, and experiencing communal musical events outside more formalized teaching contexts.

For educators who seek to employ African idioms outside African contexts, it is useful to think of the ways in which we can bring a range of practices into the classroom, avoiding entanglement with the myth of authenticity. No matter how accurate the performance, context will always dictate the impossibility of a truly authentic rendition of another culture's music. The need for sensitivity and awareness when appropriating styles for educational use persists, but we shouldn't feel paralyzed by the impulse to mirror musical culture in educational settings. In my practice, I seek out opportunities for pedagogical syncretism. African music games, predicated on the combination of movement, rhythm, and singing, provide such an opportunity and meld nicely with an Orff approach that unifies music, movement, speech, and improvisation.

Amoaku (1982) proposes parallels between traditional African systems of music education and the Orff-Schulwerk method, which closely resembles indigenous instructional practices. Amoaku prescribes African music for classrooms as a means of reinvigorating African traditions. Just as Orff was inspired to make an African instrument, the xylophone, a cornerstone of his pedagogy, Amoaku contends that the foundations of Orff Schulwerk—speech, rhythm, movement, and improvisation—are entirely compatible with traditional African approaches to teaching. His book of transcriptions was supplemented by the Folkways recording, *African Songs & Rhythms for Children: Orff-Schulwerk in the African Tradition* (1978) on which Dr. Orff collaborated.

One prime example of a pedagogical extension of Amoaku's recording can be found in a workshop conducted by Robert Kwami for the World Music Centre in 2001 (Kwami, 2001). There, Kwami introduced teachers to the "3M" approach, comprised of mnemonics, movement, and music using an aural-oral teaching process. This approach is significant because it closely reflects indigenous African music pedagogy. Mnemonics constitute an integral method employed by traditional African music teachers. For Kwami, considerations of classroom compatibility are mediated by the impossibility of replication. Therefore, he advocates an approach based on cultural transposition, utilizing appropriate teaching strategies and resources with respect to social and cultural context.

The following procedures are used to teach the song "Tse Tse Kule," which can be heard on Amoaku's *African Songs & Rhythms for Children*.

1. Use the rote method to recite words, line by line, and then sing the song. Lead the group with the gradual addition of simple dance movements (eg. marching, raising hands above the head and down at the sides) that the class can copy.
2. Once the students are confident with the song and accompanying movements, split up the class into four groups, each one with a specific line of the song and its corresponding movement.
3. Have the students recite their parts, one by one using LIFO (last in first out) or FIFO (first in first out) method, with the possibility of dynamic modulation.
4. Once fluent, divide the class further and introduce instruments with a variety of pitches.
5. For more advanced students, apply or have the students create variation techniques and dynamics.
6. Once refined, record, review, and assess with the class (Kwami, 2001).

This sample lesson exhibits a determined commitment to adapt African traditions to the elementary classroom. In terms of both engagement and facilitation technique, Kwami's "3M" technique successfully meets the demands of elementary classroom contexts through the medium of traditional African pedagogy. Kwami also recommends specific activities and exercises for the primary curriculum. The activities utilize progressive methods, encouraging pupils to compose music based on African children's stories and particular phrases from them. The exercises involve learning mnemonics for the rattle, bell, and drum parts by rote and then by applying them to the instruments.

Kwami's methodical approach reveals that even rote learning involves specific pedagogical applications. His pedagogy reflects traditional practices as it relies on mnemonic devices, offering an alternative to learning based on written forms. Though the procedures listed above are not necessarily representative of a standard practice, they show a systematic teaching technique suitable for formal educational settings.

MUSIC GAMES

One African music game that has become popular in early childhood classrooms is "Obwisana." In this game, a stone or instrument is passed along to the beat of the song. In my music classes, we pass around an egg shaker. Once students can pass around the shaker to a steady beat while singing, we try out new patterns along with the song (e.g., shake-shake-pass). As always, I solicit ideas for patterns from the students. In small groups, I will sometimes take away one shaker, so that there is always one person missing a shaker while we are passing it around. The person who is without a shaker at the end of the song must then choose an instrument to play while we sing another rendition, this time with one less shaker. We repeat this until everyone is playing an instrument.

In an activity I adapted from Oran Etkin (2011) in which we sing along to Babatunde Olatunji's "Jingoloba," students are to bring their shakers to the ground with the syllable "ba." To keep the children engaged, once they have become aware of the structure of the song, I try to trick them by changing the movements and/or syllables. Then I offer students the opportunity to trick their peers and me. Such opportunities for student leadership are not always easy to conduct in large classes, but they are effective in keeping everyone engaged and listening actively. One of the students' favorite games is Master Shaker/Master Drummer, which is basically "Indian Chief" adapted to instruments. Though parameters must be set, the children whom I work with consistently amaze me with their creativity. Even more inspiring is the way that they will incorporate items that they have learned into their own creativity.

In order to maximize student engagement and induce participation, it is best to introduce improvisation activities as games. Some of my favorite games incorporate elements of logic and mathematics, in which students must count beats. With dominos, partners can invent call-and-responses based on the number of beats on each side of a domino.

In Drum UNO, students select UNO cards and have to invent a rhythm with the number of notes on the card. Colors can indicate dynamics (e.g., mellow yellow is soft, mean green is loud, blue is slow, and red is fast) and students can make up rules for the wild cards. In a large group, students can guess the card that the composer used to invent his or her rhythm. Older students can be split into small groups to compose a poly-rhythm based on their cards.

In the visual realm, students can be asked to match recorded music to images, or they might be responsible for composing a score to a given movie clip. By introducing improvisation and composition in a palatable and structured way, students are provided a framework to achieve musical competence and compose on their own terms. Instead of a prescribed curriculum, these activities are subject to renewal and reinvention, and I invite teachers to stay true to themselves and discover the repertoire that best reflects their own sensibilities in a way that will motivate everyone in the classroom to be enthusiastic.

MULTICULTURAL CREATIVITY: TENSIONS BETWEEN PROGRESSIVISM AND TRADITIONALISM

The creative music strategies that I employ are carried out on mostly African instruments and structured by the stylistic traits of African music, namely, mindful repetition of rhythmic patterns in concert with one another, and a one-to-one relationship between musical notes and speech syllables. This leads us to the more salient issue of musical creativity in the multicultural classroom. Even if a student creates a rhythm that is not derived from Africa, it can reflect African style, meter, and timbre in its conception. A purposeful exploration of the different aspects of music making within the confines of African instruments and idioms can yield important insights into the music, so long as they are supplemented by actual rhythms and conversations about culture. Traditions should not be confused with the compositions and improvisations that emerge from creative music activities. The refined rhythms of West Africa must remain distinct from the accidental or purposeful improvisations of a drum circle, but both should be available to students.

Each of the creative strategies that I have devised and implemented can be perceived to run counter to the distinct West African traditions that inform the content of the music classes that I facilitate. With respect to both instruments and repertoire, the activities do not reflect any one tradition. Rather, I borrow from recreational styles that I have learned in order to instill first a sense of pulse, and then a sense of rhythm. The call for social justice makes it imperative that we move beyond the notion of a supposedly neutral drum circle and engage in musicking that is, at least partially, culturally specific and infused with critical histories. Drum circles are nevertheless a compelling avenue for exposition because they beckon students to participate without any restrictions.

I consistently seek to find a happy medium between the facilitation techniques of drum circles and the didactic methods of African drumming instruction. My own pedagogical efforts fall within a larger debate, between proponents of progressive and traditional teaching practices, which has preoccupied educators for the past century. Progressive education can be compared to a drum circle. Through its process-oriented approach, each participant is free to engage in a group project at his or her level of competence and willingness, testing out rhythmic and timbral possibilities in percussion. Traditional education, on the other hand, is predicated upon the notion of repertoire, in which students are grouped by ability and expected to excel individually. My experience as an educator and my budding philosophy of education lead me to the conclusion that, far from mutually exclusive, the progressive and traditional approaches are complementary and mutually reinforcing. They constitute integral components of a creative approach to African percussion in American elementary school contexts.

The games and activities that I have developed borrow from traditional African pedagogies and progressive techniques. Progressive aspects are meant to suit the needs and learning styles of American students who are taught to express their individuality. The model thus rejects a strict adherence to traditional African musical pedagogy, which tends to ignore or reject improvisation as anathema to amateur practice of African music. The model also averts a purely progressive approach, which takes the act of improvisation for granted and assumes that children will know how to motivate themselves to compose in real time in relation to an underlying groove-referent. Despite the pitfalls of progressive approaches, it is important to give pupils the opportunity to express their creativity through improvisation and composition.

CODA: ENGAGING COGNITION

This chapter has established some of the different ways that musicking can engage cognition. Percussion music is remarkably accessible during childhood because the gross motor skills that are necessary for playing percussion instruments tend to be available to most young children, and their facility with drums, shakers, and bells allow for musical and imaginative explorations that might be more difficult to achieve on instruments that demand finer motor skills. I have argued that elementary percussion instruction would benefit from the inclusion of repertoire from Africa and the African diaspora.

From both a humanist and social justice perspective, I cannot help but argue for educational endeavors that effect learning about (and from) other cultures so that children emerge with diverse ways of thinking and doing. Educators must seek to rectify past and present injustice through curricular and pedagogical choices. One activity that I conduct with older students is a musical recounting of the history of the conga. In small groups, students must come up with three to five musical phrases that depict a short piece of writing on the way that enslaved, black Cubans had to exchange their wooden pegs for metal tuners to convince Christian colonizers that their drums were no longer representative of African pagan traditions. Social justice and recognitions of pluralism are inextricably linked in that they can only be achieved through promoting ways of knowing and thinking that expand upon and challenge the cultural norms we have come to internalize as consumers of more conventional forms of (music) education. We are fortunate that Maxine Greene gives us such eloquent words to bridge the theoretical divide between humanism and social justice:

> Something life-affirming in diversity must be discovered and rediscovered, as what is held in common becomes always more many-faceted—open and inclusive, drawn to untapped possibility. No one can predict precisely the common world of possibility, nor can we absolutely justify one kind of community over another. Many of us, however, for all the tensions and disagreements around us, would reaffirm the value of principles like justice and equality and freedom and commitment to human rights since, without these, we cannot even argue for the decency of welcoming. (Greene, 1993, pp. 17–18)

The case for multicultural music education in early childhood should be clear. Whether we use African percussion, Japanese Taiko drumming, or South Indian Solkattu, our goal must be to educate children to be well-rounded, critical and creative artists, fluent in a most provocative and ubiquitous human form.

Music is all around us. A rich education in music demands more than the mere presence of music in school; it demands critical ears attuned to a wide array of cultural forms, from the dominant sounds that media bombard us with each moment, to the classical canons that retain such notable pedagogical prominence, to the far-reaching musical styles that arrived on our shores and made their way into our collective musical consciousness. Schools and cultural centers should not feel encumbered by the constraints of the classical curriculum. Rather, music educators would be wise to utilize the greatest wealth of musical diversity, employing an extensive artistic vocabulary to instill a sense of musical possibilities while opening pathways to a multitude of cognitive benefits conferred by such explorations.

It is especially important that music, with its capacity to engage our emotions, remains an artistic endeavor. We must not take away from music that ethereal element so mystifying, alluring, and gratifying to the soul. In an age where high-stakes testing and curriculum control find increasing prominence, music remains a respite for those willing to engage in acts of the spirit and imagination.

NOTES

1. Beyond the mere act of performing, the term "musicking" encompasses listening and experiencing; see Small, 1998.
2. The only rule for adaptation is that phrases must not sound forced; the musicality of any given phrase must come close to the natural rhythm and intonation of the phrase as it is spoken.
3. Student enthusiasm is consistently augmented when I bring in finger puppets or other visual props to support musical activities that incorporate animals. I have also found success having students make up the music and movement for monster or alien toys.

REFERENCES

Amoaku, W. K. (1978). *African songs & rhythms for children.* Washington, DC: Smithsonian Folkways Records.

Amoaku, W. K. (1982). Parallelisms in traditional African system of music education and Orff schulwerk. *Journal of International Library of African Music, 6*(2), 116–119.

Benedict, C. (2009). Curriculum. In H. Abeles, & L. Custodero (Eds.), *Critical issues in music education: Contemporary theory and practice* (pp. 143–166). New York, NY: Oxford University Press.

Campabello, N., De Carlo, M., O'Neil, J., & Vacek, M. (2002). *Music enhances learning.* Retrieved, July 1, 2011 from ERIC database.

Connors, A., & Wright, D. (2004). *101 rhythm instrument activities for young children.* Beltsville, MD: Gryphon House.

Etkin, O. (2011). *Oran Etkin's timbalooloo.* Retrieved, July 1, 2011, from http://www.oranetkin.com/kids.htm

Gardner, H. (1999). *Intelligence reframed: Multiple intelligences for the 21st century.* New York: Basic Books.

Greene, M. (1993). The passions of pluralism: Multiculturalism and the expanding community. *Educational Researcher, 22*(1), 13–18.

Isaak, C. (2006). *African rhythms & beats: Bringing African traditions to the classroom.* Burlington, VT: JPMC Books.

Iyer, V. (2002). Embodied mind, situated cognition, and expressive microtiming in African-American music. *Music Perception, 19*(3), 387–414.

Kwami, R. (2001). West African drumming, 'Tse Tse Kule' and the '3M' approach to using West African musics in the classroom: 1. Retrieved July 1, 2011 from http://www.worldmusiccentre.com/uploads/cdime/kwami2001.PDF

Levitin, D. (2006). *This is your brain on music: The science of a human obsession.* New York: Plume.

Locke, D. (1998). *Drum gahu: An introduction to African rhythm.* Tempe, AZ: White Cliffs Media.

Locke, D. (2011). The metric matrix: Simultaneous multidimensionality in African music. *Analytical Approaches to World Music, 1*(1), 48–72.

Morton, C. (2001). Boom diddy boom boom: Critical multiculturalism and music education. *Philosophy of Music Education Review, 9*(1), 32–41.

Nzewi, M. (1999). Strategies for music education in Africa: Towards a meaningful progression from tradition to modern. *International Journal of Music Education International Journal of Music Education, 33*(1), 72–87.

Patel, A. D. (2008). *Music, language, and the brain.* New York: Oxford University Press.

Sacks, O. (2008). *Musicophilia: Tales of music and the brain.* New York: Vintage Books.

Sacks, O. (2011, January 1). This year, change your mind. *The New York Times,* A19.

Small, C. (1998). *Musicking: The meanings of performing and listening.* Middletown, CT: Wesleyan University Press.

APPENDIX: CHILDREN'S BOOKS FOR THE DRUMMING CLASSROOM

Aardema, V., & Vidal, B. (1981). *Bringing the rain to Kapiti plain : A Nandi tale.* New York: Dial Press.

This rhyming story tells the tale of a resourceful bull who finds water for his thirsty herd and ends the drought afflicting the plain.

Andreae, G., & Parker-Rees, G. (2001). *Giraffes can't dance.* New York: Orchard Books.

Gerald the giraffe is clumsy and discouraged by the other animals that tease his dancing. When reading this story, I have students lightly tap the steady beat of the rhyming on their drums. We explore play a prototypical waltz and cha-cha-cha along with the story and I offer students the opportunity to invent rhythms based on the animals they see in the jungle dance.

Carle, E. (1997). *From head to toe.* New York: HarperCollins.

This classic book provides a fantastic opportunity to explore movement through a simple call-and-response structure.

Dole, M., & Eligio, A. (2003). *Drum, chavi, drum!.* San Francisco: Children's Book Press.

Chavi, undaunted by those around her who believe that girls should not drum, wins the approval and praise of her family, friends, and teachers when she performs conga at the Calle Ocho festival.

James, J., & Tsukushi. (1999). *The drums of noto hanto.* New York: DK Pub.

This story recounts the legend of Nabune villagers who ward off samurai through clever use of Taiko drums and masks. This book is filled with great rhythms from Japan that students echo throughout the telling of the story.

Krebs, L., & Cairns, J. (2003). *We all went on safari: A counting journey through Tanzania.* Cambridge, MA: Barefoot Books.

In this counting story, we learn the numbers one to ten in Swahili as well as the Masai names for animals. Each new page has an animal and a number. For each new number, students play that many repetitions of the animal rhythm that appears on the page.

Lake, M., & O'Malia, C. (1996). *The royal drum an Ashanti tale.* Greenvale, NY: Mondo.

This folktale tells the story of how animals come together to make a drum in order to communicate across great distances. I use this book as an introduction to the main jungle animals that we will perform on drums and in dances throughout the year. Each time an animal is introduced in the story, we have to perform its rhythm.

Martin, B., Archambault, J., & Ehlert, L. (1989). *Chicka chicka boom boom.* New York: Simon & Schuster Books for Young Readers.

In this class alphabet chant, students are to tap the beat of the rhyme and echo the title phrase whenever we hear it in the story.

McDermott, G. (1992). *Zomo the rabbit: A trickster tale from West Africa.* San Diego: Harcourt Brace Jovanovich.

This trickster tale follows a standard structure in which the main character must overcome three obstacles presented by other animals in order to win something from Nyame, the sky god. In this story, Zomo the Rabbit sets out to gain wisdom.

Pinkney, J. (1994). *Max found two sticks.* New York: Simon & Schuster Books for Young Readers.

In this story, a New York City boy named Max finds two stick and creates percussion instruments with various objects, including a bucket, hat boxes, and garbage cans, echoing the urban sounds around him.

CHAPTER 12

DANCE AND PLAY

Herman Jiesamfoek
Brooklyn College
City University of New York

ABSTRACT

Children naturally and spontaneously challenge themselves physically through play. Dance and physical movement have numerous physiological benefits, including enhanced core physical support, connectivity, and alignment, and increased awareness of the visceral and muscular systems. Contemporary childhood play often consists of sedentary engagement with digital screens and gadgets. Increased physical inactivity, though, is not only a result of advances in digital technology, but also often an outcome of over-protective parenting, or of parents and teachers who have little time or inclination to engage with children in dance. Cross-cultural vignettes of children engaged in spontaneous physical play are presented. Five observations—three in New York City, one in the Netherlands, and one in a Surinamese Bush Negro village—are discussed for their implications for the place of dance and spontaneous movement in childhood. Parental or other adult attention to and encouragement of a child's dance and movement can support children's willingness to seek spontaneous, natural, and creative ways to engage in physical play activities.

Young Children and the Arts, pages 195–207
Copyright © 2012 by Information Age Publishing

All children have a right to enjoy dance
—Standards for Dance in Early Childhood, 2009

Removing play from kids prevents them from developing themselves.
—Stuart Brown (Tippet, 2009)

OBSERVATION #1: NYC LINCOLN CENTER

At a New York City street crossing near Lincoln Center, I spotted a boy and girl, perhaps ages five and six, respectively, waiting to cross with an adult female. The adult crossed the street quickly with determined strides; the children, on the other hand, recognized a playful opportunity in the zebra stripes of the crossing and instantaneously created a rhythmical play—skipping, turning, and hopping over the stripes as they moved across the street. The adult, not atypical of most adults, reprimanded them and told them to cross in a quick, orderly, and safe manner. Once the children arrived at the other side, the adult firmly took their hands and dragged them along to their destination with determined adult-sized strides.

Most parents can identify with the above observation. For professional dancers, movement is closely and immediately connected to their physical and inner selves. When children become physically animated in play, they also reveal much about their bodies, particularly how they feel about their bodies and about their relationships to themselves and their world. Dance, says Edward Villella (2003), is an extension of that childlike physical activity.

Motivating Movement

When children utter their first words, it is much to the delight and pride of their parents and grandparents. From that moment on, language skills are continuously encouraged at home and in schools. The idea of stimulating a child with dangling toys, animated books, and other mediating learning tools is well-established; however, it is as important to pay attention to, motivate, and stimulate the child to physically engage in movement and dance.

Physical growth and development are often taken for granted. Once the period of enthusiasm and encouragement has passed—when young children first attempt to crawl and take their first steps—it is expected that a child will automatically continue a healthy physical development without further encouragement. Physical growth and development proceed, of course, but physical and even mental shortcomings that often surface later in life are, according to Gilbert-Green (2006), often due to the improper wiring of the nervous system as a result of inadequate physical activity at a younger age. Continued engagement in healthy physical activity from the earliest ages onward is therefore important, especially in this technological era when we as a society are becoming increasingly sedentary.

Another argument can be made for movement and physical expression through play and dance following Mahler, Pine and Bergmann's (2000) line of human development, which considers it necessary, natural, and unavoidable to allow children opportunities to process personal frustrations and painful situations. This does not imply that children need to be deliberately exposed to frustrations, but rather that the period after birth and during early childhood is accompanied by frustrations as children progress toward independence and psychological separation. Children from birth to age seven go through a period of tremendous growth and learning—physical, intellectual, and social. To process resulting frustrations and feelings means for them to relive impressions repeatedly; to do so, they must develop the particular attribute of play (Foks-Appelman, 2009).

Grown-ups also process their frustrations, according to Foks-Appelman, by actively engaging not only in creative and artistic activities, but also in visits to museums, theater, sports, and games. For children especially, the activities of play and dance act as natural releases for daily frustrations and responsibilities and are physical expressions of their inner feelings (Foks-Appelman, 2009). Very young children who have had opportunities to engage meaningfully and continuously with the arts will most likely as adults also engage creatively, actively, and participatory in the arts and in society.

OBSERVATION #2: CHILDREN'S DANCE IN THE BUSH NEGRO SOCIETY OF SURINAME

In the technologically less advanced society of the Surinamese Bush Negro people, I observed how children at very young ages were encouraged and "teased" by the elderly to dance and express themselves aesthetically. I observed two village girls, ages four and five, showing off village songs and dances with accurate precision, mastery, and grace. They told me they had learned these by observing adults perform, but I also saw them spontaneously improvise dance movements as reactions to the adults' teasing and encouragement.

Dance in this culture is as highly regarded as other forms of artistic aesthetic expression, including needlepoint, wood carving, music, and theatrical engagement. Mastering the skills of their aesthetically gracious and creative dances not only contributes to supporting social cohesion, but also to children's healthy physical growth and development and their ability to close in on prey during a hunt with graceful agility or to skillfully maneuver canoes on the country's treacherous rivers.

These observations of the Bush Negro society in the Surinamese jungle made me aware of how these children at very young ages were included and encouraged to dance, sing, and act out real or imagined stories, and then to transform these artistic ventures to suit their particular cultural style and aesthetic. Price and Price (1999) also arrived at similar findings of children participating from a very young age in the world of artistic production and performance. Babies, as Price noticed, as soon as they can stand, are frequently and enthusiastically encouraged to dance to the rhythm of hand-clapping or thigh slapping. The learning of artistic skills and aesthetic judgment is achieved without systematic formal instruction, as an unstructured "by-product" of the communal settings in which adults engage in making art. Artistic production is generally a sociable affair, with advice and commentary flowing freely.

Dance and Movement Education

Much as with the children in the Bush Negro society today, American children in the past were mostly taught skills necessary for day-to-day living; in fact, according to Ozmon and Craver (2008), education was targeted toward survival. Today, however, education in our technologically advanced society, according to these authors, is for a different kind of survival: obtaining employment, improving our thinking, enhancing the quality of our leisure time, and refining our social and cultural lives. While dance and creative movement continue to support these requirements today, our schooling and educating culture seems to have become fully comfortable in accepting *illiteracy* in movement and dance.

American sociologist Sarah Laurence-Lightfoot, in a June 2009 interview with Bill Moyers on PBS, made a useful distinction between schooling and education to illustrate that teaching and learning are not only matters important to schools, but also to education in general. Lawrence-Lightfoot noted that education takes place everywhere in society and culture, including schools, but that *schooling* only takes place in schools. This distinction is especially useful when discussing societal and cultural views on dance on the school's curriculum. It also provides a useful distinction when discussing ways to stimulate and support children's needs for physically acting and playing out imagined or real ideas and stories in various environments, thereby challenging their own physical movement boundaries—in other words, finding relationships to their body parts, discovering new forms of bodily expression, and learning physical movements to associate with and relate to the outside world.

Beyond the cognitive, emotional, kinesthetic, and aesthetic learning that occurs, there are clear health and nutritional benefits that surface when children engage safely in dance or creative movements with their own bodies. Thus, it is important that regular movement, rhythmic movement, and dance be nurtured from its first manifestations and continued throughout schooling and education. Honing (in Mayesky, 2009) found that by the fourth grade, creativity takes a nosedive if it is not nurtured. The innovation and invention that we would like children to engage in as adults and that become the engine driving society, according to Mayesky (2009), arise from the burgeoning curiosity that young children express, and this curiosity is kept alive by nurturing their creativity.

Dancing at School

A growing sedentary society is not beneficial for the well-being of society. In addition to requiring children to become literate in digital technology and achieving dexterity in computer labs at increasingly younger ages in both home and school, we should just as equally and urgently promote free expression through movement, dance, and play in schools and homes.

It is obvious that schooling and education in dance contribute to better use of leisure time, but survival in our technologically advanced society also means developing physically and mentally agile adults, who can creatively and swiftly involve with new technological developments, and can synthesize large amounts of available information at the touch of a button. To link this to dance may seem a long stretch; however, research has shown that engaging in dance can significantly contribute to physical agility, and following the mind-body line of thinking, also an agile mind.

The pioneering research of Irmgard Bartenieff (Bartenieff & Lewis, 2000) and Bonnie Bainbridge Cohen (1993) has shown how physical and mental skills can be easily nurtured by engaging in dance and movement activities from early childhood years. Bartenieff, a physiotherapist who looked at the progression of human growth, developed a method to re-educate the body by connecting to their internal and external environment, thereby increasing movement efficiency and expressiveness. Bainbridge Cohen, an occupational therapist, certified neurodevelopmental therapist, and dance and movement therapist, developed embodied and integrated approaches to movement, touch and repatterning. Embodied integrated approaches facilitate learning through exploratory internally-experienced rather than imitated externally-experienced movements and allow the child to engage actively with his or her environment using all the senses.

Current work of Gilbert-Green's (2006) provides a rationale for how dance as a form of communication can increase connections between brain cells and reduce cognitive decline. Similarly, Joyce (1994) advocates creative dance activity in public schools to help children build skills in the areas of self-respect, responsibility, concentration, and self-discipline, particularly given their constantly changing family and neighborhood situations. She also provides useful information for classroom teachers on how to incorporate dance into the curriculum. A final example of current work of researchers and educators is Lynch-Fraser (2000), who relates children's physical development, curiosity for learning, continuous exploration, and apparent insatiable energy to their intellectual and social lives and to developmental perspectives, with a focus on intellectual, social, emotional, and sensory motor development.

Schools should therefore, in spite of pressures to perform according to continuously changing state and local educational policies, put dance and creative movement classes as core academic subjects on their curriculum. However, dance and creative movement engagements should not only be thought of as the schools' responsibilities. Parents also have to take up their part and designate the time and create an environment that promotes and motivates safe physical play and dance with their children and stimulate their creative natural and spontaneous movements.

What Parents Can Do

To complement what schools can do, parents could create specific activities that can also enhance the use of dance at home. The first of two most pressing parental activities is paying attention to children's natural need to safely explore physical body movement and potentials, through acting out imagined or real ideas, stories, and feelings through movements that exponentially expand on their functional daily routines. The second is to actually engage with children when they spontaneously engage in movement and dance play. This can be achieved by creating a physical space, time, and atmosphere at home that allow unencumbered spontaneous movement and invite learning through playfully designed movements. By engaging in dance and physical activity with their children, parents also regain lost opportunities to enrich themselves and relearn the language of play.

OBSERVATION #3: OUTSIDE A MANHATTAN
APARTMENT RESIDENCE

He must have been about five years old, jumping up and down on a two-foot high wall in front of my apartment building that separates the pedestrian sidewalk from a flower garden. His mother walked steadily determined towards an unknown destination, gesturing to the boy to follow her. The boy, however, remained totally immersed in a balancing act on the wall, stretching his leg behind him, arms to the side, and changing his supporting leg as he moved along the wall. Seemingly stressed and not paying attention to the boy's play, the mother walked over, grabbed his hand, and impatiently pulled him off the wall to continue on to their destination.

Children, says Davies (2003), learn from exploring movements in particular ways when they play, and this includes challenging their physical potential in natural and human-made environments. It is natural for young children to spend much energy in seemingly purposeless physical activities. Rather than just walking the most efficient direct path to their destination as an adult would, children often manage to seek, find, and create playful situations in which to challenge themselves physically. Although such short movement outbursts allow children to playfully test out their balance or try new movements, there is far more going on than simply the observable physical activity.

From birth through age one, according to Gilbert-Green (2006), physical activity is in fact an absolute necessity for the child's healthy neurological growth. Baby movements are not yet "dance" per se, but they aid the proper wiring of the nervous system and development of a physical frame to continue physical activity and exploration at later ages. Engaging in dance at later ages includes additional aspects such as imagination, creativity, and the ability to examine, question, act on, and associate in new ways beyond cultural or personal norms.

The cognitive development of young children goes hand in hand with their movement development. Movement, according to Stuart Brown (Tippett, 2009), accelerates learning and aids children's academic performance. Recess time on the playground, he says, is therefore as important as academic performance. When children engage in activities such as climbing, balancing, and jumping, they tap into information concerning their cognitive development. The children's movement activities in structured environments, says Davies (2003), provide children several possibilities of learning through movement, such as how to orient themselves in space, understanding that climbing up precedes falling down, the symbolic meaning of activities (e.g., a fireman sliding down the pole), and the verbalization of their actions and activities with words. This stringing of activities together in the brain, are, according to Calvin (in Davies, 2003, p. 95), core activities of the brain and useful for language development, storytelling, planning ahead, games, and ethics. Moreover, following the notion of Singer and Singer (cited in Davies, 2003), children become good learners by developing their cognitive skills when they are able to play openly and freely investigate what is immediately at hand to design their activities.

Furthermore, since children use their bodies as major frames of reference before other external contexts, such as playing with blocks, are established Davies (2003), they can benefit from their free expression through bodily movement that explores range, rhythm, and dynamics and creates spatial awareness and knowledge for responding actively to their environment. Such playful explorations of movement also cultivate learning about strength, flexibility, height, width, weight, proximity, and distance. Finding similarities in movement, classifying or arranging them in succession, and employing composition (seriating) all reflect Piaget's stages of development, according to Davies (2003). Davies also found that children who used movements based on their own experiences could seriate earlier. Calvin (cited in Davies, 2003) similarly found that stringing activities together in the brain—a core activity critical for language development, storytelling, planning, games, and ethics—occurs when children engage in movement activities such as dance and free physical play.

Thus, to nurture the child's physical and cognitive development, parents need to allow this play to happen and unfold according to the child's own interest, but they also should encourage and accompany their actions and activities with words that preserve actions through time (Gerhardt cited in Davies, 2003). Through free and guided movement exploration, children construct their own knowledge and a series of self-set challenges that help them construct spatial notions of direction (e.g., up-down, jump-land); extension and contraction (e.g., long-short); size (e.g., big-little); distance (e.g., near-far); zones (e.g., above-below); and levels (e.g., high-low) (Davies, 2003). Through seriating, children learn to classify and see similarities, associate, and make connections to areas in their physical world.

Parents can therefore do a lot at home by paying attention to the child's spontaneous movements and providing a safe environment in which movement can be explored. The parent engaging with the child in this way additionally has the benefit of creating a special bond with their child and awareness that physical engagement and expression is natural. The following section will give suggestions for engaging with the child through dance and physical play.

Tips for Creating Occasions to Learn through Dance and Play

We can't fail play; therefore, it is an optimal state for learning.
—Stuart Brown

Young children should at first be able to explore creative dance movements without rules. Structure can be imposed when children are ready to learn the rules and skills of the trade. Their youthful lack of inhibition, creativity, and curiosity can be used to great advantage to explore a wide range of movements and set a pattern and consciousness that dancing and creative movement exploration are natural. This is especially suited to young children who naturally love to discover new things about the world and to imagine without hesitation or inhibitions.

The first suggestion is for both parents and children to wear comfortable clothing after setting aside a special time to spend together. Lynch-Fraser (2000) suggests that this dedicated time does not have to be extended, since the attention span—especially for children under three—is extremely short. Similarly, it is suggested that parents be aware of children's natural curiosity and their mental and physical readiness. When executing a planned movement session, another suggestion is to begin slowly, repeating the exercise until both parents and children are comfortable. This requires patience, continuous response to the child, balancing exercises to keep interest alive, and allowing the child to imitate without expecting exact interpretations of your movements. In fact, children may concoct surprisingly delightful movement renditions of their own, imitating yet interpreting something unique. Stuart Brown (Tippet, 2009) stated that children in general solve their own problems by learning about themselves through the challenges they place on themselves.

Setting up the circumstances involves allowing children to express themselves freely and creatively and building with children a sense of acceptance and encouragement to continue exploring. Creativity, according to Mayesky (2009), is recognized in children's behavior if they are solving problems, redefining situations, demonstrating flexibility, and being adventurous. Another important, yet often overlooked point raised by Lynch-Fraser (2000) is that each child is an individual and so they may be reluctant to do certain exercises, not because they are intellectually unprepared, but because they are not at that point interested in the subject matter. Therefore, it is best never to pressure children into what they do not want to do and to switch when they indicate they have had enough. Children may quickly and unexpectedly change to other activities and insist on repeating the same movement repeatedly—to the utter boredom and exhaustion of the adult. In such a case, Lynch-Fraser recommends quieting them down with more relaxing exercises towards the end of the session, convincing them that these are equally enjoyable substitutes. Or perhaps, it is a good time for another sibling or spouse to take over to inject a new perspective and interest in a new activity.

OBSERVATION #4: BROOKLYN AFTERNOON

A young girl around five years old shouted "Look at me!" to an older woman, perhaps her grandmother, who responded, "I am watching you." Thus confirmed, the child executed a series of movements around an upside-down U-shaped bicycle pole, spinning around it, crawling through it, first face-down, then backwards while holding on to the sides of the bar, and finally balancing to the side while grasping with one hand. This incredible burst of creatively challenging movements to discover how she could move her body through and around the poles happened within only a minute and resulted in the happy, satisfied, and proud smiles of the child and the grandmother.

When children play, they innately know how to impose self-made rules or self-imposed boundaries. They may show off and ask for attention for their particular activity, as did this little girl in my observation.

Elaborating on Schirrmacher's (2002) and Smith's (1984) recommendations on responding to children's art, it is also important to respond to what is seen and to have children respond in their own ways on what they are doing. This encourages children to continue thinking in terms of dance—in this observation, on physical movements—whereby children are developing appropriate movement vocabulary and the ability to classify and seriate. Responses to play and dance demonstrations could include: "I see you are crawling backwards through the loop. How are you holding your body up?" "I see you are swiveling in one direction. How does that feel?" "You are balancing on one side, your head is held upright and one arm is stretched to the side. How far can you go without losing your balance?"

Similarly, the focus could be on a particular body part or relations to other body parts, such as, "I see that your legs move slowly when you are balancing. What are your arms doing?" Or the adult could remark on the child's ability to focus: "How does concentrating on firmly holding on to the pole while you create your off-balance pose help you make your pose?" Or the focus could be on a particular quality of movement such as, "I see how amiably, smoothly, and graciously you crawled through the U-shaped pole. How would it be different if you did the same with an angry feeling?" Focusing on the process rather than the end project develops creative habits of mind and creativity and a personally high level of positive self-awareness that continues to develop as the child grows up.

When children have the opportunity to physically play or dance freely in a safe, encouraging environment, they connect new ideas to personal experiences. They thus learn that movement feels good and they can express themselves kinesthetically as well as verbally. They notice that their individual movements have value and that experiences build upon earlier established ones to develop new skills. Perhaps most important, they learn they can have fun in experiencing the joy of movement.

Expressing Natural Creative Tendencies

Mayesky (2009) offers suggestions to help children express their natural creative tendencies. Children, she says, should be familiar with the environment; worrying or becoming upset in new situations hampers expression of creative potential. Children should learn to accept change and be supportive when no immediate answers can be found to a question or problem; encouraging them to seek answers shows them that a problem can have various acceptable answers. Children should feel safe to express freely and learn to judge and accept their own feelings, which can happen in an environment that respects and tries out all ideas. Parents should demonstrate that children's ideas are valued and children are rewarded for creative solutions. Children should feel that finding answers for themselves is fun and rewarding, especially if allowed to work through problems independently. Children should be encouraged to follow through and persevere on all activities. Because rewarding for conformity discourages creativity, it is useful to help children appreciate themselves for their uniqueness and persist with an activity, even if others have moved on to other things.

OBSERVATION #5: A PARK IN HOLLAND

In a children's section of a park, a little girl (six or seven years old) separated from her class group and ran towards a two-foot high concrete pole jutting from the ground. The top was about 10 x 15 inches and rounded off on both sides. The girl jumped on it, balanced on both feet, and stretched her arms out to the sides, smiling happily and proudly. Alarmed by what she saw, the adult leader of the group shouted in fear: "Be careful, your feet will slide off, the sides are rounded." Another adult, perhaps the mother, with an imperative tone shouted, "Get off now!" She walked over, briskly took the girl by the hand, and pulled her down from the pole.

Here, again, is an example of a lost opportunity for exploration, challenge, and play. Understandably, grown-ups need to be concerned and care for children's physical well-being. However, adults could also tame their fears enough to find a positive substitution for the opportunity in a safer circumstance without losing the rich potential exploring in the moment. Perhaps the grown-up in this observation could have allowed the child to examine and replicate her movements once she was back on the ground. Perhaps she could challenge the girl to explore in words further movement possibilities embedded in such an experience. The important aspect is to avoid setting fear and negativity in the child's mind. Removing kids from play and play from kids ultimately prevents them from developing, according to Stuart Brown, and exaggerated safety frightens children out of obtaining the freedom they need. For that matter, says Brown, playgrounds are too sterile, swings do not go far enough, and monkey bars can be too low to be sensible for play. At the same time, parents need to find a balance between what is reasonable and what is overly challenging, but in conjunction with what a child seeks to do.

CONCLUSION

Play is nature telling us who we are and what we are. Going back to what gives joy is to allow us to get a glimpse, a clue, on what our innate talent is.

—Stuart Brown

In short, dancing and physical movement has numerous physiological benefits for many body systems and organs. It enhances core physical support, connectivity, and alignment, while also increasing awareness of the visceral and muscular systems that support the body and lead to correct use of body structures. Thus, children (and adults) can remain injury-free, move with ease, and coordinate their actions gracefully. Dancers have always found that movement deepens their understanding of particular elements of dance technique and that fundamental movement patterns are integral parts of dance technique. What they know as dancers is information that should be shared with parents, teachers, and children as a way to extend the art of dance into the everyday life of each and every child. As Stuart Brown suggests, without dance and play, "the essence of life is missed." Parents and teachers have responsibility to their children—and to themselves—to rediscover this essence and maintain it.

REFERENCES

Bainbridge Cohen, B. (1993). *Sensing, feeling, and action: The experiential anatomy of body-mind centering*. Northampton, MA: Contact Editions.

Bartenieff, I., & Lewis, D. (2000). *Body Movement: coping with the environment*. New York: Routledge

Davies, M. (2003). *Movement and dance in early childhood* (2nd ed.). London: Paulo Chapman/Sage.

Foks-Appelman, T. (2009). *Kinderen geven tekens (Children give signals)*. Delft, The Netherlands: Eburton.

Gilbert-Green A. (2006). *Brain-compatible dance education*. Reston, VA: National Dance Association.

Joyce, M. (1994). *First steps in teaching creative dance to children*. Mountain View, CA: Mayfield.

Mahler, M. S., Pine, F., & Bergman, A. (2000). *The birth of the human infant: symbiosis and individuation.* New York: Basic Books. (Original work published 1975)

Mayeski, M. (2009). *Creative activities for young children* (9th ed.). Clifton Park, NY: Delmar, Cengage.

Moyers, B. (2009). *Bill Moyers Journal.* Interview with Sarah Laurence-Lightfoot. PBS. Retrieved from http://www.youtube.com/watch?v=yBm6-CsrUws

Ozmon, H. A., & Craver, S. M. (2008). *Philosophical foundations of education.* Upper Saddle River, NJ: Merrill/Prentice-Hall.

Price, S., & Price, R. (1999). *Maroon arts: Cultural vitality in the African Diaspora.* Boston: Beacon Press.

Schirrmacher, R. (2002). *Art and creative development for young children.* Albany, NY: Delmar Gengage.

Smith, N. (1984). *Experience in art: teaching children to paint.* New York: Teachers College Press.

Standards for Dance in Early Childhood, NDEO. Retrieved July 8, 2009 from http://www.ndeo.org/content.aspx?page_id=22&club_id=893257&module_id=53060

Tippet, K. (2009). *Play, spirit, and character.* Speaking of Faith interview with Stuart Brown. NPR, June 4, 2009. Retrieved from http://being.publicradio.org/programs/2009/play/

Villella, E. (2003). Why dance? In M. H. Nadel & M. R. Strauss, *The dance experience: Insights into history, culture and creativity* (pp. xi-xiii). Hightstown, NJ: Princeton Book Company.

ARTS AND IMAGINATIVE PEDAGOGY

The Art of Classroom Improvisation

Carol Korn-Bursztyn
Brooklyn College
and City University of New York

Young Children and the Arts: Nurturing Imagination and Creativity considers the implications for teachers, parents and other adults for working within a model of arts in education that integrates high quality early childhood education with an experiential approach to the arts in classrooms, homes, and in community settings. It presents a set of principles that incorporates developmentally appropriate practice within a flexible, interactive approach that can readily be adapted for particular needs of diverse groups of children in various school, family and community contexts.

The arts provide an important vehicle for the expression of children's understanding of the world and for the complex emotions that emerge when children are faced with difficult, sometimes traumatic events. We are reminded in Chapter 6, *Museum Visits with Young Children* (Hill Bose, Korn & Ellmann), of the role of the arts in helping children to master traumatic

Young Children and the Arts, pages 209–216

events, here in response to the terrorist attacks of 9/11. In the classroom vignettes described in that chapter, engaging in the arts provided an important linking function, connecting the children's growing cognitive understanding to their affective understanding of the events that surround, and when traumatic, intrude on and interrupt the safety and predictability of everyday life.

For a brief moment, the events of 9/11 propelled the caring, supportive and mediating role of the early childhood educator into the foreground of the public imagination, a place that has come to be increasingly dominated by discourse on skill development. New York City teachers earned recognition, albeit briefly, in the public eye for their efforts to protect and care for the children in their charge both on the day of, and in the aftermath of the destruction. Like other New Yorkers who questioned their commitment to love relationships in the aftermath of 9/11, these New York City teachers began to raise questions about the work and the children they loved.

Then, as now, they raised questions about the complex role of teaching, broader than the skill development and teach-to-the-test pressures that have permeated even early childhood education in recent years. Questions about the role of education in developing the whole child, including children's intellectual development, emotional growth, and capacity to engage in reciprocal relations had a poignancy that increasingly takes on a sense of urgency today. The arts provide a means to engage children in making sense of their world by making available to educators and parents a framework within which to strengthen or even re-introduce the artistic and affective dimension of teaching and learning. This function of the arts becomes demonstrably clear in those situations where, in recent years, affective education has been driven to the margins by concerns for measured academic skill development.

Young Children and the Arts: Nurturing Imagination and Creativity takes up the primary role of educators and parents, to co-create with children experiences that are meaningful for both children and adults. I'd like to begin with a consideration of how our own experience and evoked memories enter into the classroom, shaping what we do, how we see and respond to the children in our care. It's useful here to consider three areas central to the development of early childhood teachers, and extrapolate. These are: a) the capacity for teacher imagination, b) the ability to critically reflect on teacher practice, and c) the ability to design and create educational experiences and environments.

It will be useful to briefly review the place of childhood imagination discussed in greater detail in Chapter 4, *Cultivating Imagination and Creative Thinking*, followed by consideration of teacher imagination in early childhood pedagogy. Imagination in the early childhood years fills the gaps between what is known and what one needs to know. Children's growing capacity for memory is what makes it possible to imagine. Imagining provides opportunity for children to play with what Katherine Nelson (2006) refers to as narrative scripts, at times staying close to remembered narrative sequences of experience, while at other times producing elaborated, often fictive riffs of everyday experience. Rather than escapist entertainment, imagining is a means of stepping back, reflecting on, and responding to experience. In childhood, reflection is typically reflection-in-action, a physical embodiment of understanding.

Over 75 years ago, Vygotsky (1934/1987) observed that "imagination is a necessary, integral aspect of realistic thinking" (p. 349), and also that complex forms of understanding call for more complex forms of imagining. Imagining and complexity are joined in the child's impulse to amplify and give expression to understanding and experience through creative acts. Imagination and creativity lend shape and form to private understanding, providing the ground upon which children's ability to reflect upon personal experience first emerges.

Imagination also plays another, under-recognized role in human development. The capacity to imagine provides a window into the minds, or subjective experiences of others. The child who imagines can imagine being another—having other ways of walking or talking, in short, other ways of being in the world. When children perform their understandings of others, as in dramatic play—the theater of childhood—they take on varied roles, creating the settings that frame their characters' actions. Barbara O'Neill, in Chapter 8, *Integrating the Theater Arts: Creativity and Inclusion*, however, reminds the reader that the theater arts serves not only to help children (with and without disabilities) take on the roles of others, but also by imagining themselves in different situations—and even as different beings—self-regulate, especially from a state of high- to low-arousal. Her "baba story" is a bittersweet personal tale of a young child's desire to hold on to the soothing rituals of infancy, while reaching for the developmental gain of increasing autonomy that comes with relinquishing the dependency of the very early years. The children love her story; they intuitively understand that going to school means growing up and away from home, and that school calls for emotional resources of a different magnitude than home.

The ability to imagine the other by taking on the behavior—both verbal and physical—of others is closely tied to the development of empathy in childhood. As such, it is closely linked to the process of de-centering, by means of which we develop the capacity to move beyond our own subjectivity and towards an appreciation of the other.

Imagining the other is central to developing empathy in childhood, and is also critical to teachers' understanding of children's experience. The arts can provide multiple points of entry for imagining one's own experience and that of others. This is true for children and for adults, rendering close study of works of art especially meaningful in teacher education. An example of how imagining the self and imagining the other can provide an entry point into classroom-based teacher research is illustrated by a segment of work jointly developed by Barbara Ellmann (see Chapter 6, *Museum Visits with Young Children: A Teaching Artist's Perspective*) and myself for a graduate course on teacher research that I taught.

This segment, designed around autobiographical memory, self-representation and reflection, was developed as a prelude to study of John Singer Sargent's portraits of children and Kehinde Wiley's contemporary installation "Go" at the Brooklyn Museum of Art. Its place in the course curriculum served as introduction to observing and recording, an important research tool in teacher research, where the subjectivity of the observer must always be held in mind. In advance of the first session with the teaching artist, I asked a graduate class of teacher-researchers to post on the course website a brief writing in which they described a childhood memory and its impact on their teaching practice. We asked our group of teacher researchers to bring to class two photographs of themselves as children: one solitary, and one posed with an adult.

In class we selected one of the two photographs to work with and wrote brief autobiographical sketches of the child in the photo. We exchanged photographs with partners and wrote about our partner's imagined experience. In pairs we presented our contrasting essays—one an autobiography, the other an imagined biography. Many of the autobiographical/biographical accounts were surprisingly matched, the biographies recalling the autobiographical in content and in the quality of expressed emotion. Later, beginning to build a link to the application of reflection to teacher practice, we returned to our own photographs and wrote about where the remembered child's experience is located today in our lives as teachers. Jolie, a teacher in an exclusive private school writes:

> Teaching in a private school, where many of the children are from affluent backgrounds, usually causes me to find my childhood very different... This year to my surprise, as the children began to share their family situations, I found my experience similar to that of the children in many ways. For example, there is a boy whose parents are going through a divorce. My parents were divorced when I was about his age. There is another boy whose grandmother lives in his house. I grew up with my grandmother living with my mother, my brother, and myself. For the first time I am beginning to feel a personal connection with my students, knowing that there is a part of their life which I can understand.
>
> My inability in the past to find a personal connection with my students has for a long time caused me to question my ability to reach my students on a personal level... As I began this year with the family unit, I realized there are children here who do not live fairy tale lives. They have lives with real issues

that represent the real world. This is something that I can understand. This is something with which I can connect.

May writes the following:

> I grew up in a little town named Lil Washington, in North Carolina. My grandmother's house is on a dirt road filled with deep holes. In the back of the house is a wooded area, and in front is a ditch filled with snakes, berries, vines, and water. As a child I used this ditch as a short cut to visit relatives and friends. Sometimes I picked berries when I got hungry, and I pulled vines from the ditch to create a jump rope. When I wasn't exploring the great outdoors, I was in the presence of my grandparents or aunt.

> At the age of six I entered Beauford County School for black children. I had never been separated from my grandparents or my aunt. I sat in my seat trembling. The teacher had a large bump on her forehead and a very loud voice. On her desk lay a switch. I began to cry. I ran from the class, down the corridor and outside to the building at the end of the road…where I found my aunt after searching every class. When I found her she picked me up and held me tightly in her arms. As she held me she explained that I had to go to school and that she would pick me up after school. She escorted me back to my class—even though I was still upset—but I knew she was coming back to take me home.

> As a teacher I have observed many children entering the class for the very first time crying and screaming…As a teacher and an individual I am a very caring and loving person, and I hate to see anyone in distress. Tears swell in my eyes and all I think about is trying to ease her distress…When I observe children not adjusting to school I am able to relate. I will bend down and talk to them and explain just like my aunt explained to me.

In studying our own photographs, and examining the residue of early experience on our professional practice, personal experience serves as metaphor for the experience of others, even experiences remote from our own. Teachers take such metaphoric leaps when they draw on their own lives to imagine their students' subjective experiences. This understanding is at once intellectual and visceral, recalling Jolie's "ah ha!" moment, and May's visceral response to the distress of a child.

A rough translation of how personal experience works metaphorically for the experience of others might be: "My experience can be metaphoric for yours; this can help me to imagine your experience." Teacher imagination is formed out of carefully honed skills of observing and listening to others, and by the ability to mine personal experience and memory in order to imagine, or create a mental image of the other. Teacher imagination, though, cannot end with reflective musings. The turn to practice, critical at this juncture, involves application of four foundational components. These are what teachers know about a) their own lives, b) children's particular circumstances, c) children's developmental needs, and then d) creating meaningful experiences/curriculum development and classroom design.

Pedagogy in a democratic society invites a breadth of subjective responses and must anticipate the particular subjectivities, experiences, and vantage points of diverse students. Questions of teacher practice must deliberately consider the following: a) how diverse cultural and community contexts impact on teaching in diverse settings, b) how diverse personal, social and cultural contexts are provoked by artistic expression and representation, and c) how teachers and other adults can locally develop and implement arts-suffused experiences for young children that address children's developmental needs to explore, experiment and improvise.

A challenge to the arts in early education is one that touches on archaic teacher fears of many little children, moving quickly in many different directions, all under the care of a solo practitioner. As noted in Chapter 1, *Defining a Place for the Arts in Early Education*, these often include fears that the orderly environment of the classroom will become chaotic, and that artistic license will devolve into messiness. Where cultural practice calls for clear delineation of child and adult roles, the messiness of art can provoke fear that the invisible lines that demarcate the boundaries of acceptable behavior will be blurred—and that the arts will provide license for irresponsible freedom.

In Chapter 7, *Art-Making with Young Children with Disabilities*, Freed and Bursztyn describe the importance of working with art materials with children with special needs, and argue for providing children with disabilities opportunities for working with visual media. Their chapter specifically raises the question of why the arts are especially important for children with special needs, a population that is often left out of both school-based arts enhanced programs and community arts initiatives.

Working with messy art materials and getting out of one's seat—as Herman Jiesamfoek in Chapter 12, *Dance and Play*, strongly recommends, raise questions about how we can prepare children to exercise freedom responsibly. How can we create classrooms that promote freedom to explore, learn, and express one within the parameters set by responsible teachers and other adults? Fear of children's movement is expressed both in the hesitation of teachers and parents to encourage spontaneous movement, and also in concerns about visiting museums and art galleries with young children. Chapter 6, *Museum Visits with Young Children*, opens with a frank discussion of how to prepare young children to visit a place where "Don't touch" is typically the first message children hear.

In Chapter 10, *A Journey of Musical Collaboration*, Judith Hill Bose describes a collaborative approach to designing classroom experiences that will promote children's spontaneous explorations and that also meet the criteria for meaningful experiences that reflects the children's interests as well as their teachers' understanding of the children's needs. Andrew Aprile, in Chapter 11, *Music-making with Young Children: African Orff and Rhythmic Intelligence,* describes his work with young and very young children, inspired by African drumming, in which he and the children develop and create rhythmic experiences.

Making the arts an everyday experience for children presents a challenge to teachers and other adults to draw on their knowledge of young children and best practices in early childhood education in order to create and—as Beth Ferholt reminds us in Chapter 9, *Playworlds and Early Literary Arts Education*—co-create with children meaningful experiences and curricular connections. The arts are empowering to children, serving the twin purposes of both developing individual creative capacity, as well as creating community and possibilities for the development of communal imaginings. Play provides a powerful realm for children, as long as it is owned and directed by children.

Co-creation of play experiences is a delicate balancing act: play is a source of power and confidence for children as long as children guide and adults follow. In Ferholt's chapter, she describes the way in which what began as an adult–child co-construction increasingly became child-led and dominated. The children's classroom experience clearly helped them acquire the tools to learn about literature, theater, and the art of resolving differences amicably. This enabled them to spontaneously decide to autonomously produce a play, leaving their teacher and parents to form an admiring audience.

The arts provide an avenue by which teacher imagination develops in tandem with the growth of imagination and creativity in young children. Eschewing the model of teacher anonymity that underlines the contemporary trend of "teacher-proof" curricula, this book suggests, rather, that teachers and adults engage with the arts and with the challenge of developing arts experiences suitable for young children and geared to particular interests and affinities of particular children.

The arts call for subjective responses and invite us to imagine our own selves, past and present, and consider the experiences of others. Work in the arts and in curriculum development invites teachers, parents and other adults to become researchers who observe and reflect on children and on their own ability to develop meaningful experiences with and for children, and who imagine their own continued creative development alongside that of the children in their care.

REFERENCES

Nelson, K. (2006). *Narratives from the Crib.* Cambridge, MA: Harvard University Press.

Vygotsky, L. (1934/1987). Lecture 5: Imagination and its development in childhood. In R.W. Rieber & A. S. Carlton (Eds.), *The collected works of L.S. Vygotsky, Vol.1* (pp. 339–349). New York: Plenum Press.

ABOUT THE EDITOR

Carol Korn-Bursztyn, PsyD is a psychologist and psychoanalyst, and Professor of Education at Brooklyn College and Professor in the PhD Program in Urban Education at the Graduate School of the City University of New York. She developed and led the Early Childhood Center Programs, the lab school of the School of Education from 1991 through 2007. Dr. Korn-Bursztyn began her career as an English teacher and early childhood educator, and worked as a school psychologist in New York City public and private schools, and in clinical settings before coming to Brooklyn College. She maintains a private practice with children and families and also consults with schools. Professor Korn-Bursztyn is the author of numerous articles on children's narrative, the arts in education and teacher research, and the co-author, with Alberto Bursztyn, of *Rethinking Multicultural Education: Case Studies in Cultural Transition* (Bergin & Garvey). She is series editor of *Making Sense of Psychology* (Greenwood Press).

ABOUT THE CONTRIBUTORS

Andrew Aprile, M.A. is a doctoral student in the Urban Education program at the CUNY Graduate Center. His research interests include multicultural music education (with a focus on percussion and African music); musical cognition and development; equity in arts education; sociocultural theory; and the application of indigenous knowledge and oral traditions in formal classroom contexts. Currently, Andrew teaches music at various schools, after-school programs, and community centers in Manhattan and Brooklyn. He also teaches an educational foundations course on diversity at City College of the City University of New York. Andrew's interests in diversity and ethnomusicology took shape at Wesleyan University's World Music program, where he had the opportunity to learn musical styles and experience pedagogies from a host a musical traditions. Andrew remains an active musician and plays guitar in the African-influenced funk/hip-hop band, Mamarazzi.

Judith Hill Bose, Ph.D. is currently the Director of Education Studies at the Longy School of Music of Bard College in Cambridge, MA. Now an active soprano in the Boston area, Judith has also had a long career as a teaching artist in New York City, working for organizations such as the Lincoln Center Institute and the New York Philharmonic. She received her Ph.D. in Urban Education from the Graduate Center of the City University of New York, her MM from the New England Conservatory of Music and a B.A. from Duke University.

Young Children and the Arts, pages 219–221
Copyright © 2012 by Information Age Publishing
All rights of reproduction in any form reserved.

Kirsten Cole, M.F.A. is a parent, teacher and artist who lives in Brooklyn, NY with her husband David and her sons Max and Zeke. Cole is a doctoral candidate in the program in Urban Education at the City University of New York Graduate Center, completing a dissertation on how teachers' life histories shape their approach to working with families. For the past seven years she has taught as an adjunct instructor at Long Island University and Brooklyn College, working with pre- and in-service teachers in coursework in art education, teacher research and language and literacy. She holds a Masters in Fine Arts in Textiles from the California College of Arts. For four years she was the director of an arts and literacy based afterschool program in Brooklyn. Additionally she worked with NYC public school students as a museum educator, developing and teaching curriculum that responded to the museum's collections.

Barbara Ellmann, visual artist, has exhibited in galleries and museums around the country, and is in the collections of Peter Norton, Leonard Nimoy, Walter Scheuer, the U.S. Embassy in Kampala, Uganda, and the Four Seasons Hotel in Marrakech, Morocco.

Among Barbara's accomplishments are permanent public artworks that are part of the collection of the City of New York: seven glass windscreens for the Metropolitan Transportation Authority's Arts for Transit Program at the Van Siclen Avenue station and a 10' × 48' installation of paintings for the Cambria Heights Public Library. For the city of Summit, NJ Barbara designed faceted glass windows for a bus shelter.

As a consultant for universities, orchestras, theaters, private schools, and arts programs Barbara conducts professional development for teaching artists, faculty members, and students of all ages.

She is a museum educator at the Museum of Modern Art and the Whitney Museum of American Art and a presenter in the Kennedy Center's National Partnership Program. She has been a teaching artist for Lincoln Center Institute since 1980.

More information about Barbara's work is available at www.barbara ellmann.com.

Beth Ferholt, Ph.D. is an Assistant Professor in the School of Education at Brooklyn College, City University of New York. She is interested in play and the interconnections between play and education, the role of affect in the development of cognition, and means of making dynamic relations between cognition, emotion, imagination and creativity available for empirical research.

Herman Jiesamfoek, Ed.D. is Assistant Professor at Brooklyn College, CUNY. He earned a doctorate in Art Education at Teachers College, Columbia University. He is a Fine Arts painter and has danced professionally in various European ballet companies. He holds a master's degree in dance education from Teachers College, Columbia University, and ballet/dance teaching degrees from the Vaganova Choregraphic Institute, St. Petersburg, Russia, and from the Rotterdam Dance Academy, the Netherlands.